Qualitative data analysis

Understanding Social Research
Series Editor: Alan Bryman

Published titles

Surveying the Social World
Alan Aldridge and Ken Levine

Ethnography
John D. Brewer

Qualitative Data Analysis: Explorations with NVivo
Graham R. Gibbs

Unobtrusive Methods in Social Research
Raymond M. Lee

Biographical Research
Brian Roberts

Qualitative data analysis
EXPLORATIONS WITH NVivo

GRAHAM R. GIBBS

Open University Press

Open University Press
McGraw-Hill Education
McGraw-Hill House
Shoppenhangers Road
Maidenhead
Berkshire
SL6 2QL
United Kingdom

email: enquiries@openup.co.uk
world wide web: www.openup.co.uk

and
Two Penn Plaza
New York, NY 10121-2289, USA

First published 2002
Reprinted 2004, 2005, 2006, 2007

A catalogue record of this book is available from the British Library

ISBN 0 335 20084 2 (pb)   0 335 20085 0 (hb)

Library of Congress Cataloging-in-Publication Data
Gibbs, Graham, 1948–
    Qualitative data analysis: explorations with NVivo/Graham R. Gibbs.
        p.   cm. – (Understanding social research)
    Includes bibliographical references and index.
    ISBN 0-335-20085-0 – ISBN 0-335-20084-2 (pbk.)
    1. Social sciences–Data processing.   2. Social sciences–Research.
    3. Qualitative research.   I. Title.   II. Series.

H61.3.G53 2002
300'.7'2–dc21   2001036206

Typeset by Type Study, Scarborough
Printed in Great Britain by The Cromwell Press, Trowbridge, Wiltshire

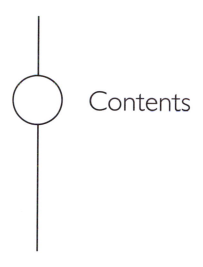

Contents

List of tables

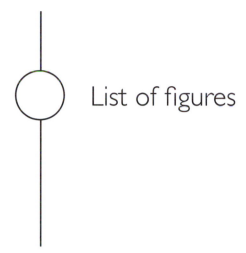

List of figures

Step-by-step guides

Series editor's foreword

This Understanding Social Research series is designed to help students to understand how social research is carried out and to appreciate a variety of issues in social research methodology. It is designed to address the needs of students taking degree programmes in areas such as sociology, social policy, psychology, communication studies, cultural studies, human geography, political science, criminology and organization studies and who are required to take modules in social research methods. It is also designed to meet the needs of students who need to carry out a research project as part of their degree requirements. Postgraduate research students and novice researchers will find the books equally helpful.

The series is concerned to help readers to 'understand' social research methods and issues. This will mean developing an appreciation of the pleasures and frustrations of social research, an understanding of how to implement certain techniques, and an awareness of key areas of debate. The relative emphasis on these different features will vary from book to book, but in each one the aim will be to see the method or issue from the position of a practising researcher and not simply to present a manual of 'how to' steps. In the process, the series will contain coverage of the major methods of social research and addresses a variety of issues and debates. Each book in the series is written by a practising researcher who has experience of the technique or debates that he or she is addressing. Authors are encouraged to draw on their own experiences and inside knowledge.

Graham Gibbs's book is concerned with the processes involved in qualitative data analysis and how to use computer software, often referred to as CAQDAS (computer-assisted qualitative data analysis software), to implement such analysis. Until relatively recently, the surge of interest in and use of qualitative research has not been accompanied by a comparable concern with how qualitative data should and could be analysed. There has been evidence of a growing interest in this issue but it has been difficult to find a comprehensive discussion of the processes involved in qualitative data analysis. Graham Gibbs's book plugs this gap by providing detailed discussions of the main steps and features of qualitative data analysis.

Students and even experienced researchers who use qualitative research often find that they are overwhelmed by the sheer bulk and complexity of the data they generate. They face at least two further problems in addition to the large volume of transcripts or field notes they typically generate. First, the data are unstructured and therefore a great deal of thought has to go into the processes whereby the data are reduced for analysis and theorized about. Second, unlike quantitative data analysis, there are no well-established principles that can be followed for conducting an analysis. Graham Gibbs's book eases the burden of finding a way of carrying out an analysis of qualitative data. Using his own research for illustrative purposes, a feature that is very much in tune with the aims of the Understanding Social Research series, he shows how qualitative data can be boiled down and conceptualized. He provides guidelines about how to make sense of qualitative data and demonstrates the role of frameworks such as grounded theory in developing an analysis of such data.

One of the most striking developments in recent years in this area has been the emergence of computer software for conducting a qualitative data analysis. Such software does not carry out the analysis for you – unfortunately, this is still the domain of humans, who must inject their own imaginative reflections into the data. Instead, CAQDAS facilitates the operation of the key phases and processes associated with carrying out an analysis. Thus, the manual labour of cutting and pasting and retrieving labelled chunks of text is greatly eased by getting the software to do the tasks for you. This book shows the reader how to conduct analyses using one of the most popular programs available – NVivo, a leader in the field. There are risks and controversies associated with using CAQDAS, and Graham Gibbs brings these out too.

This is an important addition to the Understanding Social Research series, in that it helps to address the 'what do I do with it now?' problem that afflicts so many qualitative researchers faced with a mountain of data on their desks. In combining some answers to the question with instruction in the use of CAQDAS, Graham Gibbs has made life a lot easier for all of us who conduct qualitative research.

Alan Bryman

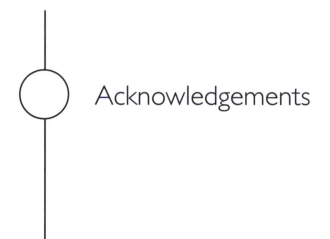

Acknowledgements

I am very grateful to Lyn Richards, Christine Horrocks, Sue Frost, Colin Robson, Raymond Lee and particulary the Series Editor, Alan Bryman, for their comments on the manuscript or selected chapters. I hope they will agree that the final version has measurably improved thanks to their feedback. Thanks also to Justin Vaughan and the Open University Press team for their encouragement and patience.

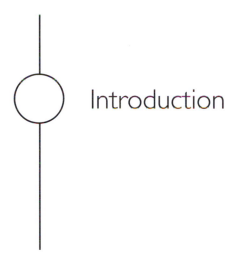

Introduction

It is often said that computers are better at numbers than people, but that people are better at understanding the world than computers. So it might seem like a contradiction that in the last 15 years computers have acquired a central role in qualitative analysis – an approach focused on interpretation, empathy and understanding and for whose practitioners numbers are usually anathema. In one sense, this amounts to nothing more than the fact that almost everyone now uses a word processor. Qualitative researchers use word processors to transcribe their interviews and write up their field notes. The more adventurous might use the Internet to acquire their data in the first place (and hence avoid transcription). Most will also use a word processor to write up their notes and theoretical ideas and to write the final thesis, report, book or paper. But between data collection and writing up many will use the traditional paraphernalia of pens, paper, photocopies, filing cards, coloured markers and floor or wall (on which to display the papers). However, it is in precisely these areas that some of the most exciting software developments of recent years have taken place.

This book explores the role of computers in such activities. Its aim is to show, at least in outline and with the use of worked examples, how qualitative researchers analyse their data. It also shows, in most cases, how the techniques they use can be carried out using one particular piece of software, NVivo. Doing both these things brings limitations. It means that it is not possible to examine all qualitative methods in detail. Consequently, I have focused on just a few, and even then I have only been able to give a taste of the full richness of their techniques. What I have selected is those aspects that I believe are core and which are well supported in NVivo. Moreover, qualitative research is an area where there is much debate both within methods and between them. I have made some reference to such debates, but in the main I have concentrated on giving a hands-on presentation of the selected approaches. At the end of each chapter are some suggestions for further reading, and you can look at these to follow up in more detail the methods I have introduced and the debates about them.

To show how the techniques work, I have used, wherever possible, a single data set. This is based on real data from a study I was involved in some years ago, but has been heavily fictionalized for the purposes of this book. That means that places have been disguised, the identities of people have been changed and even the words they used have been altered, but in such a way that the flavour (and even the Yorkshire expressions!) is preserved, rather in the way a novelist does. One advantage of a single data set in a book like this is that readers will become familiar with both data and analysis as they progress and it should, therefore, become easier to understand both the example techniques and their implementation using NVivo. Nevertheless, many will find it helpful to be able to work with the data themselves and compare what they get with what is shown in this book. For that reason, the data set (in its heavily fictionalized form) will be available for download from this book's website (see below). Using a single data set throughout has also meant that I can take the opportunity to explore the data in a cumulative fashion. This approach, I believe, captures well both the spirit and form of much qualitative work, and the software, NVivo, is well suited to this. In NVivo it is easy to be playful with the data, to try out ideas (especially in searching), to introduce new data throughout the project, and to be flexible in how the theoretical model is constructed and portrayed. That is why this book is subtitled *Explorations with NVivo*.

NVivo is an example of computer-assisted qualitative data analysis software (CAQDAS). This term, introduced by Fielding and Lee as the name of their networking project (http://caqdas.soc.surrey.ac.uk/), refers to the wide range of software now available that supports a variety of analytic styles in qualitative work. Most of these programs have been under development for many years and NVivo is the latest in a venerable line that started with NUD•IST. NUD•IST has been under development for over 10 years, and NVivo is the most recent manifestation of the approach it represents. The full name of the program is NUD•IST Vivo, NVivo for short. However, NVivo is not just an upgrade to NUD•IST. It is in fact a complete rewrite, and although it is built around many of the key ideas found in NUD•IST it also contains many new and wholly different facilities. So different in fact that QSR, the software company that produces both programs, is continuing to market both. The reason is that NUD•IST is better at some things, while NVivo is better at others. In my view, NVivo is better at supporting the kind of research that most social scientists are involved in. It is not so much that different techniques are used but rather the differences in scale and situation. NUD•IST excels in the broad-brush and large-scale. It is thus the best choice for those doing very large-scale projects (often ones linked to large-scale quantitative surveys and involving large, disparate teams of researchers) and needing to get a very broad level of analysis done quickly. Such is often the case in evaluation and applied research. The minimum text unit of analysis NUD•IST can handle is a paragraph (or a line if each ends with a carriage return). That is why the analysis it supports best is broad-brush, but that is also why it is able to handle very large data sets. In contrast, NVivo is much better at very fine-grained analyses. For example, the minimum text unit for analysis is one character. This is not to say that NVivo cannot handle large data sets. It can. But very few researchers will have the time or resources to undertake a fine-grained and intensive analysis of very large data sets. Moreover, as I suggested above, NVivo encourages an exploratory approach to analysis. It is relatively simple for those familiar with Windows to learn to use it, and its facilities encourage a constant playing with ideas and data. It is easy to ask question after question of the data and to follow up hunches about interpretation using its functions. I hope this book will show just how good NVivo is at such analytic approaches in qualitative research.

Readers who have used NUD•IST will find some familiar features in NVivo – the node and document explorers and the node tree, for instance – and some completely new functions such as assays, attributes, combined searches, sets, cases, and a graphical modeller. Moreover, they will find that the usability or interface design of the program is considerably better than in NUD•IST. (In fact the latest version of NUD•IST has borrowed some design features from NVivo.) The experience of those starting with NVivo who have little knowledge of other programs is that they find it easy to use and easy to learn. Researchers who have used NUD•IST before find it a little more of a challenge. I know, I fall into this category. There is a certain amount of unlearning you have to do. However, it is worth the effort, and now I find myself thinking 'why doesn't NUD•IST do it that way?' or 'why can't I do that in NUD•IST?'. Therein lies a small danger. The response of one researcher I know who is familiar with NUD•IST and started to look at NVivo was to get so excited about one of its facilities, the Model Explorer, that she missed most of the other new features. It is clear that the Model Explorer addresses the desire of many qualitative researchers to have a more flexible way of expressing their ideas than the node hierarchy found in NUD•IST. However, don't let that prevent you from seeing all the other functions and design improvements in NVivo. As I said above, it is worth the effort to unlearn the NUD•IST way of doing things in order to become fluent with NVivo.

Whether you have used CAQDAS before or not, this book is for you. The reader I have in mind is someone who has a background in one of the social sciences or a related applied discipline. I would therefore include those with backgrounds in sociology, psychology, health, nursing, social work, social policy, geography, anthropology, economics, criminology, politics, cultural studies and community studies. I am assuming you know a little about social research methods, though you may not know much about qualitative research. If you do know about qualitative analysis, so much the better, you will be able to focus on the parts of the book concerned with NVivo. I have also assumed that you have a qualitative research project that you need to carry out, and even that you have some data to analyse. I have made no assumption about the level of expertise you should have. I hope that readers of all kinds, from undergraduates to experienced researchers and academics as well as professionals engaged in research, will find this book accessible and that you will be encouraged to explore your data with NVivo.

There is not space, even in a book twice this size, to include all I'd like to about using NVivo. Moreover, some things are best provided in electronic form. Fortunately, this book has an associated website where you will find a copy of the data set I have used throughout the book along with further guides to using NVivo, links to websites of interest and hints and tips. The URL is:

www.openup.co.uk/gibbs

(1) What is qualitative analysis?

What are qualitative data?

The first thing that characterizes qualitative analysis is that it analyses a distinctive form of data, namely language and texts. This does not mean that there can be no qualitative analysis of other forms of cultural expression, such as images and social practices, or that there is no quantitative analysis of text. Only that language is the most common form of meaningful expression, and even if the researcher is looking at images or observing social practices, these are commonly transformed into linguistic form through descriptions and field notes. As we shall see later, most of the features of the computer programs that support qualitative analysis are concerned with text, although recent developments in software are making it easier for researchers to work with photographs, video and sound recordings.

Language is both the medium and the message – to misquote Marshall McLuhan. Language not only incorporates the terminology and vocabulary with which we understand the world, use it and transform it, but also is the medium by which we convey that meaning or interpretation to others. As well as being the tool we use to express our ideas and interpretations of the world, language contains the concepts, categories and ontologies that describe and constitute the world in which we live. Some of these refer to the physical world we inhabit, but the more interesting ones from the qualitative researcher's perspective are those referring to and representing the experiences, social organizations, institutions, activities and practices that we have created in human culture and society.

There are two consequences of this focus on language. First, qualitative analysis tends to be based on an interpretative philosophy. Second, researchers tend to take a holistic view of what they are investigating. The interpretative view is that people are constantly interpreting the world they live in. They are always trying to understand the world or to imbue it with meaning. What the qualitative researcher is doing is trying to capture these acts of interpretation and to understand them. Some, such as the philosopher Peter Winch, suggest that what the researcher is doing is something akin to clarifying the conceptual frameworks the respondents are using – an activity he concludes is close to, if not identical with, linguistic philosophy (Winch 1958).

The holistic approach of qualitative analysis follows from this philosophical position (and related ones). The proper understanding or interpretation of people's words and actions can only be achieved if these are related to the wider context in which they have been used or happened. This approach is most common in ethnography and anthropology, where it is often expressed through the researchers' need to immerse themselves in the society and mores of the people they are studying. But it is also characteristic of many key approaches in qualitative work such as biography and grounded theory. This holistic, ethnographic approach usually entails very flexible forms of data collection that are sensitive to the social situations being examined. Such sensitivity extends into theoretical areas too. Although almost all qualitative researchers will to some degree draw upon existing theories and concepts, all will to a lesser or greater extent conceptualize and formulate theory as it comes from the data.

The focus on interpretation and holism has consequences for the practical activities of qualitative researchers. Qualitative data analysis is commonly iterative, recursive and dynamic. Researchers do not feel constrained to preserve analysis as a separate stage of work that follows data collection. Typically qualitative data analysis is coincident with data collection. It is not always the distinct phase of research found in the model recommended for quantitative analysis (or at least the normative version of the model). Some, such as the grounded theorists, emphasize that analysis must take place during data collection. For them the researcher's developing ideas about the project should guide and change the form of later data collection, for instance, by suggesting new questions that respondents can be asked or by guiding the sampling strategy. On the other hand, not all qualitative analysts mix analysis and data collection in this way. It is not always appropriate to conduct data collection and analysis in parallel. For instance, if the data collection takes place across a number of different settings or cases undertaken by different researchers then it may make more sense to wait till all interviews, observations etc. are complete. But even here it can be helpful to

Table 1.1 Characteristics of qualitative research

- *Seeing through the eyes of.* . . . This involves a commitment to viewing events, actions, norms, values etc. from the perspective of those being studied. It includes a sensitivity to the differing perspectives held by different groups and introduces the potential of conflict between the perspective of those being studied and those doing the studying.
- *Description.* There is emphasis on the description of the setting being investigated to answer the question 'what is going on here?'. Detailed description can contribute to an understanding and analysis of the setting under study.
- *Contextualism and holism.* Phenomena are interpreted in relation to the context or setting in which they occur and in terms of an understanding of the whole society and the meaning it has for the participants.
- *Process.* A focus on interconnection and change and on the processes that produce them. Particularly manifest in implementation and evaluation studies where interest is in what produces changes.
- *Flexibility and lack of structure.* Favours a relatively open and unstructured research strategy. Research questions are often decided late in the study, for instance, if the original questions make little sense in the light of the perspectives of those studied.
- *Theory and concepts.* A reluctance to impose *a priori* theoretical frameworks at the outset. Instead favours an approach in which theories and concepts are developed in tandem with data collection. Theories are treated as signposts or sensitizing concepts.

Source: adapted from Bryman (1988: 60–69)

modify the work of later investigations using the experience of earlier ones. Moreover, in qualitative research it is hard, during data collection or the fieldwork stage, not to start some preliminary analysis or at least some thinking about the data. In order to emphasize the distinctiveness of qualitative *analysis* many writers on the subject avoid the term itself. Silverman (1993) prefers the term 'interpreting', Wolcott (1994) uses 'transforming' and Hammersley and Atkinson (1995) refer to 'making sense of' the data.

A further key difference between the procedures of qualitative and quantitative analysis is that the former does not seek to reduce or condense the data, for example, to summaries or to statistics. (Though at the final stage of reporting, the analyst may have to use summaries and examples from the data.) Qualitative analysis usually seeks to enhance the data, to increase their bulk, density and complexity. This distinction can be seen in the different roles of coding in qualitative and quantitative analysis. Coding in quantitative analysis is for the explicit purpose of reducing the data to a few 'types' in order that they can be counted. For instance, people's responses to a question on a questionnaire are coded into one of, say, four different possible answers. The responses are then counted so that some numerical summary can be made or so that a statistical test can be carried out. In contrast, coding in qualitative analysis is a way of organizing or managing the data. All the original data are preserved. Codes are *added* to the data. In fact, typically, text may be densely coded; not only will most text be assigned a code but much will have more than one code attached to it. The researcher does not count the occurrences of the code, rather a link between the code and the coded text is maintained so that by retrieving the code the original words can be displayed (easily done on a computer, but traditionally done by the extraction of file cards on which the text was written). Whereas quantitative analysis can be seen as a consistent move away from the original data towards a summary, qualitative analysis constantly cycles around between the original data and the codes, memos, annotations etc. that the analyst constructs. Table 1.1 summarizes the distinctive characteristics of qualitative research.

The two-paradigms approach

Another way in which qualitative data analysis may be distinguished is by reference to its underlying philosophy. This is seen most vividly in the contrasting views about the essential nature of the world being studied and in the preferred logic of analysis used to describe it. Quantitative methods are seen as reflecting an empiricist and realist view of the world and using a deductive logic of inquiry. Qualitative approaches tend more often to be idealist and to use an inductive logic of inquiry. However, although qualitative and quantitative approaches are often characterized in this way, as we shall see, the dichotomy is Procrustean, and many writers have argued that qualitative research can also be realist (e.g. Van Maanen 1988).

Realism

Simply put, realism is the view that the world has an existence independent of us. In response to the schoolchild's philosophical conundrum of whether a tree falling in a forest makes a noise if there is no one there to hear it, the realist argues that the nature of the world is unchanged whether humanity exists or not. Moreover, the form it takes and the way we perceive it are independent of how we might think about it. One might say this is the common-sense view of the world as having an independent existence. While this might seem uncontentious for objects in the material world, realists usually want to go further. There are all kinds of other things in our world that seem to have an existence yet are not simply material things. Many of them are connected with our social lives, our thinking and our communication:

> Normally to be a realist in philosophy is to be committed to the existence of some disputed kind of being (e.g. material objects, universals,

causal laws, propositions, numbers, probabilities, efficacious reasons, social structures, moral facts).

(Bhaskar 1993: 308)

Language is another good example. While language has its material form in books, recordings and so on, even if all these material expressions disappeared overnight, realists would still want to say that language is real in some sense. Yet we cannot point to where language is as we can point to a mountain, a building or a dog. We could argue that language is in people's heads – but, as linguists point out, we have the capacity at any time to utter novel sentences and it doesn't make sense to say they already existed in people's heads. Others argue that what exists are the rules for the use of language. But no one has been able to work out fully what these are – and besides, as philosophers point out, rules about the use of language need rules about their application and that leads us into an undesirable infinite regress of rules about rules.

Bhaskar (1993) offers one possible way out of this puzzle. Things are real, he says, if their effects are real and observable. He uses the example of a magnetic field to illustrate the point. We accept that the field is real yet we, as humans, cannot see or feel it. We do so because it has real effects that we can detect. We can see the compass needle turning and the aurora in the sky and hence we know of the reality of the earth's magnetism. The same is true with the more problematic social things, says Bhaskar. We can know the reality of laws, moral facts, social institutions and so on through their real effects. Those effects would be there whether we were around to experience them or not, and no amount of thinking or argument on our part could make them any different.

Such a realist view of the world is an assumption of most quantitative social research. Quantitative researchers rarely state this explicitly, but their findings are usually expressed in terms of causal efficacy and real consequences. More fundamentally, quantitative research generally assumes that, at least at some base level, we all inhabit the same world. We may have different ways of talking about our world, but essentially we are all experiencing the same things and we can come to some agreement about the nature of this world. To put it another way, there are indisputable facts about the world and the task of research is to discover them. This is something that researchers following an idealist philosophy hotly contest.

Idealism

For idealists, not only are all the contested objects such as universals, moral facts and social structures creations of the human mind but so is the material world itself. The external world consists merely of representations. Even the very idea of a real, external world is itself a representation or concept and the result of human cognition. The link between this view and the interpretative approach that underlies most qualitative research is clear. If we live in a world that we imbue with meaning and which we constantly interpret and give significance to, then it is only a short step to the view that our concepts, including those about what exists or not (and even the concept of reality) are something that humans have in some sense created. A common recent version of this view is constructivism. According to constructivists the material, social and psychic worlds we live in are constructed by us as individuals. As Guba and Lincoln, two qualitative researchers who are enthusiastic constructivists, put it:

> There exist multiple, socially constructed realities ungoverned by laws, natural or otherwise . . . those constructions are devised by individuals as they attempt to make sense of their experiences . . . constructions can be and usually are shared . . . this does not make them more real, but simply more commonly assented to.
>
> (Guba and Lincoln 1989: 86)

The task of the qualitative researcher, then, is simply to reflect as accurately as possible these constructions (shared or otherwise) without any commitment to saying anything about an underlying and shared reality. Idealists therefore reject the idea that there are facts and that the role of research is to discover them. Researchers might come up with statements that look like facts, but these are inevitably 'theory-laden'. In other words, our descriptions of the world and theories about it reflect preconceptions and prejudices that arise out of the researcher's or the respondent's construction of the world. For idealists, we cannot say how the world is, only how some people see it. Of course, the problem for the incautious idealist is that even a report of how some people see the world is making a factual claim, and others can argue that it itself is just one construction of the respondents' constructions. At this point we enter the vertiginous world of relativism, where every view of the world is relative to a society, subculture or even an individual.

Although I have presented the realist–idealist contrast in stark terms above, in practice most qualitative researchers are fairly catholic. As Hammersley points out, even though many ethnographers subscribe to the idealist philosophy, the actual language they use in their research reports gives away realist assumptions. The use of terms such as 'reveal', 'dig down to' and 'pull back the veil on' suggest an implicit belief in an underlying reality (Hammersley 1992). The point of examining the realist–idealist debate is that it illustrates well what qualitative researchers mean by a sensitivity to the social situations being examined. It is a recognition that there are different views about what really exists, and such beliefs and knowledge about the world will affect the way they act and behave. If some people think things are as they think they are then that belief will be real in its effects. In the end we may not want to support the full constructivist position, but as qualitative researchers we need to identify the kinds of reality perceived and assumed by our respondents, especially if they are not shared by others.

Contrasting logic

The second philosophical difference between quantitative and qualitative research is the logic of explanation. This is summarized by the distinction between deduction and induction. Put simply, deduction describes a logic of argument that moves from the general to the particular. In contrast, induction is the argument for general statements based upon particular observations or facts.

For example, the move from the general statement or law 'the pressure of a fixed mass of a gas is inversely proportional to its volume' to the particular proposition 'if we halve the volume of this container of gas, its pressure will double' is one of deduction. The latter, particular, statement is deduced from the former, general or universal statement.

In contrast, induction moves the other way. From a (large) number of particular observations or statements we derive a general or universal law. For example, we may observe a large number of qualified midwives in the UK and note that every one is female. From these particular statements like 'Pam is a midwife and female, Jenny is female and a midwife' and so on, we might conclude, inductively, that 'all midwives in the UK are female'. Induction clearly describes a very common type of human thinking, one that captures the form of much of people's thoughts. It could also be argued that it lies behind a good deal of the presuppositions and prejudices with which we address the world. For instance, it is on the basis of having seen so many female midwives that people come to expect that all midwives are female.

For a long time induction was thought to characterize the form of proper scientific thinking. Again, intuitively this seems to be true. Much science advances by the careful accretion of a large number of observations that eventually allow the scientist to develop some general laws or statements. However, in the early twentieth century, philosophers came to realize that not only did some science not develop this way, particularly when completely novel theories were proposed, but induction itself could never logically justify any general or universal statement. As Popper (1959) pointed out, for hundreds of years Europeans had noticed that every adult swan they saw was white. On these grounds they had inductively concluded that all swans were white, until, that is, they visited Australia, where they discovered swans that were black. As Popper argued, there is no limit on the number of observations you need to justify the general law. It is always possible that tomorrow you will make a new observation that will contradict the established view. Science based on induction was poor science, or at best provisional science, he argued.

Moreover, suggested Popper, induction does not properly capture what many scientists do, which is to test their theories. According to this hypothetico-deductive view of science, researchers have an idea of what they think is happening, a general theory or a hypothesis from which specific predictions can be deduced. Then they carry out experiments to see if the predictions are correct and hence if their hunch is right. Popper's critical rationalist stance suggested that scientists could never actually confirm their hypotheses, but it is possible to disconfirm or falsify the hypothesis if the experiment throws up a result that is not the same as what the theory predicts. In fact, for Popper, it was this very ability of their hypotheses to be falsified that distinguished true science from what he called pseudo-science, that is, disciplines that have the trappings and appearance of science but in fact are based on theories and generalizations that are not actually falsifiable.

There has been a great deal of debate in the second half of the twentieth century as to whether critical rationalism is an adequate criterion for scientific inquiry and whether it accurately describes what scientists actually do. (Popper's response to the latter question would, of course, be that they to be critical rationalists.) The work of Thomas Kuhn, a historian of science, has been much quoted and much discussed as showing that for much of their time scientists actually are not actively seeking to falsify their theories. Between what Kuhn calls revolutionary periods, which he sees as quite rare, scientists commonly operate inductively. Their major activities consist of the elaboration of existing views, not, to use Popper's term, making bold conjectures about the nature of phenomena. Besides, given the complexity and interrelatedness of scientific theories, when researchers come across something that doesn't match their expectations, it isn't immediately obvious which theory is in error, that is, which is falsified. Even if there is an error, the anomaly is usually dealt with by some   amendment to the theories on which the prediction was based.

Critical rationalism and the hypothetico-deductive methods have been very influential on the view that social scientists have of their work. Researchers in disciplines such as psychology and to some extent sociology and economics were very taken with the idea that this is how research should proceed. Deduction has become identified with the quantitative method in these subjects, and hypothesis testing is seen as the gold standard form of empirical research. The social survey, perhaps the most common research strategy, might seem to contradict this when used to generalize to a wider population. However, the results of surveys are rarely couched in terms of universals, and are usually expressed as tendencies or restricted with statistical probabilities. In contrast, several qualitative researchers have claimed their area as the domain of induction. The classic formulation of grounded theory by Glaser and Strauss (1967) seems to fit this well. The notions of eschewing pre-existing theory and grounding ideas in the data, which Glaser and Strauss promote, are a rejection of deduction and an adoption of induction as the approved approach. At the same time, the adoption of induction brings with it the problem, noted by Popper, of how we can be sure that the next observation won't undermine any generalization we are trying to make. This is why Glaser and Strauss pay such attention to activities such as saturation, which is a form of repeated sampling carried out until no further variations are discovered, in an attempt to ensure that (at least for the data collected) no contradictory phenomena are missed.

It would be quite wrong to conclude simply that quantitative analysis is deductive and qualitative is inductive. Not only is much quantitative social research actually inductive in tenor, but qualitative analysis commonly involves both deductive (especially hypothesis testing) and inductive reasoning. As we shall see in Chapter 8, the procedural approach to analysis is essentially one that tries to test the accuracy of predictions made on the basis of pre-existing theory. Also, as Bryman and Burgess (1994: 6) note, even those claiming to do grounded research rarely follow its strict inductivist prescriptions. Actually, social research is often simultaneously inductive and deductive. Some writers refer to this as retroduction:

> A theory is not pieced together from observed phenomena; it is rather what makes it possible to observe phenomena as being of a certain sort, and related to other phenomena. They are built up 'in reverse' – retroductively.
>
> (Bulmer 1979: 660)

Strategies of qualitative research

Qualitative strategies are characterized by diversity. There are manifold methods and with them a variety of views, of what are the most significant kinds of qualitative data. Creswell (1998), for example, identifies five traditions: case study, biography, phenomenology, grounded theory and ethnography. Harré (1997), starting from a more psychological perspective, includes conversation analysis, discourse analysis, narrative, life history, and even conceptual analysis, repertory grid analysis and account analysis. In her book on qualitative analysis, Tesch (1990) reviews the enormous number of approaches researchers have taken and reduces them to four major categories: investigations of the characteristics of language; investigations of the discovery of regularities; investigations of the comprehension of the meaning of text or actions; and varieties of reflection. The first, the investigation of the characteristics of language, has become very popular in the last decade or so. It includes such approaches as conversation analysis, discourse analysis and the analysis of narrative. There is not space in a book of this length to cover all these approaches, but in Chapter 8 I look at how to use software to undertake a basic analysis of narrative. Investigations that try to discover regularities sound rather like quantitative approaches. However, the regularities are rarely of a numeric or statistical kind. Rather they are based on the kinds of systems and functional relationships to be found in organizations and institutions. One of the most common uses of this approach is in evaluations of social, educational or organizational programmes. Chapter 8 provides a brief examination of such approaches, particularly focusing on analytic induction and the analysis of case studies. The third category, investigations of the comprehension of the meanings of texts or actions, is perhaps the most common approach in qualitative analysis. Key examples of this approach are phenomenology and grounded theory. Grounded theory and related approaches will also be examined in Chapter 8. Tesch's fourth category, that of reflection, is a more literary approach to the analysis of texts. In recent years this has become important in two ways. The first is the focus on literary forms, such as the use of metaphor, that can reveal underlying meaning and intentions. We shall examine some of these ideas briefly in Chapter 6. The second reflects the recognition that how qualitative data are written about is as important as how they are analysed. In fact, one can argue that writing about qualitative data is analysis. Such a poetics of qualitative analysis is discussed in Chapter 10.

Computer-assisted qualitative data analysis

The exciting evolution of analytic styles since the 1980s has been complemented by the development, especially during the 1990s, of a wide range of software to assist qualitative analysts. Initially these were rather intimidating programs, based on command line interfaces (where users had to type in commands as sequences of letters and numbers), but all now take full advantage of the windows, menus and icons of modern operating systems.

It is important to recognize from the start that although computer-assisted qualitative and quantitative analysis share the same term, analysis, the computer supports the analysis in very different ways. In the case of quantitative analysis, principally using statistics, the computer does the hard work of calculation in the creation of statistics, which many people will see as the fundamental part of analysis. In the case of qualitative analysis there is no real equivalent to the calculation of statistics, though most programs will produce simple counts. The real heart of the analysis requires an understanding of the meaning of the texts, and that is something that computers are still a long way from being able to do. Essentially the function of qualitative analysis software is more akin to that of a database, though it supports ways of handling text that go well beyond most databases. It enables the researcher to keep good records of their hunches, ideas, searches and analyses and gives access to data so they can be examined and analysed. However, in much the same way as a word processor won't write meaningful text for you, but makes that process of writing and editing a lot easier, using computer-assisted qualitative data analysis software (CAQDAS) can make qualitative analysis easier, more accurate, more reliable and more transparent. But the program will never do the reading and thinking for you. Moreover, just as in quantitative analysis any statistics produced need to be interpreted, so the parallel is true in qualitative analysis. CAQDAS has a range of tools for producing reports and summaries but the interpretation of these is down to you, the researcher.

In his discussion of qualitative analysis, Wolcott (1994) makes a distinction between analysis that is data management (in other words, that is concerned with the more effective handling of data), and analytic procedures (where features and relationships are revealed). The first programs developed tended to focus on data management. It was the common experience of researchers carrying out qualitative analysis in the days before computers that such work required careful and complex management of large amounts of texts, codes, memos, notes and so on. In fact one could argue that the prerequisite of really effective qualitative analysis is efficient, consistent and systematic data management. Traditionally, researchers had to use a variety of paper management techniques, such as photocopiers, filing cards and cabinets, and coloured pens. In this way they could manage the large amounts of data they created, maintain links between the chunks of data and ensure that important ideas could always be tracked back to the interviews, observations and so on from which they originated. Some researchers realized that these tasks were just the kind of things that computers could do very well. The combination of word processor and simple database enabled researchers to search texts and store the results of any extracted chunks in a way that could be easily manipulated. The key development was the introduction of software that could manage the coding and retrieval of texts. The attaching of labels to chunks of text, called coding, is a central activity in much qualitative analysis. Such code-and-retrieve programs make it easy not only to select chunks of text and apply codes to them, but also to retrieve all similarly coded text without losing any information about where it came from and to work with it in further analyses. In Wollcott's terms all this can be seen as just using the computer to support a more effective way of handling data. However, some programs try to assist with analytic procedures too. These programs, of which NVivo is a key example, provide a variety of facilities to help the analyst examine features and relationships in the texts. They are often referred to as theory builders – not, it should be noted, because on their own they can build theory, but because they contain various tools that *assist* the researcher to develop theoretical ideas and test hypotheses. Table 1.2 summarizes the categorization of CAQDAS provided by Weitzman and Miles (1995).

Table 1.2   Types of computer-assisted qualitative data analysis

- Text retrievers – search for words or phrases
- Textbase managers – sort and organize data
- Code and retrieve – support coding and reporting by codes
- Code-based theory builders – coding and the ability to build conceptual structures and test hypotheses
- Conceptual network builders – diagrams, concept mapping, charts

: Weitzman and Miles (1995)

While there are many benefits to be gained from using software like NVivo, there are dangers too. Some of these are discussed in the recent book by Fielding and Lee (1998). They examine the history of the development of qualitative research and its support by computers in the light of the experience of those interviewed in their study of researchers using CAQDAS. Among the issues they identify is a feeling of being distant from the data. Researchers using paper-based analysis felt they were closer to the words of their respondents or to their field notes than if they used computers. In part I suspect this was because many of the early programs did not make it easy to jump back to the data to examine the context of coded or retrieved text. Improvements in software mean that NVivo excels at this. At the same time, the ease with which a user can start to manipulate node trees and models in NVivo means there is still a danger of forgetting that all analysis should be well grounded in the data. A second issue, as many users and some commentators have suggested, is that much software seems too influenced by grounded theory. This approach has become very popular among both qualitative researchers and software developers. Certainly NVivo would fall into this category. However, as Fielding and Lee point out, most other software is equally influenced. Moreover, as programs have become more sophisticated, they have become less connected to any one analytic approach. A related danger that some have pointed to is the overemphasis on code-and-retrieve approaches. As we shall see later in this book, these are core activities of NVivo. Some commentators have suggested that this militates against analysts who wish to use quite different techniques (such as hyperlinking) to analyse their data. It is clear that coding is central in the kind of analysis best supported by NVivo, and although it does have some linking facilities, these are not as well developed as those that support node construction and coding.

The quality of qualitative research

CAQDAS has become very successful, not always for the best of reasons. As some commentators have noted, there has been a tendency for researchers to try to give their proposals some kind of gloss of rigour by suggesting in research bids that the data will be analysed using NVivo or some such program. It is as if the use of software will somehow alone improve the quality of their work. As will, I hope, become apparent from the rest of this book, CAQDAS alone cannot do that. It is just a tool for analysis, and good qualitative analysis still relies on good analytic work by a careful human researcher, in the same way that good writing is not guaranteed by the use of a word processor.

Much of the thinking about the quality of research originates in ideas about quantitative research. Here there is a strong emphasis on ensuring the validity, reliability and generalizability of results so that we can be sure about the true causes of the effects observed. Validity is the concern that the theories or explanations derived from the research data really are true, that they correctly capture what is actually happening. A reliable result is one that is consistent across repeated investigations in different circumstances with different investigators, and a generalizable result is one that is true for a wide range of (specified) circumstances beyond those studied in the research. In quantitative research, techniques such as experimental design, double blind testing and random sampling are used to guarantee valid, reliable and general results from which causality can be inferred.

In recent years there has been much discussion about whether such ideas can be applied to qualitative data and, if they are applicable, what alternative techniques might be available to qualitative researchers to help ensure the quality of their analysis. From the discussion earlier in this chapter, it is clear that the issue of validity cannot be separated from the idealist–realist debate. Validity makes best sense if you are a realist, in which case the attempt to ensure that your analysis is as close as possible to what is really happening is worthwhile. In contrast, for those taking an extreme idealist or constructivist position, there is no reality against which to check the analysis, only multiple views, and hence little point in asking the question in the first place. However, as I suggested above, even idealists, in the end, want to make realist claims about the multiple views of the world they are reporting on. Thus the issue of whether the representation of the objects of qualitative research are valid cannot be escaped.

The issues of quality in qualitative research have been tackled in part by recognizing that, in the absence of the techniques available to quantitative researchers, qualitative analysts have to pay more attention to how they write about their data and present their reports. This is an issue we shall return to in Chapter 10.

Another response by those undertaking qualitative analysis has been to focus on the possible threats to quality that arise in the process of analysis. There is a variety of such threats, including biased transcription and interpretation, the overemphasis on positive cases, a focus on the exotic or unusual, the ignoring of negative cases, vague definitions of concepts (or codes), inconsistent application of such concepts to the data and unwarranted generalization. As Dey suggests:

> We tend to make more of the evidence that confirms our beliefs, and pay less attention to any evidence that contradicts them. This is a particular problem in qualitative analysis, because of the volume and complexity of the data. Because the data are voluminous, we have to be selective – and we can select out the data that doesn't suit. Because the data are complex, we have to rely more on imagination, insight and intuition – and we can quickly leap to the wrong conclusions.
>
> (Dey 1993: 222)

It is therefore not surprising that it is easy to produce partial and biased analyses. As we shall see in later chapters, the use of CAQDAS can make a positive contribution here, not least because it takes away much of the sheer tedium of qualitative analysis. Using the software it is easier to be exhaustive in analysis and to check for negative cases, and there are some techniques for ensuring that text has been coded in consistent and well-defined ways. Much of the paper chase that constituted the pre-computer qualitative analysis described above can be eliminated. However, no software can read and understand text – yet – so the use of CAQDAS still requires the researcher constantly to read and reread the texts to check interpretations.

Conclusion

Qualitative data are distinguished by their meaningfulness, and hence interpretation is a key aspect of qualitative data analysis. Not surprisingly, the reliability and validity of such interpretation is a major concern of analysis and something where CAQDAS has an important part to play. The two traditions of analysis, induction and deduction, both appear in qualitative data analysis, and although it is often seen by many as merely inductive, typically researchers use both deductive and inductive procedures in their analysis. This is something we shall explore in later chapters.

Further reading

Bryman, A. (1988) *Quantity and Quality in Social Research*. London: Unwin Hyman. (A classic text that examines many of the philosophical and methodological issues underlying the qualitative–quantitative contrast.)

Coffey, A. and Atkinson, P. (1996) *Making Sense of Qualitative Data Analysis: Complementary Research Strategies*. London and Thousand Oaks, CA: Sage. (A general introduction to qualitative analysis that contains a good discussion of the nature of qualitative data.)

Creswell, J.W. (1998) *Qualitative Inquiry and Research Design: Choosing among Five Traditions*. London and Thousand Oaks, CA: Sage Publications. (A highly structured comparison of five key traditions in qualitative research. Compares their analytic approaches and gives some ideas about using software in each case.)

Dey, I. (1993) *Qualitative Data Analysis: A User-Friendly Guide for Social Scientists*. London and New York: Routledge. (An exploration of how to do qualitative analysis with the use of computers in mind. Contains a good discussion of the nature of qualitative data.)

Murphy, E., Dingwall, R., Greatbatch, D., Parker, S. and Watson, P. (1998) Qualitative research methods in health technology assessment: a review of the literature, *Health Technology Assessment*, 2(16). (Designed to address the need for benchmark standards in assessing qualitative research proposals and reports. It provides an excellent review of the methodological issues underlying the nature of qualitative analysis and judgements about its validity.)

Seale, C. (1999) *The Quality of Qualitative Research*. London: Sage. (This is a comprehensive discussion of the issues that affect the quality of research, including issues of validity and reliability as they apply to qualitative research. There is a useful discussion of involving participants in the validation of transcripts and analysis in Chapter 5.)

Weitzman, E. and Miles, M. (1995) *Computer Programs for Qualitative Data Analysis: A Software Source Book*. Thousand Oaks, CA: Sage. (Although now somewhat dated (since publication most software mentioned has been replaced by updated versions), it does give a good idea of the range of tools available to the analyst.)

2 Getting started with NVivo

To run NVivo you will need a fairly modern, well-equipped PC running Windows 95, 98, NT, ME or 2000. You will find it beneficial to have a fairly large monitor or screen. Use of the program involves opening a large number of windows and sometimes you need the space to display windows without overlapping them. To use the instructional videos that are included on the CD with the program you will need a sound card. NVivo has no Macintosh version, though some users have reported success in running the program under software emulation on a fast Macintosh. This book assumes you are familiar with the Windows operating system and know how to cut and paste, move between active programs, open, move and resize windows and use menus, dialog boxes and the file manager. If you are preparing your documents using a computer you will need to be familiar with a word processor. Most word processors can produce files that are compatible with NVivo. NVivo can read files in plain text or rich text format (RTF).

Documents and nodes

Fundamentally, NVivo does two things: it supports the storing and manipulation of texts or documents; and it supports the creation and manipulation of codes, known in NVivo as nodes. Around these two basic functions the program also provides tools for creating and examining new ideas about the data – for example, through searching, linking and modelling – and for reporting results. The dual functions of supporting documents and nodes are reflected in two major tools in NVivo, the Document Explorer and the Node Explorer. The first is used to manage the collection of documents, information about all documents including proxy documents, and anything linked to them such as other documents, annotations and memos. Passages of text in documents can be coded, and NVivo will keep a track of the codes and associated text. Documents can also be edited, formatted and reported on. The Node Explorer is used to manage nodes. Nodes are names or labels for a concept or idea about your data. Coding text at a node is the process of establishing a relationship or connection between a node and one or more passages of text. Nodes can be free nodes – just kept as a list – or organized into a tree, or hierarchical structure. The Node Explorer enables you to create, delete, merge and move nodes and to change the text to which they refer. At any time you can browse the text coded at a node and change that coding or view it in context. Nodes can also be searched and in this way, along with an inspection of linked data, such as memos, the researcher can ask questions of the data and build and test theories.

New project

All the facets of the NVivo database are collected together into a 'project'. The first thing you must do when starting up NVivo with data from a new research study is create a project. Once you have started NVivo from the **Start:Programs** menu or by double-clicking the NVivo icon, you will be presented with the Launch Pad (see Figure 2.1). From here you can open an existing project, create a new project or open one of the tutorial projects provided with the software.

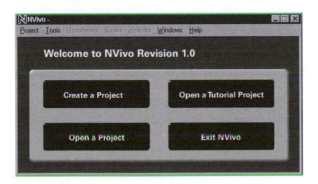

Figure 2.1   The NVivo Launch Pad

If you choose to open an existing project you will be presented with a dialog box with a pull-down menu of your recent projects (Figure 2.2). By default these are kept in a folder called QSR Projects on your C: drive. You can choose to store the files elsewhere if you take the **Custom** option when setting up the project. The last project you used is usually displayed in the pull-down menu, so it is easy to reopen it. Just click on the **OK** button.

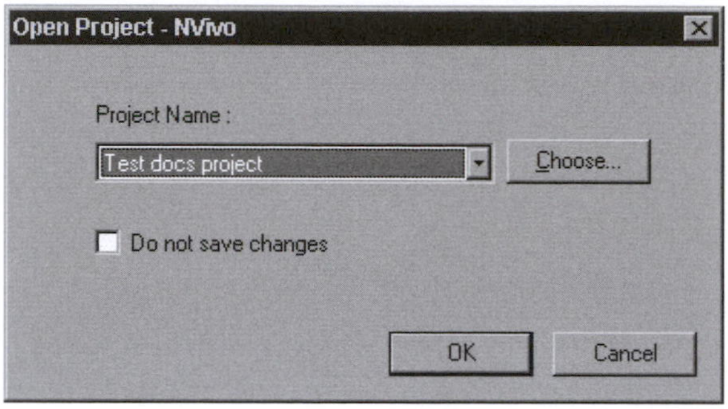

Figure 2.2 The Open Project dialog

However, if you are starting from scratch, you will need to set up a new project. For the purposes of illustrations throughout most of this book, I shall use a project called 'Job Search'. This contains a set of files from a project about job searching by people in West Yorkshire, UK, in the mid-1990s. It involved a large number of interviews, of which just a few are included in this test project.

To create a new project

1 Click on the **Create a Project** button on the Launch Pad. This will open the New Project Wizard.
2 Choose **Typical** and click on **Next>**.
3 Give a name to your project and a description. Click on **Next>**.
4 If everything looks fine, click on **Finish**.

If you choose **Custom** in the New Project Wizard you can choose where on your hard disk you want to store your files and you can change the name of the project owner and password protect the files.

You will now be presented with the Project Pad for your new project (see Figure 2.3). This divides up the major functions of NVivo into six groups and two extra overall functions – search and model. These are summarized in Table 2.1. Move from one group to another by clicking on the appropriate tabs. All these functions can also be accessed from the standard menus at the top of the Project Pad.

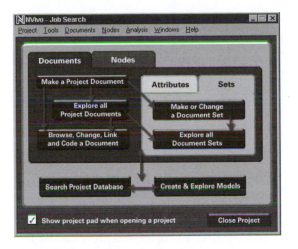

Figure 2.3   The Project Pad

Table 2.1   Functions available from the Project Pad

Things to do with documents	Make a project document
	Explore all project documents
	Browse, change, link and code a document
Things to do with document attributes	Make or change a document attribute
	Explore all document attributes
Things to do with document sets	Make or change a document set
	Explore all document sets
Things to do with nodes	Make a project node
	Explore all project nodes
	Browse, change, link and code a node
Things to do with node attributes	Make or change a node attribute
	Explore all node attributes
Things to do with node sets	Make or change a node set
	Explore all node sets
Two global functions	Search project database
	Create and explore models

Backing up

As you build your database and develop your analysis, you will create files and structures you won't want to lose. NVivo itself does regular saves of your data, so that if the program or the computer crashes at any time, you will only lose work done since the last automatic save of your project. You can change the frequency of the automatic save by accessing the dialog from the **Tools:Options** menu item. The default is 15 minutes. But you do still need to keep your own back-up copies of your project.

Most of the data you create in NVivo is very compact. Only documents and reports will take up lots of space. Information about codes and links takes only a little space by comparison. But you may well find all the files are too large to fit onto a floppy disk – and besides, floppy disks are not a safe medium. They easily corrupt. I recommend the use of a Zip drive that uses 100 or 250 MB disks for backing up. However, any high-capacity removable storage device will do, including rewritable compact discs (CD-RWs). Even though modern hard disks are very reliable, never rely on just one copy. Hard disks   fail. Your computer may be stolen or someone may acciden-tally delete your files. After months of working on your project you don't want to lose all your work.

Figure 2.4 shows the hierarchy of folders in a project – in this case the Job Search 1997 project. The All Users folder and the folders in it are available for use by any users and are a suggested way of keeping your reports and other files tidy. You can add other folders to those in All Users if you wish to. The folder Database.nv1 is reserved for files created by the program and you should   attempt to change or delete any of the folders and files inside it. Autosave.nv1 is where the automatically backed-up file is saved and is only there while the project is open in NVivo.

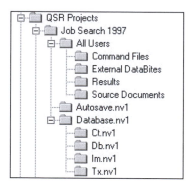

Figure 2.4   The NVivo folder hierarchy in the default folder, QSR Projects

If you need to restore your project from a back-up or you need to copy the project to a new machine, then you should re-create the folder hierarchy of Database.nv1 exactly as in Figure 2.4. Although your project may still appear in the pull-down list when you open NVivo, you may need to use the **Choose. . .** button to tell the program where the files have been moved to.

If you are backing up to a high-capacity removable drive (e.g. a Zip drive) and there is already an old copy of the project on the drive, then rename the existing, old project first (or move it into a folder or even delete it), then either copy the new one across or from within NVivo select **Save As...** and save it to the drive.

Job Search project

When you start a new project you have a choice of what to do first: import new documents or set up a coding structure. It might seem perverse to do the latter first, but if you already have some ideas, from previous theory or the project remit, about what nodes you will need then there is no reason why you cannot set them up without any documents to work on. The documents can be added afterwards. In most cases, however, you will probably want to work on documents and generate some, if not all, your nodes from them.

There are several ways to get documents into NVivo. You can just create a new blank document and start typing some content. You could do this to enter your field notes or transcribe a taped interview directly into the program. Alternatively, if you have prepared documents in a word processor then you will need to ensure they are in RTF or plain text format. A third option is to make proxy documents referring to the external data. These can be created and edited at any stage either in NVivo or as templates in a word processor. One of the features of NVivo is its flexibility. You can add new documents at any time and edit any that have already been added.

For the purposes of this introduction all the documents for the Job Search project were typed in Word and saved in RTF format in the Source Documents folder (see Figure 2.5). In addition to the 12 interviews there are documents on the data collection: one is an outline interview check list with prompts used by the interviewers, and one is a set of notes produced by the transcriber. There are also four documents that are committee minutes from meetings of the local government Employment Committee. These have been scanned from the originals and saved as RTF. The project also used a government report. This will be referred to by a proxy document. The template for this is stored here too. Finally, the Codes document is a list of possible nodes based on the principal questions used in the interviews and there is a document containing the brief for the original study.

```
Source Documents                          _ □ ×
File  Edit  View  Help
Name                            Size   Type
June.rtf                        51KB   Rich Text Format
Harry.rtf                       50KB   Rich Text Format
Susan.rtf                       26KB   Rich Text Format
Pauline.rtf                     25KB   Rich Text Format
Dave.rtf                        22KB   Rich Text Format
John.rtf                        21KB   Rich Text Format
Andy.rtf                        20KB   Rich Text Format
Mary.rtf                        18KB   Rich Text Format
Ahmed.rtf                       14KB   Rich Text Format
Jim.rtf                         14KB   Rich Text Format
Tom.rtf                         13KB   Rich Text Format
Sharon.rtf                      12KB   Rich Text Format
Emplymt Cttee mins 10 95.rtf    11KB   Rich Text Format
Proxy Templ Govt Report.rtf     10KB   Rich Text Format
Emplymt Cttee mins 1 96.rtf      9KB   Rich Text Format
Emplymt Cttee mins 2 96.rtf      9KB   Rich Text Format
Emplymt. Cttee mins 12 95.rtf    9KB   Rich Text Format
Unemplymt Study Brief.rtf        6KB   Rich Text Format
Codes.rtf                        6KB   Rich Text Format
Job Search prompt list.rtf       4KB   Rich Text Format
Transcription notes.rtf          3KB   Rich Text Format

21 object(s)          343KB
```

Figure 2.5   Files for the Job Search project

To import new documents into a project

1 On the Project Pad click on the **Documents** tab and then the **Make a Project Document** button, or from the menu bar choose **Documents:New Document Wizard**. This opens the New Document Wizard (see Figure 2.6).

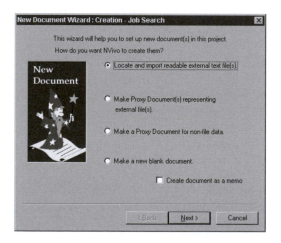

Figure 2.6   The New Document Wizard

2 There are four options. To create documents from Word files (transcribed interviews, minutes etc.) make sure the first button **Locate and import readable external text file(s)** is selected. Click **Next>**.

3 A standard Windows file selector dialog appears (see Figure 2.7). Use this
   to select the folder where you have stored your files and select the file
   you wish to import. You can use Ctrl-click to select more than one file. If
   you are importing plain text files you may need to change the pull-down
   file type menu at the bottom of the dialog to show .txt files. Click on
   Open.

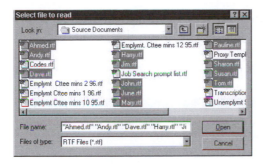

Figure 2.7   Windows file selector dialog in NVivo showing several files selected

4 The New Document Wizard now presents a choice of how the name and
   description for the file should be established. The options are:
   (a) Use the source file name as document name and first paragraph as
        description.
   (b) Read the first paragraph as name, second as description.
   (c) Read marked-up title and description paragraphs.
   (d) None of these, NVivo will prompt for a name and description.
5 Choose appropriately, depending how you have set up your original file(s)
   – see Chapter 3.
6 Click on **Finish**. An Import Documents progress dialog shows briefly
   while your documents are imported and then the Wizard closes.

When you import a document a copy of it is created in the
project and the original is left intact. You can store, move, back
up etc. these originals as you wish without affecting the NVivo
project. You can also make a new document in the project
(either a proxy or an empty document for working on later)
that does not come from a file you have already produced. This
will be stored in the project with all the other documents. You
can create new documents or delete existing ones at any time in
the life of a project.

The Document Explorer

To inspect the documents you have imported you will need to use the Document Explorer.

To open the Document Explorer

1 On the Project Pad click on the **Documents** tab and then the **Explore all Project Documents** button, or from the menu bar choose **Documents:Explore Documents**.
2 The Document Explorer will open (see Figure 2.8).

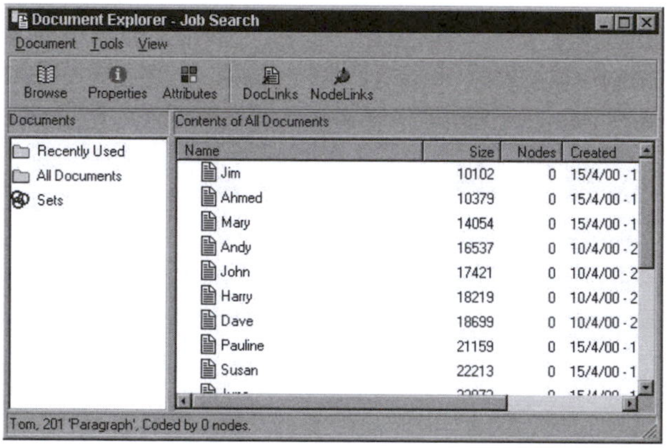

Figure 2.8   The Document Explorer

The Document Explorer acts rather like the Windows Explorer program. To the left is a list of collections of documents. Click on one of these to see what's in it in the right-hand pane and double-click to open up the hierarchy in the left-hand pane. The right-hand pane can be displayed as icons or as a list. Use the **View** menu. From the Explorer you can select a document and browse its contents (in order to code it or link it to other documents) or inspect its properties. The toolbar at the top of the window gives access to the most common functions of the Document Explorer (see Figure 2.9).

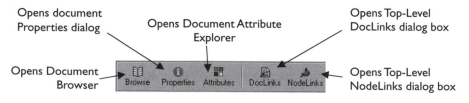

Opens document
Properties dialog

Opens Document Attribute
Explorer

Opens Top-Level
DocLinks dialog box

Opens Document
Browser

Opens Top-Level
NodeLinks dialog box

Figure 2.9   The Document Explorer toolbar

The contextual menu

A very useful feature of NVivo is the contextual menus. These are accessed by clicking on an object with the right mouse button. Most objects in NVivo – documents, text, nodes, DataBites and so on – have an associated pop-up menu that contains the most frequently used functions associated with that object. In fact, many functions can be selected in one of four ways: menu bar, toolbar button, keyboard shortcut or context-sensitive pop-up menu. As you become familiar with NVivo you will find yourself using a combination of these methods best suited to your own style.

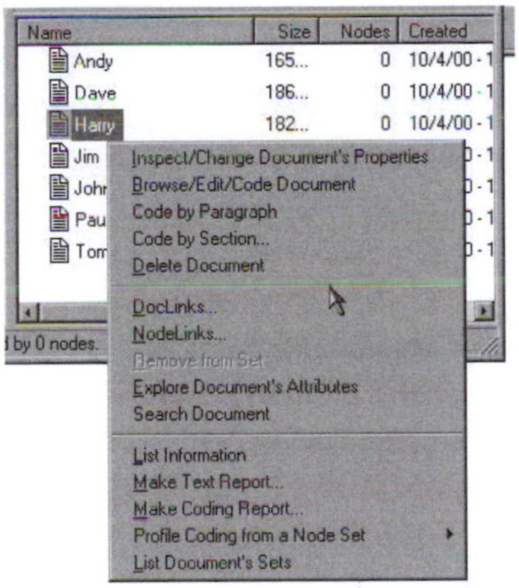

Figure 2.10   Document contextual menu

For example, Figure 2.10 shows the contextual menu for a document in the Document Browser. This reproduces most of the functions found in the Document menu in the Document Explorer menu bar. To show when you can use the contextual menu a small icon, will appear in the text.

The Document Browser

To inspect and edit the contents of a document

1   In the Document Explorer click on a document to select it. Then either:
   (a)   click on the **Browse** button in the toolbar; or
   (b)   use the right mouse button to get the document's contextual menu and choose **Browse/Edit/Code Document**; or

(c) choose **Document:Browse/Edit/Code Document** from the menu bar; or

(d) press Ctrl+B on the keyboard.

2 The Document Browser opens (see Figure 2.11).

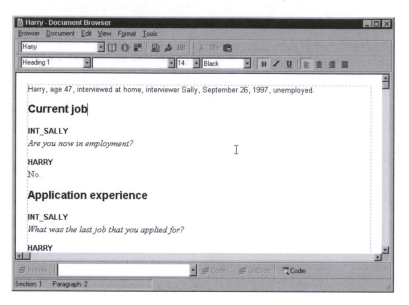

Figure 2.11 The Document Browser

The Document Browser is a mini word processor. You can edit and format your document with many of the facilities you will be familiar with in your usual word processor. In addition, there are several other features that can be accessed from here (see Figure 2.11). Just below the menu bar is a toolbar of frequently used functions (see Figure 2.12). The first of these is a pull-down menu of other documents, showing the most recently used at the top of the menu. This is a quick way of moving from one document to another as you are browsing their contents or coding text. Below this is a toolbar of formatting tools. This allows you to apply fonts, text size, text colour, to make bold, italic or underlined selected text and to apply styles and set the justification of paragraphs (see Figure 2.13).

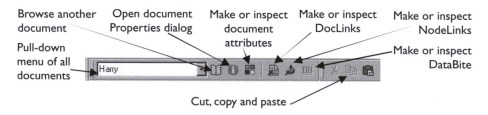

Figure 2.12 The Document Browser functions toolbar

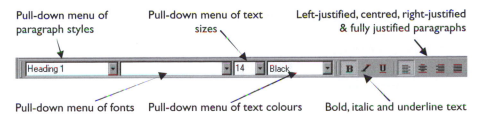

Pull-down menu of paragraph styles

Pull-down menu of text sizes

Left-justified, centred, right-justified & fully justified paragraphs

Pull-down menu of fonts   Pull-down menu of text colours   Bold, italic and underline text

Figure 2.13   The Document Browser formatting toolbar

At the bottom of the document browser window are tools for coding text. We shall return to these later in this chapter.

The parts of the document

The interviews that have just been imported to the project were formatted before saving as RTF. They were divided into subject sections and the section titles were inserted into the interview and given the style 'Heading 1'. Before each question the name of the interviewer was inserted and before each answer by the respondent the name of the respondent was inserted, each as a separate paragraph and each with the style 'Heading 2'. The text of the questions and of the answers was given the style 'Normal'. The short description at the start of the file was given the style 'Description', so that it would be recognized as such by NVivo when the document was imported. The use of styles will be discussed in more detail in Chapter 3. NVivo interprets the heading styles and their implicit hierarchy when importing the documents and can display this in the Document Explorer. See Chapter 4 for more detail on how to do this. Double-click on the All Documents folder and then click once on the appropriate document to see the hierarchy in the right-hand pane (see Figure 2.14). The link between these document sections, their appearance in the Document Browser and the styles applied to the paragraphs is shown in Figure 2.15. If you have structured documents such as structured interviews, sectioned reports and so on then this sectioning of the document in NVivo can be of great assistance. The sections of documents displayed in the Document Explorer act like chapter headings for the document. You can jump straight to that section of the document.

To jump to a document section

1 Click on the required document in the left-hand pane of the Document Explorer.
2 Right-click on the appropriate section in the right-hand pane of the Document Explorer.

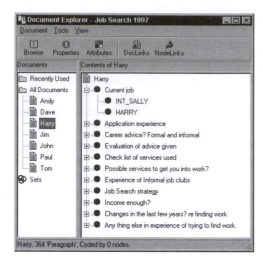

Figure 2.14   The Document Explorer showing document sections

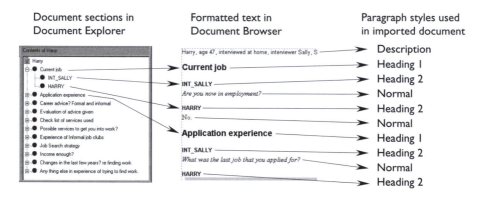

Figure 2.15   Relationship between document sections, document display and styles applied

3 Select **Browse/Edit/Code** from the one-item contextual menu 🔲.
4 The Document Browser is opened, the document is scrolled down to the required section and the section title is highlighted (selected).

Browse the document, edit and change style

The Document Browser can be used to read and edit the document. It is also used to code text, as we shall see later. Use the Document Browser like a word processor. You can delete, add and edit text. If you change the heading styles of a document that has sections indicated by headings, then this will be reflected in the section contents in the Document Explorer. For example, if you change a paragraph from 'Heading 1' style to 'Normal' then not only will the display in the Browser change but the contents in the Explorer will no longer show a section for that paragraph. Changing back the text will reinstate the section.

Sometimes in NVivo the display does not update immediately. You need to close the window and reopen it, or switch to another node or document and then back again. That is normally sufficient to update the display.

Document properties

You can use the Document Explorer to inspect the properties of a document, such as its description, last date edited and icon colour.

To inspect the properties of a document

1 Select the document in the Explorer

2 Click on the **Properties** button Properties .

3 The document Properties dialog opens (see Figure 2.16).

Harry - Properties

General | Icon Color |

Name:
Harry

Description:
Harry, age 47, interviewed at home, interviewer Sally,
September 26, 1997, unemployed.

Created: 10/4/00 - 20:17:44
Modified: 10/4/00 - 20:17:59

Owner: Administrator

☐ This document is a Memo

OK   Cancel   Apply

Figure 2.16   The document Properties dialog

From here you can inspect and edit the name and description of the document, inspect when it was created and last modified, who owns it (important in team projects) and (by clicking on the tab at the top of the dialog) change the colour of its icon. The latter might be used to indicate the state of coding for the document. One colour could indicate no coding done, another could indicate outline coding done, and another indicate detailed coding done, for instance.

 If you have created the description automatically when the document was imported using the 'Description' style, then changing the description in this dialog will not update the paragraph(s) that appear in the document seen in the Document Browser and vice versa.

Make a report on a document

If you want to have a copy on your hard disk of a document in the project (e.g. if you have edited it in NVivo) or want to do some coding away from the computer and need a hard copy, then you will need to produce a report on the document.

To make a document report

1 In the Document Explorer select the document you want to make a report for.
2 Either from the Document menu or from the document's contextual menu △ choose **Make Text Report**.
3 In the dialog that appears make sure all three tick boxes are selected. Click on **OK**.
4 A progress bar appears while the program creates the report, and then opens it in a text editor.
5 The text editor has some simple word-processing functions, including the ability to print the document. Alternatively, you can save it to disk and then print it. By default it will be saved in the Results folder of your project folder.
6 If you want to save to disk you can choose to save as plain text or RTF. Use the pull-down menu at the bottom of the File Save dialog to choose your required format.

The report includes paragraph numbers at the start of each paragraph, followed by section numbers if the paragraph starts a new section. The paragraph numbers are useful if you code 'off-line' and then want to enter coding by paragraph. See Chapter 4 for more details.

Nodes

A node in NVivo is a way of bringing together ideas, thoughts and definitions about your data, along with selected passages of text. Passages of text from one or more documents are connected to a node because they are examples of the idea or concept it represents. This process is called coding the text at a node. This brings together passages of text that are about the same thing or indicate similar ideas, concepts, actions, descriptions and so on. For example, by coding them at a node you could connect together all the passages of text where a surprising theme you discovered in the documents is recurring, so you can browse and think about it. Coding is a fundamental activity of most kinds of qualitative analysis and will be discussed in more detail in Chapter 4.

As well as its name and the passages of text to which it is connected, a node can have a definition and any number of memos that contain ideas, hunches and other notes about the node or the text it codes. As I noted above, you can create nodes even before you import any documents. This is possible where you have some ideas beforehand about what the significant themes of your analysis will be. Having established the node in NVivo, you could then start to look for examples in the text that could be linked with the node. Alternatively, you can discover significant ideas in the texts while reading them and create nodes from them. Typically, most qualitative researchers do both.

NVivo distinguishes three ways of keeping nodes: free nodes, tree nodes and case nodes. Free nodes are the simplest and appear as a simple list in the program. Like all nodes, they have a title, icon (with colour), description, and one or two other properties such as the dates when created and modified. Tree nodes, which we shall examine in more detail in Chapter 4, have all the properties of free nodes, but in addition are organized into a hierarchy or tree shown in the Node Browser like the file and folder hierarchy in Windows Explorer. Free nodes can be made into tree nodes (and vice versa). The process of constructing a hierarchy of nodes is often a central activity in qualitative analysis, as we shall see in Chapter 7. Case nodes are used for organizing coding about cases. They can refer to all the text for a particular case or can be used to organize these cases into case types (e.g. unemployed interviewees). We shall look in more detail at the use of case nodes in Chapter 8.

Node Explorer

You can create nodes and generally manipulate your system of nodes using the Node Explorer.

To open the Node Explorer

1 Either:
  (a) from the Project Pad, click on the **Nodes** tab and then the **Explore all Project Nodes** button; or
  (b) from the menu bar choose **Nodes:Explore Nodes**.
2 The Node Explorer opens (see Figure 2.17).

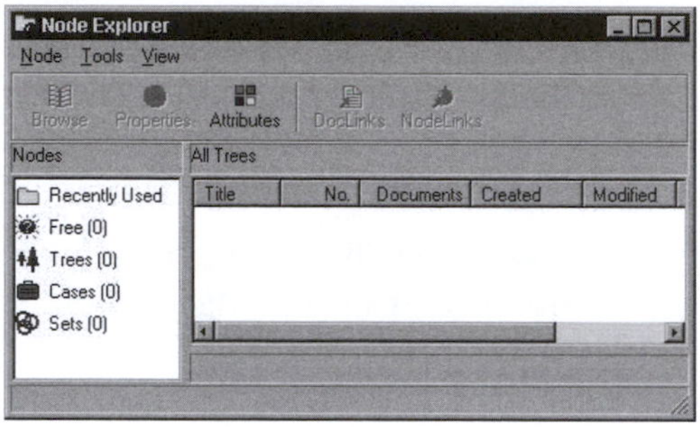

Figure 2.17 The Node Explorer

Like the Document Explorer, this operates like the Windows Explorer. On the left is a list of nodes. This is an expandable and collapsible listing and will reflect the hierarchy of any tree nodes you have established. For a new project this will show no nodes against each category (indicated by the 0 in brackets against each node type). As well as the three types of nodes discussed above, you will see icons for Sets of nodes and for Recently Used nodes. The latter is a quick way of getting to nodes that you have just used and is particularly useful when you have developed large numbers of nodes. Sets of nodes are a way of organizing your nodes into thematic groupings that can be used, for example, in searching.

From the Node Explorer you can quickly create some nodes at which you can later code some text. However, the node doesn't have to have any text coded at it. You can simply use it as a way of recording your theoretical ideas about the data, for example in linked memos.

To create a free node in the Node Explorer

1 Select **Create Free Node** from the contextual menu 🄰 on the Free node folder.
2 A new node is inserted below the Free node and indented one level.
3 Click once on the name. You can now type in a name for this node (see Figure 2.18).

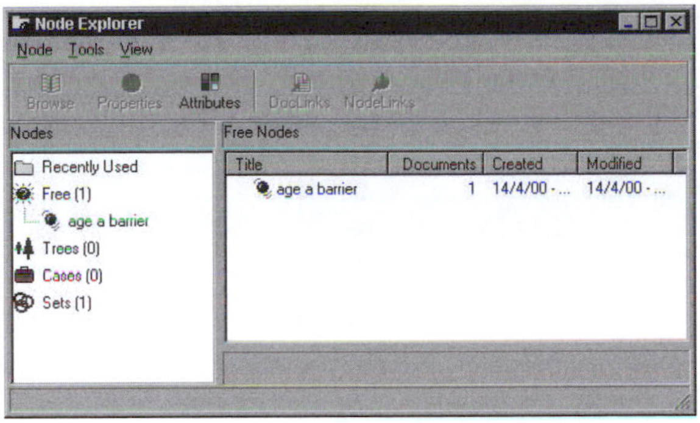

Figure 2.18 Node Explorer with one new free node

Alternatively, you can create new nodes from the Create Node dialog that is accessed from the Project Pad or from the Node Explorer. This gives you an opportunity to save a description of the node as you create it. If you have used the method shown above you can add a description using Properties dialog window (see the instructions in Chapter 4). It is important to write a description, especially as you create more nodes and if you are working as part of a team. As the number of nodes grows you will find not only that you need to refer to the description to remember exactly what the node was meant to be referring to, but also that you start to create very similar nodes. You can use the descriptions as one way of telling whether the nodes should be combined or are really about different ideas.

To create a new free node using the Create Node dialog

1 Either:
   (a) click on the Node tab in the Project Pad and then on the **Make a Project Node** button; or
   (b) in the Project Pad, select **Nodes:Create Node** from the menu bar; or
   (c) in the Node Explorer, select **Tools:Create Nodes** from the menu bar; or
   (d) in the Node Explorer, press Ctrl-N on the keyboard.
2 This opens the Create Node dialog (see Figure 2.19).
3 Click on the **Free** tab.
4 Type in a title for the node (e.g. Careers Information Service) and a description.
5 Click on **Create**.
6 Repeat stages 4–5 for any further free nodes you want to create.

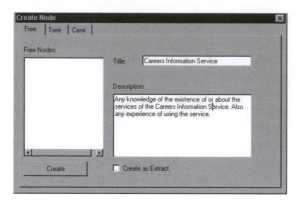

Figure 2.19 The Create Node dialog

Other ways of creating nodes

The key to much qualitative analysis is keeping close to the data, the texts, documents etc. you have collected and transcribed. NVivo provides a way of creating nodes and linking them with coded text that starts from the document on view in the Document Browser. This uses the speed coding bar at the bottom of the Browser window (see Figure 2.20).

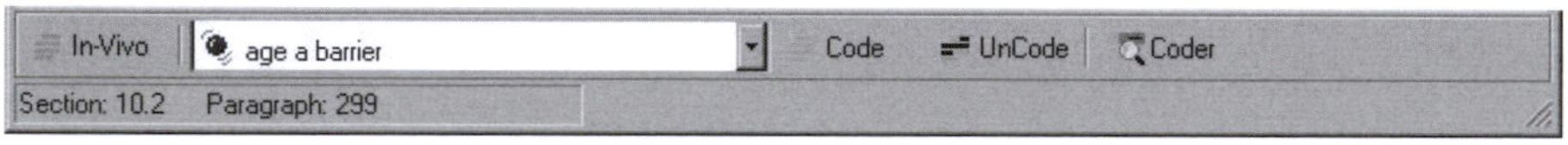

Figure 2.20 The Document Browser speed coding bar

The simplest procedure is the creation of in vivo codes. The term 'in vivo' comes from grounded theory (Glaser and Strauss 1967). It refers to the use of words taken directly from actors in the setting to name the nodes used. For instance, respondents might use the term 'at my age' to refer to the idea that they have found age a problem in getting a job; 'at my age' can then be used as the name of the node. In vivo nodes have two characteristics, analytic usefulness and imagery. The first arises in part in the same way that any node is analytically useful because it can be related to other categorizations of the data, but it also arises because generally in vivo nodes have a very clear meaning assigned to them by people in the setting. Imagery is useful because it quickly indicates to the analyst and the reader what the node refers to. Their colour and vividness mean they are seldom forgotten by readers (or analysts!).

To create an in vivo code

1 From the Document Explorer, select a document and click on the
   Browse button to open it in the Document Browser.
2 Read the text until you find the word or words you want to use as the
   name of an in vivo code.
3 Select these words in the browser (see Figure 2.21).
4 Click on the **In-Vivo** button at the left of the speed coding bar.
5 A new free node named with the text you selected is created and it
   appears in the speed coding bar just to the right of the **In-Vivo** button.

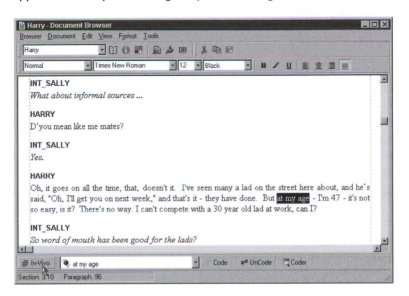

Figure 2.21   Using the Document Browser for in vivo coding

At the moment only the words you highlighted in the text are coded at the
node you have just created. Commonly you will want more than just those
words coded. For example, you may also want the surrounding sentences
that constitute the context of the in vivo phrase coded at the node. To do this
you use the same process as you would to code some text at any node that
already exists.

To code text at an existing, recently used node

1 In the Document Browser find and select the text you want to code. You
   now have two choices:
   (a) If the node you want to use is showing in the pull-down list in the
       speed coding bar at the bottom of the window, just click on the
       Code button in the speed coding bar (see Figure 2.22). This will be

the case if you have just created an in vivo node and are now extending the text to which it refers.

(b) If the node is not showing in the pull-down list, then click on the list and select the node you want to use. Then click on the **Code** button.

2 The selected text is now coded at the selected node.

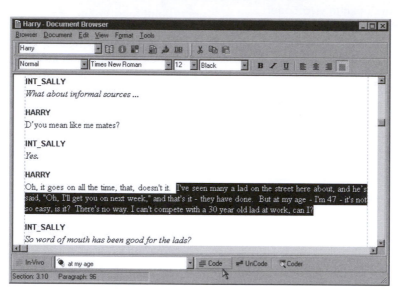

Figure 2.22 Coding selected text to an existing node

On the other hand, you might be reading the text when you come across a passage you want to code, but where you haven't yet created a node. In this case do the following.

To create a new node and code text from the Document Browser

1 In the Document Browser find and select the text you want to code.
2 Type the name of the node you want to create. You will find that if you have some text selected and then you type, what you type is entered into the node pull-down menu in the speed coding bar (see Figure 2.23).
3 Click on the **Code** button in the speed coding bar.
4 A new node is created and the text you had selected in the document is coded at that node.

When you create a node from the Document Browser, you don't have a chance immediately to give it a definition. You can do this by using the Properties dialog from the Node Explorer (see Chapter 4).

From the Node Explorer you can also display the text that has been coded

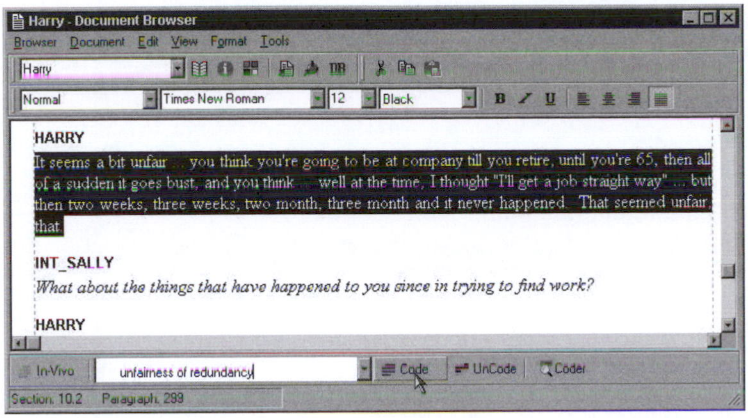

Figure 2.23 Creating a new node and coding selected text to it

at a node. This is a key activity in qualitative research as you can begin to see the range and variation in views and expressions. You can look for significant relationships with other aspects of the data set such as case-by-case variation and differences by attributes such as gender and age. This is done using the Node Browser. This looks similar to the Document Browser and you will find similar buttons in the toolbar at the top as well as the speed coding bar at the bottom.

To open the Node Browser

1 Select a node you want to browse, then either
   (a) click on the **Browse** button, or
   (b) select **Node:Browse/Code Node** from the menu bar, or
   (c) press Ctrl-B.
2 The Node Browser opens, showing all the text that has been coded at the node, along with headings indicating the documents they come from and what section and paragraph is coded (see Figure 2.24).

Initially the Node Browser shows just the text that you have coded at the selected node. On reading through the text you might decide you want to see more or less of the text than just the phrases you have coded. In the Node Browser you can extend or reduce the text displayed.

To extend or reduce the text displayed from one passage of coding

1 Click in the piece of text you want to extend or reduce your view of. Then either:
   (a) from the menu bar select **View:Passage Contents Display** and

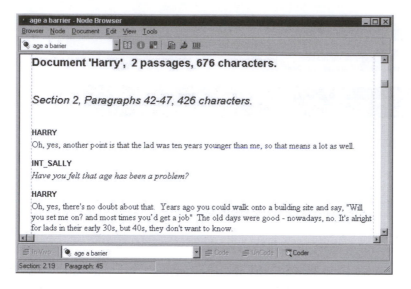

Figure 2.24 The Node Browser

from the pull-down menu that displays select the spread or reduction you want. For instance if you want to see the entire section of which the coded text is a part, select **In Enclosing Section**; or

(b) select the spread or reduction you want from the selected text's contextual menu .

2 The text displayed in the Node Browser changes to reflect your choice.
3 If you have chosen to display more text, then the extra is displayed in green or grey to indicate that it is not actually coded at the node in question.

Coding on

If, having displayed more text in the Node Browser, you want to extend the text that is coded, you can select it and click on the **Code** button. Alternatively, if you decide that not all the text currently coded should be, you can select the text you want to remove from coding and click on the **UnCode** button.
Moreover, just as in the Document Browser, you can create new nodes using the speed coding bar for further coding.

Another way of seeing the context of the passages you have coded that appear in the Node Browser is to jump to the text of the document from which the coded text comes.

To jump to the document from a passage of coded text in the Node Browser

1 Click in the piece of text you want to investigate the context of. Then either,
   (a) from its contextual menu △, select **Browse/Edit/Code Document**, or
   (b) from the menu bar select **Document:Browse/Edit/Code Document**.
2 The Document Browser opens with the required document displayed. The contents are automatically scrolled to the point where your coded text begins and the actual coded text is highlighted (selected) – see Figure 2.25.

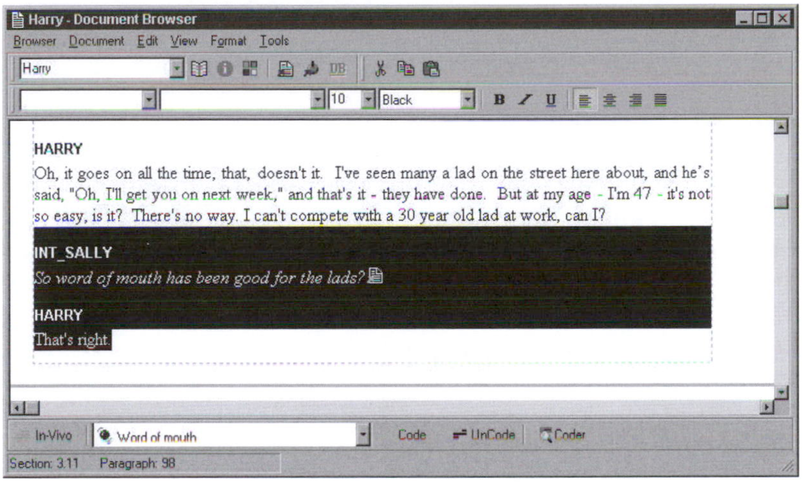

Figure 2.25   The Document Browser, showing coded text highlighted after a jump from the Node Browser

Another common activity when analysing coded text is to compare the passages coded at two or more nodes. From the Node Browser, you can quickly jump to browse the text coded at another node.

To jump to another node from the Node Browser

1 If the node is one you have used recently, either:
   (a) select the node from the list in the **Browser** menu. A new Node Browser window opens showing the text coded at the chosen node; or
   (b) select the node from the pull-down list of recently used nodes in the button bar just below the menu bar. The contents of the current

Node Browser window are replaced with those for the text coded at the chosen node.
2 If the node you want is not displayed in either list – only up to the last 10 are shown – then, either:
   (a) go back to the Node Explorer and select the node from there and click on the Browse button; or
   (b) use the Coder. This will be discussed in Chapter 4.

Node report

As in the case of documents you may want to have a copy of the text coded at a node so that, for example, you can include it in the report of the analysis you are writing. You can, of course, cut and paste text from the Node Browser window into your word processor, but sometimes it is more convenient to create a computer file.

To create a node report

1 From the Node Explorer, select the node you want a report on. Either:
   (a) select **Node:Make Coding Report. . .** from the menu bar; or
   (b) select **Make Coding Report. . .** from the node's contextual menu .
2 This opens the Node Coding Report Setup window (see Figure 2.26).

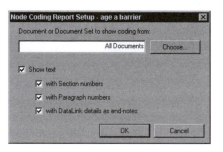

Figure 2.26 The Node Coding Report Setup window

3 You can choose to include coding from all documents or just a subset of them. Click on the **Choose** button and select those you want.
4 You can also choose whether to include the text and other information in the report.
5 Click on **OK**.
6 A progress bar appears while the program compiles the report, then a text editor window opens with the report showing (see Figure 2.27).
7 You can print or save this document using the **File** menu. If you save it you need to select where. By default reports are saved in the Results

subfolder of your project folder in RTF. They can be opened again in NVivo or with any word processor.

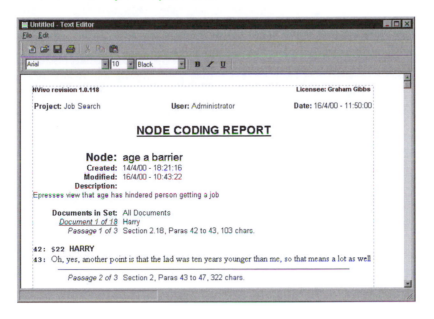

Figure 2.27 A node coding report in the Text Editor

The report shows all the information you asked for, along with all the properties of the node (what you get in the node Properties dialog) and the coded text, if you asked for it.

Searching

NVivo has a wide range of facilities for searching text and nodes. Searching texts will be covered in more detail in Chapter 6 and searching nodes in Chapter 7. For now we shall just look at one simple example. The most important thing to recognize about searching in NVivo is that when you do a search of whatever kind, a new node is created and the results – the text that is found – are coded at that new node. (The one exception to this is where you create a new document set of the finds – we shall examine this option in Chapter 6.) Thus, for example, if you search for a word, say 'wages', across all documents then the program creates a new node or, if you request it, codes at an existing node. If you opt for a new node the program creates one called 'Single Text Lookup' as a subnode of the top level node 'Search Results'. (The latter is created if it does not already exist.) As we shall see in later chapters, in NVivo the results of almost all analytic activities like searching will create a new node or set that can itself be the subject of further analysis. This is an important aspect of NVivo and is referred to as 'system closure' by the authors of the program.

To do a simple text search

1 In the Project Pad, click on the **Search Project Database** button.
2 This opens the Search Tool (see Figure 2.28). At the top of this is a text box that will contain the description of the search you have specified. Below this are five buttons that determine the search operation and enable you to set up the search criteria.

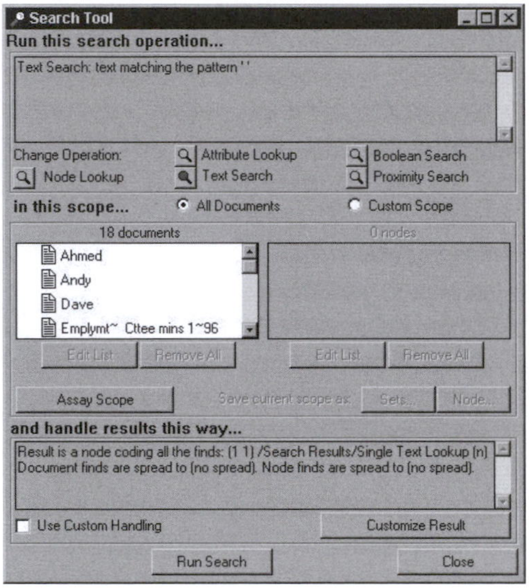

Figure 2.28   The Search Tool

3 Click on the **Text Search** button.
4 This opens the Text Search window (see Figure 2.29). Text searching has some very powerful features, and we shall look at them in more detail in Chapter 6.
5 For now just type in the word you want to find into the text box at the top of the dialog, 'children' in this example. Note that this is a pull-down menu of the most recent items you've searched for and it gives a quick way to redo a search.
6 Ensure that in the advanced options, **Regular Search** is selected and that, at the bottom of the window, the results are specified as being returned as **All finds as a node**.
7 Click on **OK**.
8 You are returned to the Search Tool. You will notice that the description at the top now specifies the word(s) you have just entered.

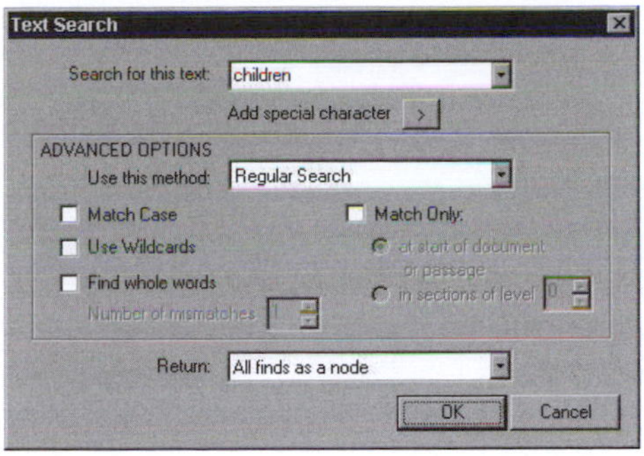

Figure 2.29   Text Search specification window

9 Below the Change Operation buttons is an area of the window where
   you specify the scope of the search – what documents or nodes will be
   searched. For the moment ensure that the **All Documents** radio
   button is selected.
10 At the bottom of the dialog is an area where you specify how you want
   the results of the search to be handled. If you are searching for just one
   word, what gets coded at the new node is just the text of the word. If
   you want to code, say, the whole paragraph where the word occurs then
   you will need to customize the result. For the moment ensure that the
   Use Custom Handling tick box is not selected.
11 Click on the **Run Search** button at the bottom of the window.
12 A dialog appears showing the search has been completed and asking
   what you want done with the results. You can choose to **Show Node
   in Explorer** or not and to **Browse Node** or not. Choose both.
13 Click **OK**.

The Node Browser is opened showing the text now coded at the new node
created by the search, and the Node Explorer is also opened showing the
new node that has been created as a child of the node Search Results (see
Figure 2.30). It is called 'Single Text Lookup *n*' (where the *n* is a number
which is omitted if it is the first search you have done). Notice that in the
bottom right-hand part of the Node Explorer the node definition shows how
many documents are coded, and that the node was the result of a text search
with details of how it was done.

The Node Browser shows that the new node is coding just the words that
were searched for and found. Sometimes this is just what you want. You
may, for instance, be searching for a technical term and are interested in just
the fact it was used. However, more commonly you will use the search tool
as a way of quickly finding text that discusses a topic of interest. In that case
you may well want to code more than just the text you have found. You can
do that one find at a time by using the technique explained above, namely

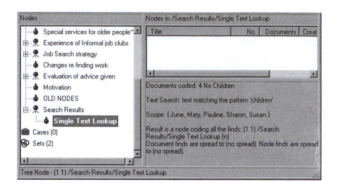

Figure 2.30   Part of the Node Explorer showing a new search result node

click one of the found words, then from its contextual menu ⌂ select **View Enclosing Paragraph** (or **Section**). However, you can show the context of all the finds at once. Select all the text in the Node Browser window. Do that using the **Edit:Select All** menu item (or press Ctrl-A on the keyboard). Now if you choose to view the enclosing paragraph (using the **View** menu or the selected text's contextual menu ⌂), this will be done for all the finds at this node. (This may take a few seconds.) See Figure 2.31. Notice the found words are still in black and the surrounding text (that is not yet coded) is in green or grey.

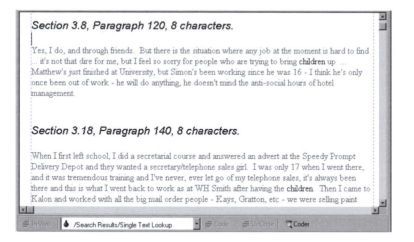

Figure 2.31   Part of the Node Browser showing finds with enclosing paragraphs

Refining the coding at a node

As I argued earlier, qualitative research involves the constant review and development of ideas. Using NVivo encourages this as it is easy to display and review text coded at a node in its context. The text search just described just codes single terms at a node. What you need to do now is review these terms in their context in order to determine whether additional passages surrounding the terms should be coded at the node in order to develop a more meaningful node.

Do this immediately after a text search. First, show the context of the finds in the manner just described. You can now read the text and select the part of the phrase or sentence(s) that you want to code at the node. Select the text and click on the **Code** button in the speed coding bar. If a find is irrelevant you can take it out by selecting the found word (in black) and clicking on the **UnCode** button. If you extend the coding the text turns black to indicate it is now coded and if you uncode a find it turns green or grey to indicate it is no longer coded. If you have reworked the coding at a node in this way then it will make sense to rename the node and move it somewhere else in your node system.

To rename and move a node

1 In the Node Explorer, click twice (slowly) on the name of the node.
2 You can now edit the name. Type in something appropriate, e.g. 'Children work break'.
3 Press ↵. The node is renamed.
4 To move the node elsewhere in the node tree, first find a place for it to go.
5 Drag the node (or its name) to the node under which you want to attach it ('Changes re finding work' in the example). Notice the cursor changes shape to a white arrow with a small grey box as you move over the nodes where you can attach it, and has an extra small box with a plus sign in it if you can add it to a different folder such as Cases. See Figure 2.32.

There are several other ways you can use text search to set up new nodes. We shall look at those in Chapter 6. As I mentioned at the start of this section, text is not the only thing you can search for. The Search Tool enables you to look for text, nodes, attributes and even DataBites and linked documents. All these can be combined so that you can, for example, search for any one of a selection of words in passages coded at a specific node that occurs in documents with a particular attribute. When combined with sets and node trees the Search Tool is a very powerful and central support for qualitative analysis. We shall examine such uses in more detail in Chapters 7, 8 and 9.

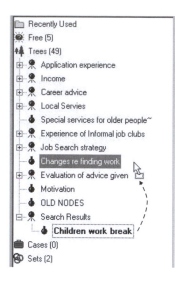

Figure 2.32 Moving a renamed search node to become a child of another tree node

 From this point on, for the sake of brevity, the step-by-step instructions will not show the alternative ways in which tasks can be initiated in NVivo. Bear in mind, though, that there may be many different ways of doing something. You can use the main window menu or an item's contextual menu ⌂, and there is often a toolbar button or a keyboard shortcut available. Many actions can start from the Project Pad, and most users find they continually go there to begin activities.

Conclusion

We have covered a lot of ground in this chapter. You should now have a grasp of the key features of NVivo such as the Node and Document Explorers. You have seen how both documents and nodes can be browsed using their respective Browsers, how to import and make documents, how to create new nodes, modify text coded at nodes and how to undertake simple text searching. NVivo is a flexible and open program and allows you to do things in a variety of ways. This allows you to add documents when you are ready and create nodes whenever you want. You can use the software to bring together documents, coding and your theoretical ideas and add to them in any order. This flexibility in how the program can be used encourages exploration of the data and an iterative approach to analysis. We shall look at what this means for qualitative analysis in more detail in succeeding chapters.

Further reading

Bazeley, P. and Richards, L. (2000) *The NVivo Qualitative Project Book*. London: Sage. (A guide to using NVivo on a provided project. Assumes you have a good knowledge of qualitative analysis.)

Coffey, A. and Atkinson, P. (1996) *Making Sense of Qualitative Data Analysis: Complementary Research Strategies*. London and Thousand Oaks, CA: Sage. (A general introduction to qualitative analysis that demonstrates approaches using a single worked example project.)

Dey, I. (1993) *Qualitative Data Analysis: A User-Friendly Guide for Social Scientists*. London and New York: Routledge. (An accessible guide to analytic techniques, especially suitable for those using CAQDAS.)

King, N. (1998) Template analysis, in G. Symon and C. Cassell (eds) *Qualitative Methods and Analysis in Organizational Research*. London: Sage. (A concise, step-by-step explanation of one kind of phenomenological analysis based on themes.)

Miles, M.B. and Huberman, A.M. (1994) *Qualitative Data Analysis: A Sourcebook of New Methods*, 2nd edn. Beverly Hills, CA: Sage. (A weighty, but classic text on qualitative analysis techniques. Relatively weak on approaches focusing on language use, but very strong on techniques using tables and diagrams.)

Richards, L. (1999) *Using NVivo in Qualitative Research*. London: Sage. (This is a version of one of the guides that is provided with the software and can also be purchased separately. It is full of suggestions and hints on how to use NVivo in analysis.)

Richards, L. (1999) Data alive! The thinking behind NVivo, *Qualitative Health Research*, 9(3): 412–28. (For those familiar with qualitative analysis software, this explains some of the new features of NVivo.)

Silverman, D. (ed.) (1999) *Doing Qualitative Research: A Practical Handbook*. London: Sage. (A very accessible general text that includes some discussion of analysis and computer use.)

Willig, C. (2001) *Introducing Qualitative Research in Psychology: Adventures in Theory and Method*. Buckingham: Open University Press. (A very readable introduction to methods of relevance to psychology, and contains several worked examples of qualitative analysis.)

3 Data preparation

In the past, qualitative researchers preparing their word-processed files for use in CAQDAS had to give thought to a lot of issues. They had to strip out of the text any use of fonts, colours, styles etc. as most programs could only read plain text, and they had to decide what their hermeneutic unit would be. This means they had to decide whether the chunks of text they coded would be lines, sentences or paragraphs. None of these restrictions applies to files used in NVivo. You can include fonts, sizes, styles and colour and you can select and code any number of words or letters (see Figure 3.1).

Nevertheless, you still need to do some preparation before moving the texts into the program, and it is wise to do as much preparation in a word processor as possible as they have a much wider range of facilities for editing than NVivo. Although it is less fussy about the format of the text, NVivo does require the files to be in a particular format. This is rich text format, and many word processors can save files in this format. Sadly, RTF is a variable standard and the only software guaranteed to work directly with NVivo is Microsoft Word. Although programs like Ami Pro and WordPerfect can save in this format, they are not always compatible with NVivo. If one of these is the main software you use for your transcription (or is used by your audio typist), then you have two options. Complete all the preparation detailed below in that program and then either find someone with a copy of Word or use your copy of WordPad (supplied with the Windows operating system). Save as RTF from the original program then open and resave each

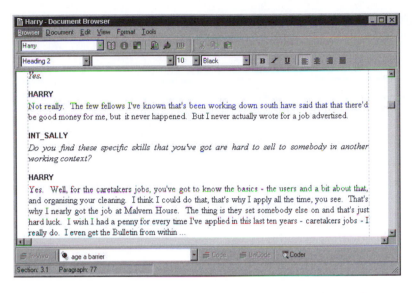

Figure 3.1   The Document Browser in NVivo, showing how a document appears

file using the copy of Word or WordPad. Alternatively, you can save as plain text and then embed the special symbols that indicate the various styles etc. in RTF using a text editor like WordPad. The NVivo manual explains how to do this. With this in mind, the discussion below will assume you are using Microsoft Word 97 or later for your document preparation.

To save your document as RTF in Word

Once you have finished preparing the text and have formatted it along the lines discussed below, you need to save it in RTF format.

1 Select **Save As. . .** from the **Edit** menu in Word.
2 At the bottom of the save file dialog that appears (Figure 3.2) pull down the **Save as type:** menu and select **Rich Text Format (*.rtf)**.
3 Give your document an appropriate name (this may be the same as you have used so far) and save it in an appropriate place. You may like to save all the RTF versions of your documents in a folder you have created for that purpose.

Along with checking for accuracy of transcription, you should use the word processor to check the spellings and grammar of your text as NVivo has neither facility. Not only should common English words be spelled correctly and consistently, but proper names and dialect and jargon terms should also be spelled consistently.

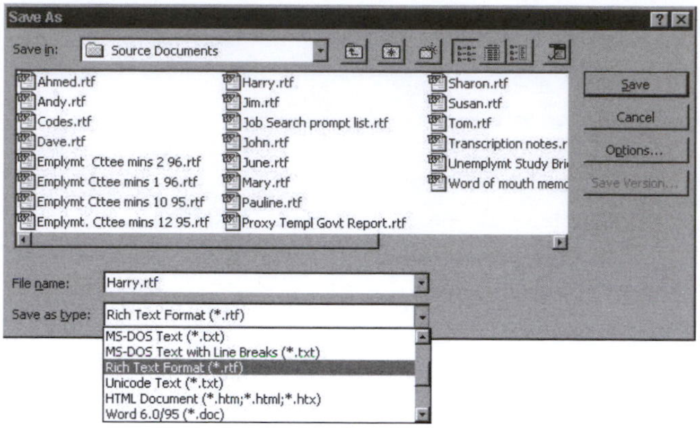

Figure 3.2 Save As dialog in Word

Styles

Not all the styles and formats available in Word can be used in NVivo documents. You can use any font, font size and bold, italic, underline and coloured text. You might use colour to indicate text of a certain kind, such as what was said in an interview when someone else was present (as opposed to when you were alone with the interviewee). Use bold, italic and underline as you would in a normal document to indicate structure, emphasis and significance. NVivo does not require you to keep a strict division between original data – the interview or field notes – and any comments, annotations and additions you make later. You can therefore include annotations in your document. You might want to use a different font and a different colour to indicate these.

To make good use of the section facility in NVivo, it helps if you are familiar with the use of styles. A style is a whole collection of text attributes together; when you apply a style to a passage of text, all these attributes are applied at once. For example, when you apply the built-in paragraph style 'Heading 1' to text, the whole paragraph will appear as Ariel font, size 14 points, bold text with 12 points spacing before the paragraph and 3 point spacing after it. Styles in Word are accessed from the pull-down list in the standard toolbar or from the dialog box produced by selecting **Style. . .** in the **Format** menu (see Figure 3.3).

NVivo uses styles in a similar way, but uses only a limited number of paragraph styles. These are:

Description
Normal
Heading 1 to 9 (i.e. you can have up to 9 levels of heading and sub-heading)
Title
Plain text

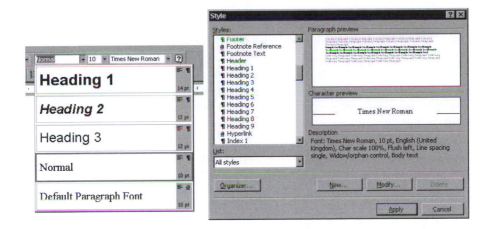

Figure 3.3 Styles in Word

Most of these are built-in Word styles, but Description is special to NVivo and if you want to use that style in Word you will need to create it.

There are several other features of Word's formatting of text that NVivo cannot use. For example, NVivo cannot recognize footnotes, page numbers and multiple columns and if you use them the program will ignore them. Tables and embedded objects such as pictures will cause the importation of documents to stop. Check with the Reference Guide that comes with NVivo if you are in doubt. If you have embedded objects such as images, sounds or video in your document, save them separately. You can then use DataBite links to connect them to the document in NVivo and open them from there. See Chapter 5 for details on how to do this.

Parts of the document

NVivo recognizes various parts of the document as significant for different purposes. In part this is to help select various sized chunks of the text. Thus the program provides a facility for selecting a word, a sentence, a paragraph or a section in the document. Paragraphs and sections are significant in other ways too. Both can be used for special kinds of coding and both can be used to extend the text displayed after a text search and for specifying nearness in proximity searching. It is therefore important to consider beforehand how you set up paragraphs and sections.

Paragraphs

As in Word, NVivo uses the hard carriage return (done by pressing the ↵ or **Enter** key on the keyboard) as an indication of where paragraphs end. In

Word you can see where these are by clicking on the ¶ button in the Standard toolbar. Paragraphs are of particular importance if you wish to code your documents 'off-line'. In most cases, researchers using CAQDAS code their documents while sitting at the computer. Techniques for this were introduced in Chapter 2 and will be examined in more detail in Chapter 4. However, in some circumstances you may want to be able to read, think about and code your texts away from the PC. For instance, you may want to distribute the text to members of a team, not all of whom have PCs or NVivo, or you may just want to mark up your coding ideas using a printed version of the documents. This is what I refer to as 'on the beach' coding, since you can sit on the beach with the printed documents and some coloured pens and code the text. Sunny, sandy beaches are not good places for laptop computers! NVivo has a special way of enabling you to enter text coded this way as long as you have coded only paragraphs. If you want to do this you need to ensure that the way you have divided the document into paragraphs gives you reasonably sized, meaningful components. For example, you may want to divide up some of the longer speeches into shorter paragraphs that reflect the move to a new topic within the speech.

Sections

The division of the document into sections in NVivo is achieved by the use of heading styles, 'Heading 1', 'Heading 2' and so on. These can be applied either when preparing documents or after importing a document into NVivo (use the styles pull-down menu in the Document Browser). Sections are most useful where you want to do some automatic coding (for example, recognizing different speakers throughout the documents) or where the document is structured (as in a semi-structured interview). One example is where your document records a focus group discussion. In this case you should indicate each speaker with a unique name in a paragraph of its own and give this a style of, say, 'Heading 1'. The speech that follows should be in the 'Normal' style. It is common practice to put names used to identify speakers in uppercase letters and to use upper and lower (title) case for names used by respondents in their speeches, so you can distinguish them when using text search (see Figure 3.4). You might find it best to use real names in the documents you analyse but don't forget to anonymize them before inclusion in any published reports. Notice the use of JOHN_2 in Figure 3.4 to distinguish this speaker from another John, who appears elsewhere, and the use of INT_SALLY to indicate that the speaker was the interviewer, Sally. When laid out in this way, you can use NVivo's 'Code sections by title' facility (select **Code by Section...** from the document's contextual menu 🔔; this opens a Section Coder dialog window). This will set up a code for each paragraph that is in a heading style and use the first 36 characters of the paragraph (including spaces) as its name. It is then a simple matter to code at it all the text in 'Normal' style up to the next paragraph in a 'Heading' style. For example, using the document in Figure 3.4 the program will set up a code called INT_SALLY and will easily code at it the text 'Have you found age a really big problem?'

Document	Style
INT_SALLY	Heading 1
Have you found age a really big problem?	Normal
FRED	Heading 1
I think age is a problem in most jobs now. That was the impression I got from the interview I went to with the Employment Exchange.	Normal
JOHN_2	Heading 1
Yes, I agree with Fred. But they don't tell you straight out. I went after one job as a labourer and they were saying, "Oh, yes, yes, it'll be alright. How old are you?" I told him and he just threw away what he'd been writing.	Normal

Figure 3.4   Using 'Heading' styles to indicate sections in a focus group

Another example is where your document is structured. For instance, you may have scanned in a highly structured report. If the document's section headings have heading styles, 'Heading 1' for the top level heading, 'Heading 2' for the next level down and so on, then NVivo will establish a hierarchical coding system based on the heading hierarchy (see Figure 3.5). When you use NVivo's 'Code sections into tree-nodes...' facility (select **Code by Section...** from the document's contextual menu ⬛) you will get a hierarchical tree with a node '1, Teaching and learning' with two subnodes, '1,1 Raised Quality' and '1,2 Increased Teaching Effectiveness'. The two chunks of text in Normal style will be coded at the latter two nodes. Note, by the way, I have used commas in the section numbering. This is because NVivo doesn't like full stops in node names and replaces them with the tilde (~) character.

A third, common example is where you are using semi-structured interviews and each interviewee gets exactly the same question (at least at the start of the topic). Then you can divide up the document with a section for each of the standard questions by putting each question into a heading style (see Figure 3.6). Using NVivo's 'Code sections by title' facility would set up codes for question 1 called 'Q1 What kind of services would help' (note:

Document	Style
1, Teaching and learning	Heading 1
1,1 Raised Quality The provision will be judged as being of high quality by peer review and will be a high quality learning experience for students.	Heading 2 Normal
1,2 Increased Teaching Effectiveness There will be greater emphasis on independent learning along with improvements in the efficiency and effectiveness of support services. Institutions will make greater use of technology-based learning systems.	Heading 2 Normal

Figure 3.5   Using 'Heading' styles and numbers to indicate sections in a structured document

Document	Style
Q1 What kind of services would help you as an individual to get back into work? As far as being a plumbing contractor, and the work you do is just in houses, I can't see that anybody really can, because it's something where you are generally employed by the public, and you can't force the public to come along to you and say you've got to have your house plumbed by this bloke. An up-turn in the economy would help - but the one big disadvantage I've got - I've nothing against the locals at all, but as soon as I speak, I think people think "He's an outsider."	Heading 1 Normal
Q2 Is there anything else that would help you get work? . . . etc.	Heading 1 Normal

Figure 3.6   Using 'Heading' styles to indicate sections in a semi-structured document

only the first 36 characters). You can then easily spread the coding to include both the following paragraphs under that heading. The program will do the same for question 2 and so on. If all your documents are structured in this way then every section on the same topic can quickly be coded at the same node. If you use this facility, then you need to make very sure that the standard questions (Q1 and Q2 in the example) are all typed in the documents in an identical way as this is how the program determines what to code together. The best way to ensure this is to cut and paste the headings in Word at the document preparation stage.

Document metadata

The term 'document metadata' refers to a collection of information about the document, its contents and its provenance. Some researchers refer to this information as the document description, the document header, the session summary or the cover sheet – reflecting the time when this information was kept on a sheet of paper attached to the front of the transcript. In NVivo this information can be included in a variety of ways, as document description, as document attributes, as linked documents and as annotations.

The kind of information recorded includes the following (as appropriate):

- date of interview;
- topic and circumstances of interview;
- name of interviewer;
- source of field notes relevant to interview;
- linked documents (e.g. previous and subsequent interviews);
- source of document (full reference);
- initial ideas for analysis;
- pseudonym of person interviewed and other anonymizing references.

The document description in NVivo

Conventionally this is a piece of descriptive text at the start of the document. It can include any of the document metadata just discussed, including simple information that could be entered as document attributes. If you're not sure if you want to keep some information put it here to start with in a short paragraph. If you want to write more then use a linked document such as a memo. (See Chapter 5 for more on attributes and memos.)

When you introduce a new document, NVivo needs to know where to find its title and description. The default is that the title of the file is kept as the document title and the description is the first paragraph of text in the Normal style. Alternatively, using the Description and Title styles on the appropriate text in the document means the program will recognize the appropriate paragraphs automatically. Figure 3.7 gives an example of a document description and this should either be:

Harry, age 47, interviewed at home, interviewer Sally, September 26, 1997, unemployed. Real name - Richard (Rick) Smith.
Mentions informal sources of job information such as word of mouth. Could this be an important real source of work opportunity information, or is it more of an 'urban myth'?

Figure 3.7   Document description

- the first paragraph in the document;
- the second paragraph in the document, where the first is the title of the document you want to use; or
- anywhere in the document (though usually near the start), but marked in the Description style.

Conclusion

When you start a new project and start preparing documents for use in NVivo there is a lot to think about: how to lay out the document, whether it can be done in a form that makes initial coding easier, what metadata you should assemble. Unless you are very experienced it is unlikely you will be able to make the right decisions, right from the start. The best policy is to have a go with one or two documents. Try out a layout, create a small pilot project, introduce the documents into NVivo and try out some coding, searching, retrieval, annotation and data links. See if it works. If not you've not lost too much if you go back and start again. Fortunately, NVivo is very flexible. It is designed so that documents can be changed throughout the life of the project. Sometimes this is time-consuming and would be easier if things had been set up correctly from the start, but there is almost nothing that cannot be changed if needed.

Further reading

QSR (1999) *NVivo Reference Guide*. (This is the reference guide provided with the program; it includes a discussion of how to create RTF documents.)

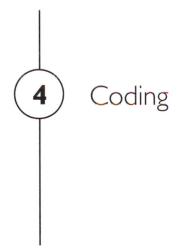

4 Coding

'Coding . . . is an essential procedure. Any researcher who wishes to become proficient at doing qualitative analysis must learn to code well and easily. The excellence of the research rests in large part on the excellence of the coding' (Strauss 1987: 27). Although some might disagree (Coffey *et al.* 1996), for most purposes coding remains one of the central activities in qualitative research. For most researchers, coding starts almost as soon as they start thinking about the first set of data they have collected and continues until they have finished writing the research report.

Nodes and coding

Coding is the process of identifying and recording one or more discrete passages of text or other data items (e.g. parts of a picture) that, in some sense, exemplify the same theoretical or descriptive idea. In NVivo coding is done by connecting each of the passages or items to a node. Figure 4.1 shows, in a short extract from the Job Search project, how passages may be coded at three different nodes. Each node has a name and it might, therefore, seem that coding is simply the connecting of a name with passages of text. Far from it. A node is not *just* a name or label. It is in fact a way of connecting a theoretical concept or idea with passages of text that in some way exemplify that idea. The name is actually just shorthand for an idea or concept

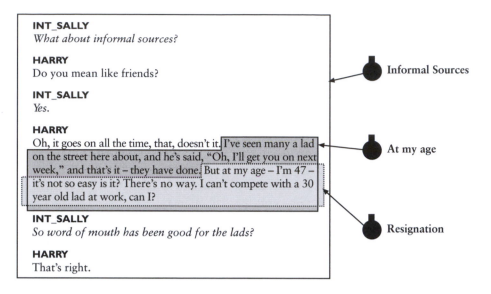

Figure 4.1   A sample of text showing overlapping passages coded at three nodes

that the passages share. Thus in NVivo a node doesn't just code passages of text (or other objects, such as audio and video, via proxy documents), it also has a definition and can be linked to other nodes and to documents and memos. The node definition and the links to memos and so on can be used to record the concept or idea the node represents and to keep any theoretical and associated thoughts about the idea. The node in NVivo is thus the focus of a lot of the analytical thinking that goes on in qualitative analysis. Recording such thinking is essential both to the process of analysis and to its validity and reliability. Figure 4.2 summarizes these relationships between node, concept, properties and documents.

The activity of coding text at a node is therefore different from the activity of coding in quantitative research, where it is merely the giving of a name to extracts, usually so that they can be counted. The names given commonly reflect pre-existing theoretical ideas. In contrast, in qualitative analysis, the very process of identifying and connecting the passages of text and clarifying the concept or idea represented by the node they are coded at is an important part of analysis. Not only that, but, crucially, qualitative researchers also examine the relationships between the actual text coded at different nodes.

A second reason for confusion about coding is that different authors have used different words to describe a similar process. For example, the terms node, index, category and code have been used by writers. In the case of NVivo matters are kept clear and simple, and only the terms node and code are used. Node refers to the place where reference to text passages may be kept along with the node's name, definition and so on. Not all nodes have to

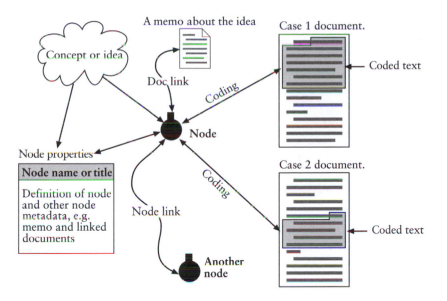

Figure 4.2 A node and its links

have text coded at them. In NVivo nodes may have other functions. For instance, they may play a structural role in a node tree or they may simply be a way of keeping together the text produced by a search. Code is always used as a verb to refer to the process of identifying passages of text that exemplify a certain idea or concept and then connecting them to a node.

Data-driven or concept-driven?

The construction of nodes and a node structure is an analytic process. It is the building up of a conceptual schema. It is possible to do this without initial reference to the data collected. The categories or concepts the nodes represent may come from the literature, previous studies and so on. It is possible to construct a collection of nodes and even a hierarchy of nodes without, at first, using them to code the data. On the other hand, there is often much to be gained from approaching the data with an open mind, with no preconceptions about what analytic framework might be appropriate. In this case the nodes would be constructed through the close reading of the text (or the examination of other media if relevant). These two approaches to generating nodes are not exclusive. You don't have to do either one or the other or even one and then the other. Most researchers move between both sources of inspiration during their analysis. The idea of constructing nodes before or separately from an examination of the data will reflect, to some extent, the inclination, knowledge and theoretical sophistication of the researcher. If your project has been defined in the context of a clear theoretical framework then it is likely that you will have some good ideas about what potential nodes you will need. That is not to say that they will be preserved either as nodes or in their definition throughout the project, but at least it will give you a starting point when reading the text for the kinds of phenomena you want to look for. The trick here is not to become too tied to the initial nodes you construct. Fortunately, as we shall see, NVivo has some good tools that enable you to manipulate nodes and coded text during your analysis.

The opposite of starting with fixed ideas of nodes is to start with none. Of course, no one starts with no idea. As I suggested in Chapter 1, the researcher is both an observer of the social world and a part of that same world. We all have ideas of what we might expect to be happening in the social situations examined by qualitative research. As social scientists we are likely to have more than most as a result of our knowledge of theoretical ideas and other empirical research. Nevertheless one can try, as far as possible, not to start with preconceptions. Simply start by reading the texts and trying to tease out what is happening. Such an approach is taken by the advocates of grounded theory (Glaser and Strauss 1967; Strauss 1987; Strauss and Corbin 1990, 1997; Glaser 1992). They suggest many techniques for teasing out nodes from the reading of texts that do not rely on any pre-existing theory. Yet even they accept that a complete *tabula rasa* approach is unrealistic. The point is that, as far as possible, one should try to pull out from the data what is happening and not impose an interpretation based on pre-existing theory. For the grounded theorists qualitative analysis is about generating *new* theory. It is only at a later stage of the analysis that one needs to relate these new ideas to existing theory. We have already seen in Chapter 2 one of the techniques that Glaser and Strauss suggest, the identification of in vivo nodes. But as we shall see later in this chapter and in Chapter 8, there are many more heuristics or rules of thumb for generating nodes.

The node definition

Whatever approach is taken, one danger to guard against is reproducing too closely what is in the data. Nodes should reflect the data but not merely reproduce them. As Dey (1993) suggests, the categories they represent should mirror the data and serve some analytic purpose. Nodes are not merely a simple categorization of passages of text. Nodes as much as anything form a focus for thinking about the text and its interpretation. The actual text coded at the node is just one aspect of that. Just as important is all the thinking and rethinking that goes on around the concepts or ideas the node encapsulates. It is important that in this process you write ideas down, and that is why NVivo provides such a variety of ways in which you can link memos, documents, annotations and definitions to the node. The starting point for this is the node definition.

The definition or description of a node can contain many things. When working with paper and index cards in the past, qualitative researchers recorded the following about new nodes:

- the label or name of the node;
- the actual text coded;
- where the text comes from (which case or document and where in the document it is to be found);
- who coded it (the name of the researcher);
- the date of coding or change of coding;
- the definition of the node (a description of the analytic idea it refers to and ways of ensuring that the coding is reliable – i.e. is carried out in a systematic and consistent way).

Most of this information is kept in NVivo in the node properties.

To open the node Properties window

1 Select a node in the Node Explorer, then click on the **Properties** button.
2 The node Properties window opens (see Figure 4.3).

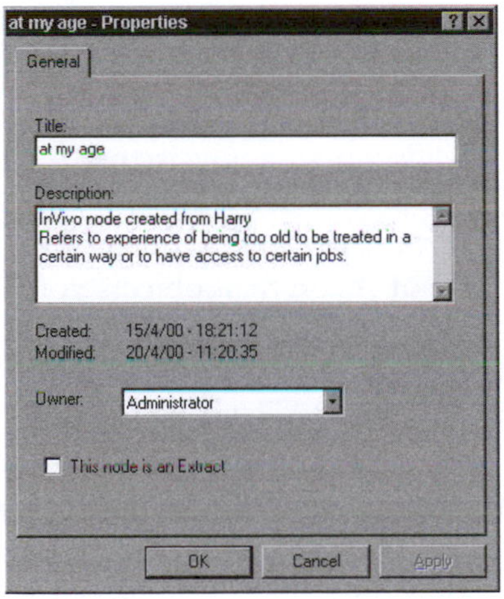

Figure 4.3   The node Properties window

At the top is the title of the node. This can be changed if necessary, but all the text coded at this node remains unchanged. Below the name is the node description. In Figure 4.3 the node is an in vivo one. So the program has inserted the text 'InVivo node created from Harry' where 'Harry' is the document from which the in vivo term came. Below that the researcher has inserted a definition of the node. That definition might be refined through the life of the analysis as the researcher gets clearer ideas about what this node refers to or as it is combined with other similar nodes and the description needs broadening to reflect that. If you edit or change the node description click on the **OK** or **Apply** button before closing the window to save your changes.

Not all the information about the node is kept in the node Properties window. Of course the text that has been coded at the node is in the documents and can be browsed in the ways seen in Chapter 2 using the Node Browser. It is also possible to link a node with other kinds of information such as memos and documents. Here you might keep a discussion of the node and its definition and perhaps some notes to yourself about how this node might relate to other parts of the data set. We shall look at such linked documents in more detail in the next chapter.

What can nodes be about?

Let us assume that, rather than setting up some nodes based on prior theory and ideas, you have decided to start reading through the documents to discover categories from the data. What kind of things can you look for and what can you code? The answer depends to some extent on the kind of analysis you are intending to do. Some disciplines and theoretical approaches will require that you pay special attention to certain kinds of phenomena in the texts you are examining.

For instance, if you are undertaking a discourse analysis then you will tend to focus on the detailed aspect of how people use language to interact and express themselves. There will be certain theoretical ideas from discourse theory that will highlight what kind of theoretical objects you might find in the discourse you are examining (Potter and Wetherell 1987, 1995; Billig 1997). Many discourse analysts undertake the deconstruction of texts and accounts by reference to their rhetorical nature. They examine the discourse for the way that people present issues and marshal their ideas and use metaphors to categorize and characterize their views and the views of others. Other discourse analysts look for interpretative repertoires such as people's use of metaphors, grammatical constructions and figures of speech in constructing accounts of their actions and the actions of other people. All these are candidates for nodes.

On the other hand, analysts taking a phenomenological perspective are interested in people's perspectives of their world. They attempt to describe in detail the content and structure of people's consciousness, to capture the qualitative diversity of their experiences and to explain their essential meanings (Giorgi 1970, 1985; Moustakas 1994; Kvale 1996). For example, in interpretative phenomenological analysis, a recent version of phenomenology (Smith 1995), after taking unfocused notes that include associations, questions, summaries, comments on language use, absences and descriptive labels, the analyst is recommended to identify and label themes that characterize each section of the text. Themes are conceptual and capture something of the essential psychological quality of what is represented in the text. Each of these themes can be made into a node.

What about other approaches? Fortunately, as it happens, for a very wide range of types of qualitative analysis there is a common ground of phenomena that researchers tend to look for in their texts. Some typical examples are listed in Table 4.1. I have illustrated each idea with an example from the Job Search project. Different authors have a different emphasis, but many of the ideas in the table will be useful to any analyst of texts.

These examples of thing to code are not mutually exclusive. A passage of text may exemplify several different ideas on different dimensions of analysis or different levels. The text coded at one node can be of any length, and within each passage sections of it (or even the whole passage) can also be coded at other nodes (see Figure 4.4). For example, text concerned with looking for work by 'word of mouth' (a strategy) may also be coded at a node on keeping in touch with professional contacts (relationships). This is possible because of the nature of the data. The text being analysed itself is rich and dense and capable of multiple levels of understanding and interpretation. For instance, when people use language they not only explain things, they tell stories, they express their opinions and views, they exemplify attitudes and values, they obfuscate, they avoid issues, they try to influence others' actions and views and so on. All of these different kinds of acts may require different kinds of coding.

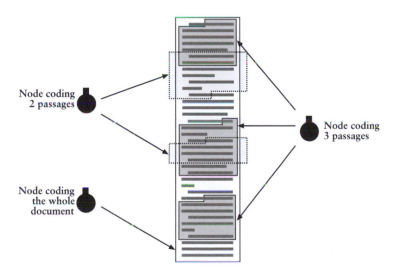

Figure 4.4 A multiply-coded document

Table 4.1 What can be coded? Examples from the Job Search project

1 *Specific acts, behaviours* – what people do or say.

> Avoiding the question. Getting the opinions of friends.

2 *Events* – these are usually brief, one-off events or things someone has done.

> Being rejected at job interview. Promised a job by a mate.

3 *Activities* – these are of longer duration than acts and often take place in a particular setting and may have several people involved.

> Attending a Job Club. Visiting the library to read the vacancies in the newspaper.

4 *Strategies or tactics* – activities aimed towards some goal.

> Word of mouth to find jobs. Taking up work with a relative.

5 *States* – general conditions experienced by people or found in organizations.

> Resignation, e.g. 'At my age the chances of finding any work aren't good'.

6 *Meanings* – A wide range of phenomena at the core of much qualitative analysis. Meanings and interpretations are important parts of what directs participants' actions.

  (a) What concepts do participants use to understand their world? What norms, values, rules and mores guide their actions?

> The idea of 'front-of-the-house work' as a way of describing dealing with customers in the hotel trade, as distinct from working in the kitchen, office etc.

  (b) What meaning or significance it has for participants, how do they construe events?

> Guilt about using government unemployment services, e.g. 'I always think that they'll think I'm after something for nothing, and I'm not'.

7 *Participation* – people's involvement or adaptation to a setting.

> Challenge to status, e.g. 'At a sales meeting, . . . I said, "I'd just like to say a few words." He said, "We haven't time for that now." That was demeaning. So I resigned.'

8 *Relationships or interaction* – between people, considered simultaneously.

> Enjoying the family, e.g. '. . . they're 26 and 21 and most boys of that age are married, but mine aren't and they like to come home, have friends to stay. I like that.'

9 *Conditions or constraints* – the precursor to or cause of events or actions, things that restrict behaviour or actions.

> Firm's loss of markets (before lay-offs). Divorce (before financial difficulties).

Table 4.1 Continued

10   *Consequences* – What happens if . . .

> Experience gets jobs, e.g. 'So what you get is, people that haven't got no
> qualification, but have got a few months' experience are walking into jobs'.

11   *Settings* – the entire context of the events under study.

> Using a range of informal networks for finding jobs.

12   *Reflexive interventions* – the researcher's role in the process – how
intervention generated the data.

> Expressing sympathy. 'It must be hard for you in that situation.'

Sources: adapted from Bogdan and Biklen (1992), Strauss (1987) and Mason (1996)

Thinking about the text

Even with a computer program to help, there is no substitute, in the end, for close reading of and a thorough familiarity with the text. There are several different approaches you can take to reading the text so that you can identify passages to code. With the list in Table 4.1 in mind, you can read your text looking for examples of the types given. Some researchers suggest reading the text line by line, thinking carefully about each line and asking a series of questions of it. Are there any examples of the things in Table 4.1? Do any of the prompts and questions in the interview schedule suggest things to look for? Do the criteria for selection of sites, cases, events etc. suggest what might be happening? Can I imagine what might be happening? Is there previous research that suggests significant phenomena? There are also several contrasts one can construct to help understand what might lie behind the surface text. For example, you can ask what if . . . questions: what if the circumstances, order of events, characteristics of the people, places, settings etc. were different? You can ask how the events and so on are like and unlike others. You can take a key element and free associate or read the parts of the text in a different order to try to stimulate ideas of what is in the text. The idea behind the contrasts is to try to bring out what is distinctive about the text and its content. All too often we are so familiar with things that we fail to notice what is significant. The contrast questions and the 'what ifs' can be used to try to stimulate you to recognize what is already there.

Selecting the text

One issue that taxes many researchers, especially when starting out, is how big the passage of text to be coded should be. This can vary from whole documents down to just one word. Most coding is done in the middle range though, on passages from a few words to a few sentences long. The longer the passage, the easier it is to understand its content and to include some contextual material. Shorter passages are easier to code because, unlike long ones, they usually only exemplify one idea; however, they can easily lose their context and it is easy to start making too many different nodes. Table 4.2 summarizes the pros and cons of large passages and small passages of text when coding.

A key process in coding in qualitative research is the extraction of text from its original document and its comparison with other like passages. This is often referred to as decontextualization of the text. The process supports the easy comparison of one passage with another coding the same issue, but it removes each passage from its context in its parent document. The process of taking this passage back to its document to see its surrounding context is called recontextualization. Fortunately, the technology comes to the rescue in recontextualization. As we saw in Chapter 2, in NVivo it is easy to jump from a passage of coded text displayed in the Node Browser to the document from which it came with the selected coded text highlighted. Moreover, no coding is fixed for ever. In NVivo it is simple to change what particular text is coded at a node. So you can start with passages that are too long and then uncode sections when you have refined your ideas of what the node is about. To this extent decontextualization can be delayed. Alternatively, you can start with very short passages and then extend the coded text later. Extending the coding becomes a kind of recontextualization.

Once you have spotted one or two passages to code and have an idea of how to define the node they are coded at, you can use the Search Tool to find occurrences of similar terms. Then check to see if the containing passage can be coded at that node too. We shall look at this in more detail

Table 4.2   Pros and cons of large and small passages for coding

Size of passage	Pro	Con
Large/wide/high level	Maximizes usefulness of coding – applied to enough passages to justify recontextualization. Avoids prejudicing later analysis.	Few episodes can be identified to match the node. Includes lots of less relevant material. Coding vague.
Small/narrow/detailed	Greater differentiation. Clear definition. Easier to identify passages in text.	Important contextual data may be lost. Loss of meaning. May need more nodes. Too many nodes to remember.

Table 4.3   Good practice in creating nodes

1 Become thoroughly familiar with the data
2 Always be sensitive to the context of the data
3 Be flexible – extend, modify and discard nodes
4 Consider connections and avoid needless overlaps
5 Record the criteria on which coding decisions are to be made
6 Consider alternative ways of categorizing and interpreting the data

Source: adapted from Dey (1993)

in Chapter 6. As you code passages you should consider whether the text fits with the node definition (see above) and whether the definition is still adequate or whether it can be refined. One tendency, if you don't check often, is for the criteria you use to select passages of text for coding to drift progressively away from the original ideas you had when you started. Checking and refining the definition will minimize such 'definitional drift'. Sometimes this divergence of ideas indicates that you may actually have two nodes that you have been conflating. In this case you might consider going back and checking all the coded text to see if it can be split into two (or more) nodes. Any notes you have made about the node (the node memo – see the next chapter) may help you make these decisions. Table 4.3 summarizes good practice in coding.

Coding at already created nodes

In Chapter 2 I introduced a couple of simple methods for coding text in NVivo: using the 'In-Vivo' facility and extending the text coded; and starting a new free node by entering its name into the speed coding bar in the Document Browser. Early in a project, most coding is likely to be done in these ways. You read the document either in the Document Browser or in the Node Browser and when you spot a passage you want to code, you select it and code it using the speed coding bar. However, as time goes by you will build up a long list of nodes. The pull-down menu in the speed coding bar only shows the last 10 nodes used. So what do you do if you want to use one outside that list? This is where you will need the Coder.

To code using the Coder

1 Open a document in the Document Browser.
2 Find and select the text you want to code.
3 Click on the **Coder** button at the right hand end of the speed coding bar. The Coder opens – see Figure 4.5. (It is called a palette because it always floats on top of the Document or Node Browser – even if you maximize

the Browser's window. If you bring another window to the front and the
Browser window moves back, the palette moves with it.)

4 Scroll up and down the list of nodes. This works in the same way as the list
in the Node Explorer. Select the node you want to code at. Then either:
   (a) click on the **Code** button in the Coder; or
   (b) drag the selected text to the node you want to code to, or vice versa.
   The passage is now coded at that node and that node is added to the
   last 10 used in the pull-down menu in the speed coding bar.

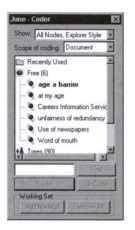

Figure 4.5   The Coder palette

 Resizing the Coder palette

This might not seem possible because there is no resize tab at
the bottom right. However, you can still drag the bottom right-
hand corner. Do this so you can see all your nodes, especially if
those low in the tree have long names or if there is a long list of
names you want to be able to pick from. Unfortunately, the
palette does not keep the size you have set after you have
closed and reopened it.

Seeing what is coded at a node

If, immediately after coding some text, you return to the Browser and de-
select the text, you will find that it is now showing a coloured background
(see Figure 4.6). This colouring only shows when the Coder is open and a
node in it is selected. It is one way of seeing what text has been coded at that
node. If you have already coded some text elsewhere in the same document

then that too will be showing the coloured background. If you now select a different node in the Coder then only text coded at that node (if there is any in the current document) will show a coloured background.

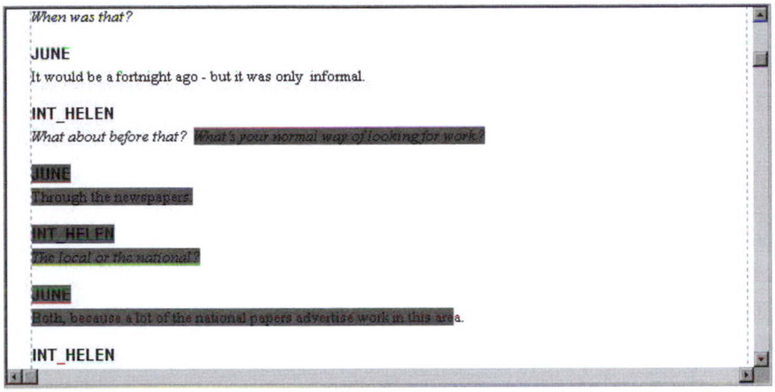

When was that?

JUNE
It would be a fortnight ago - but it was only informal.

INT_HELEN
What about before that? What's your normal way of looking for work?

JUNE
Through the newspapers

INT_HELEN
The local or the national?

JUNE
Both, because a lot of the national papers advertise work in this area.

INT_HELEN

Figure 4.6 The Document Browser showing coded text highlighted

However, this only shows what text is coded for one node at a time. A way of seeing all nodes coded in a document is to show the coding stripes. This is so called after the habit of researchers in the past of using coloured pens to put stripes down the side of their text to show what was coded. In NVivo these appear down the right-hand side of the document.

To show coding stripes in the Document Browser (or the Node Browser)

1 Select **View:Coding Stripes** from the menu bar.
2 The stripes become visible down the right-hand side of the window – see Figure 4.7. (You may need to resize the window and move the border between the text and the stripes to see both clearly. To move the border, move the mouse over it till it turns into a two headed arrow with a vertical line through it ⊞, then drag the border to its new position.)

Notice that the coding stripes only show the lines that are coded. They do not show if the actual passage started in the middle of a line or not. In contrast, the background colouring you get when a node in the Coder is selected shows exactly the text that is coded at the node. This is more useful if you want to refine the text that is coded after some automatic coding, say. (See later in this chapter.) On the other hand, the coding stripes do show all the nodes that have been applied to the document at the same time. If your screen is big enough you can display the coding stripes and use the Coder at the same time.

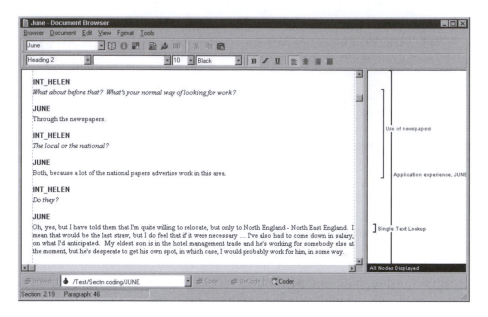

Figure 4.7 The Document Browser showing coding stripes

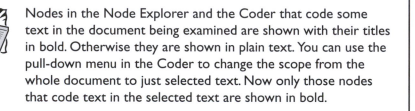

Nodes in the Node Explorer and the Coder that code some text in the document being examined are shown with their titles in bold. Otherwise they are shown in plain text. You can use the pull-down menu in the Coder to change the scope from the whole document to just selected text. Now only those nodes that code text in the selected text are shown in bold.

Hierarchy of nodes

In Chapter 2 I introduced the process in NVivo of creating nodes and coding text at them using free nodes. These appear just as a list of nodes in the Free nodes folder in the Node Browser. However, NVivo also supports nodes arranged hierarchically, called tree nodes. The advantage of arranging nodes hierarchically can be seen by examining the following example.

In the Job Search study, respondents were asked to evaluate a number of services for the unemployed. Text was coded at nodes indicating discussion of a service and at nodes to indicate positive, negative and neutral views about any service. The following free nodes were established:

- Positive views
- Neutral views
- Negative views

    🕷️ Service 1 – Youth training

    🕷️ Service 2 – Training access points

    🕷️ Service 3 – Worklink

      etc.

Typically, these nodes would be scattered throughout the list of free nodes as free nodes may only be displayed in alphabetical, creation date or modification date order. The evaluation nodes could be more clearly displayed by using a tree or hierarchy of nodes such as that in Figure 4.8. This has introduced some 'placeholder' nodes, 'Evaluation', 'Service' and 'Type of View'. These might not code any text at all. Their purpose is to clarify the relationship of other nodes in the tree.

```
Evaluation
    ├── Service
    │       ├── Service 1 – Youth training
    │       ├── Service 2 – Training access points
    │       ├── Service 3 – Worklink
    │       └── Other Services etc.
    └── Type of View
            ├── Positive views
            ├── Neutral views
            └── Negative views
```

Figure 4.8   An example node tree

In this case the hierarchy is shown by spreading downwards and to the right. The 'tree' is effectively lying on its side with its root at the top left. The node 'Evaluation' at the top left is the root or top-level node. Going down and to the right, it has two nodes connected to it, 'Service' and 'Type of View'. These are known as children of 'Evaluation' and 'Evaluation' is referred to as their parent. This nomenclature follows throughout the tree. Thus the node 'Type of View' has three children, 'Positive views', 'Neutral views' and 'Negative views'. Nodes with a common parent are called siblings. Thus 'Service' and 'Type of View' are siblings, as are 'Positive views', 'Neutral views' and 'Negative views'.

NVivo allows the construction and maintenance of such trees of nodes. The tree in Figure 4.8 would appear in the Node Explorer as in Figure 4.9. The tree can be opened and closed just as the folder and file hierarchy can in Windows Explorer. Double-clicking on a node icon will open up the tree to show any children or close it if they are already visible. The small icon showing a plus sign in a square ⊞ indicates the node has children that aren't currently displayed. A minus sign in a square ⊟ indicates there are children currently visible. A single click on ⊞ will open the tree below, a single click on ⊟ will collapse the tree below with its children.

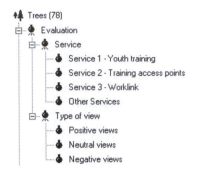

Figure 4.9 Node tree in NVivo

Functions of the node tree

The tree structure serves several purposes. First, it keeps things tidy. As your analysis proceeds you may generate a large number of nodes. Initially most of these will be free nodes, but some might be in a tree, perhaps because they are derived from an initial theoretical viewpoint. But a long list of nodes, especially free nodes, is not very helpful. It therefore makes sense to move them into a tree where their relationships can be seen more clearly.

Second, it can constitute an analysis of the data in itself. In the process of categorizing responses you develop an understanding of respondents' view of the world. For instance, in their evaluation of services, respondents in the Job Search project actually talked about how the services helped them or not: 'helped me see what I was qualified for', 'never heard of it', 'showed me how to fill in applications', 'wasn't relevant to me', 'went but they weren't helpful', 'told me about the places to look for job adverts', 'made me think about more training', 'helped with interviews and forms', 'gave me confidence', 'good service, but I'm still unemployed' etc. These go beyond a simple positive–neutral–negative dimension. Some are about skills learned, some about lack of help, others about other gains. Thus a tree like that in Figure 4.10 could be constructed in NVivo. The interesting thing is that in constructing this tree you are coming to an understanding of how your respondents categorize and conceptualize the services they used.

Third, it can be used to gain an overall view of the way your conceptual framework is growing, as can be seen in Figure 4.10. By collapsing branches of the tree low down you can hide some of the detail and thus get a view of the framework as a whole. Examining the tree also shows how the conceptual framework could be modified or improved. For example, we might realize that there could be other nodes under 'Skills gained' that would be worth creating and looking for. We shall examine this procedure more fully in Chapter 7.

Fourth, it prevents the duplication of nodes. This is especially likely

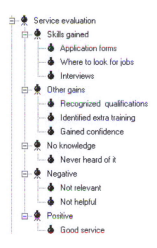

Figure 4.10   Node tree for 'Service evaluation' in NVivo

where you have a set of responses to a variety of phenomena such as in the 'Evaluation' example in Figure 4.9. The tree enables you to see such duplicates easily.

Finally, it forms the basis for further investigations. Trees are especially useful in producing matrices or tables. We shall look at these in detail in Chapter 9.

Types of node in NVivo

NVivo essentially distinguishes three ways of treating nodes: as free nodes, tree nodes or case nodes. In terms of how they relate to the text they code, their definitions and so on, there is no real difference between free nodes and tree nodes. Both free nodes and tree nodes may be used for any type of coding. The main difference between them lies in how tree nodes relate to each other, as we have seen in the preceding section. Tree nodes have a place in a tree structure, whereas free nodes just appear in a list. Case nodes are rather different. A case node is a way of coding together all the text that belongs to a case. The case node itself has no children, but it can belong to a hierarchy of case node types. Typical examples of case nodes might be each of the interviewees in the Job Search project, or each of the job centres used by these respondents. We shall look at the use of case nodes in more detail in Chapter 8.

Each of these node types is arranged into a folder that appears at the top of the listing of those nodes in the Node Explorer. In addition to the three types of nodes, the Node Explorer contains two other folders, one where the 10 most recently used nodes (of any type) can be found and another for making sets of nodes. Sets of nodes are a handy device, for example, when

Table 4.4 Icons for nodes and node folders in NVivo

Icon	Colour	Meaning
Folders		
	Yellow	Recently Used
	Purple	Free (*n*), where *n* is the number of nodes in the folder
	Green	Trees (*n*)
	Brown	Cases (*n*)
	Red/green/blue	Sets (*n*)
Nodes		
	Purple	Free node
	Blue	Root or branch tree node with no children
	Blue	Tree node with parent and child or children
	Blue	Root tree node with child or children
Cases		
	Dark blue	Case type
	Green	Case
Sets		
	Yellow	Set of nodes
Aliases/shortcuts		
	Purple	Alias or shortcut to free node
	Blue	Alias to root or branch tree node with no children
	Blue	Alias to tree node with parent and child or children
	Blue	Alias to root tree node with child or children

doing a search to restrict its scope. Nodes and their containing folders are displayed with distinctive coloured icons. They and their colours and meaning are listed in Table 4.4.

Organizing tree nodes

In Chapter 2 we saw how to create free nodes using the Node Explorer and the Project Pad. You can also create tree nodes and case nodes in a similar way. And once created, there are ways of rearranging the tree nodes along with any text that has been coded at them.

To create a new top-level tree node

1 In the Node Explorer select **Create Tree Node** from the Trees contextual menu ⬕.
2 A new top level node called 'Tree Node' is created. Click on its name to make it editable so you can type in the name you want.

However, when creating nodes below the top level node you have a choice. You can either create a child of that node or a sibling.

To create a child node of a tree node

1 Select **Create:Child Node** from the contextual menu ⬕ (and submenu) of the tree node where you want to create a child.
2 A new node called 'Tree Node' is created one level down from the start node. Click on this to make it editable so you can type in the name you want.

To create a sibling node of a tree node

1 Select **Create:Sibling Node** from the contextual menu ⬕ (and submenu) of the tree node where you want to create a sibling.
2 A new node called 'Tree Node' is created at the same level as the start node. Click on this to make it editable so you can type in the name you want.

A common process in using NVivo is to read the text and start creating free nodes. Eventually you will have a large number of them and it will become clear that they can be arranged into a more logical scheme. This is the time to start constructing a node tree and to move nodes from the free nodes area into the tree. There are several ways this can be done.

To move a node by dragging and dropping

1 Use the mouse to drag the node from the Free node list (see Figure 4.11a).
2 Drop it on to the node you want to be its parent in the node tree. As you move over a node where you can attach the node as a child the node title is highlighted and the pointer turns into an arrow with a box and plus sign (see Figure 4.11b).
3 A copy of the node is moved to become a child of the selected tree node (see Figure 4.11c).
4 You can, if you wish, now delete the node from the free node area.

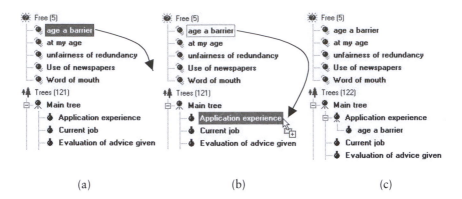

| (a) | (b) | (c) |

Figure 4.11   Moving a copy of a free node in the node browser

 Dragging to move a node between node areas (free node, tree node, cases and sets) will add a copy in the destination and leave the original node intact. This is indicated by a plus sign on the pointer. Moving nodes within these areas does not leave a copy in the original place and the pointer does not show a plus sign.

To delete a node

1 In the Node Explorer, select **Delete Node** from the node's contextual menu △.

You may find that as your list of free nodes grows and your tree gets bigger and bigger, there is not enough space on screen to show all the nodes as in Figure 4.11. In that case you have three options.

To move a node where the target is not visible

1 Either:
    (a) drag the node to or from the node list on the right-hand side of the Node Explorer window; or
    (b) drag the node to just above the bottom edge of the frame (or just below the top edge) so that the node listing scrolls till you can see the destination you want; or
    (c) open a second copy of the Node Explorer.
        (i)   Resize it and the first copy so both can be seen on screen at once.
        (ii) Scroll the node list in one window so the target is visible.
        (iii) Drag the node you want to move across from the other window into that with the target node showing.

Coding away from the computer

Sometimes it is useful to be able to read through your documents and think about the coding away from the computer. To do this you will need a list of the nodes you have constructed so far and a printout of the documents you want to code.

To get a printed list of nodes

1 In the Node Explorer select one of the node folders (Recently Used, Free, Tree, Case).
2 Either:
   (a) select **Tools:List the Nodes:Descriptions also** (if you want descriptions); or
   (b) select **Tools:List the Nodes:Titles and Addresses only** (if you don't).
3 A report containing a list of all the nodes (of the type selected) is produced (with or without descriptions taken from the node properties as chosen).
4 This can be saved to disk as an RTF file or printed out.

To produce a printed copy of a document to facilitate coding

1 Select a document in the Document Explorer.
2 Select **Document:Make Text Report. . .** from the menu bar.
3 There are three options for details with the document. If you want to use this for coding turn off the option to **Show Section Numbers** and to **Show DataLink details as end-notes**.
4 Click **OK**.
5 A Text Editor window opens showing the document with paragraph numbers (see Figure 4.12).
6 Print this file (**File:Print** from the menu bar or click on the print button) or save as an RTF file and then print later (e.g. from Word).

You can now take away the list of nodes (with definitions) and the documents printed out with paragraph numbers and do some reading and coding away from the computer. You should mark up on the printout how you want the paragraphs coded. Bear in mind, though, that there are two disadvantages of this approach. First, the printout gives you no idea of what has already been coded. For this reason the approach makes best sense early on in a project before you have coded much text in the documents you have printed. Second, you still need to transfer the coding you have marked up on the paper into your project on the computer. Fortunately, there is a method that makes this a little easier. Essentially you use the paragraph numbers to

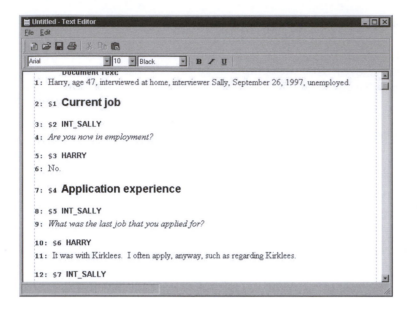

Figure 4.12   A document report in the Text Editor showing paragraph numbers

code the text and then later on refine the text coded using the methods described in the next section.

To enter coding using paragraph numbers

1 In the Document Explorer select **Code by Paragraph** from the contextual menu ⌂ of the document you want to code (the same as the printout you are working from).
2 This opens the Paragraph Coder (see Figure 4.13).
3 The right-hand list is of the last 10 nodes used. If the nodes you want are not shown, add them from the complete list on the left using the **Add** button.
4 Type in at the bottom the paragraph numbers you want to code. It makes sense to code all the paragraphs for the same node at one time. You can type in a list of paragraphs, such as 6,11-16,21-23,31-36,45,47-51.
5 Select a node from the Recently Used nodes list and click on **Code**. (If you make a mistake type in the erroneous paragraph numbers and click on **Remove Coding**.)

If you code this way then inevitably there will be some passages of text at the start of some paragraphs and the end of others that aren't relevant to the node. You have a choice here. Having done some paragraph coding, you can now go through the coded text and uncode these irrelevant passages. Do that using the Coder in the Node Browser, in the manner discussed below.

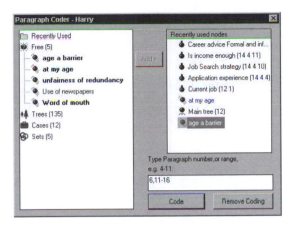

Figure 4.13 The Paragraph Coder

Alternatively, you could just decide to leave the coding as it is. For many purposes, and for some kinds of nodes, coding whole paragraphs is good enough. This may be the case if your paragraphs are quite short – just a sentence or two – so that the whole paragraph can meaningfully be classified as being about a single topic. It may also be that the kind of things you are looking for in coding are broad or high-level, so that it is unlikely that you will want to code very short passages. This will depend on your overall approach to analysis or whether such broad categorization is good enough at, say, the early stage of analysis.

Refining the coding

After having done some rough, broad-sweep, manual coding, you will need to go through the text again to refine what has actually been coded at the node. You may well have large passages of text that were in the section and thus picked up by the automatic section coding but are in fact nothing to do with the issue indicated by the heading. This can happen if the respondent wanders off topic or the interviewer suddenly remembers something they forgot to ask earlier. On the other hand, you may remember other discussions of the topic that aren't coded at the nodes you have created so far. This refining of the coded text, and indeed the refining of the node system itself (such as when looking through the text you discover the need for a new node), goes on throughout the life of the project. You should feel free to change the coding and the nodes at any time, though remember any reports you have created will only reflect things at the time you created the report, so you may need to redo them. There are several techniques for refining coding. The first described is where you have done some automatic coding or broad-sweep manual coding and where you now want to reduce the text that is coded at the node as some is not relevant.

To reduce text coded at a node

1 Select the node in the Node Explorer.
2 Browse it (e.g. click on the **Browse** button).
3 The Node Browser opens. Notice that the node in question is showing in the speed coding bar.
4 Read through the text until you find a passage you want to uncode.
5 Select this passage.
6 Click on the **UnCode** button in the speed coding bar.
7 Continue in this fashion to the end of the document.

This approach works well where you have long passages of the document coded, so that as you scroll through the document you can easily see the context of the text you are reading. If the passages are too short to give sufficient context you can show the context in the Node Browser as discussed in Chapter 2 (use the passage's contextual menu ⬛). That way you can not only see the full context of any passages you uncode but also extend the text coded at the node or even code additional passages you spot as you go through the document. An advantage of this approach is that you can deal with all the coded text from all documents in one go. However, you can only deal with one node at a time.

On the other hand, if the passages you have coded are short, just a sentence or two, and if there are several such passages coded throughout the documents, it makes more sense to start the revision process from the Document Explorer. Although this restricts you to dealing with one document at a time, it does mean you can adjust the text coded at other related nodes.

To extend or reduce text coded at a node for one document

1 From the Document Explorer, select the document you want to work on and open the Document Browser (click on the **Browse** button).
2 Open the Coder (click on the **Coder** button in the speed coding bar).
3 In the Coder, select the node you want to work with. Now, as you scroll through the document you will find that the text coded at the node is highlighted in colour.
4 To uncode some of this highlighted, coded text, select it (the highlighting turns black for the selected text) and click on **UnCode** in the Coder.
5 To extend some of this highlighted, coded text, select the extra text you wish to code and click on the **Code** button in the Coder (see Figure 4.14).
6 Continue working through the rest of the document.

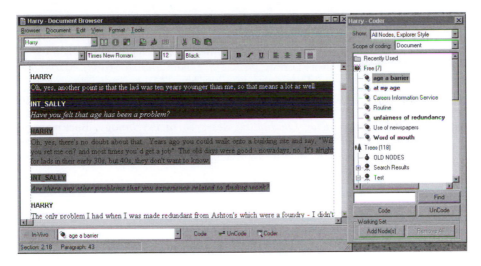

Figure 4.14   Extending text coded at a node using the Coder

Conclusion

Coding text at nodes is probably the most common activity in qualitative data analysis. What I have tried to show in this chapter is that coding requires some careful forethought. There are different kinds of things in the text that can be coded and there are different types of nodes. As we saw in this chapter and shall see in later chapters, nodes are not static things, they can be modified throughout the analysis. Such modification reflects the current state of your understanding of the data. Important aspects of this are how you record the development of your thinking and how the nodes relate to each other. The next chapter will look at how the development of theoretical ideas can be recorded in NVivo, and how the program supports the linking of documents, nodes and other information.

Further reading

Burr, V. (1995) *An Introduction to Social Constructionism*. London: Routledge. (An accessible introduction that includes some discussion of how to undertake a discourse analysis.)

Dey, I. (1993) *Qualitative Data Analysis: A User-Friendly Guide for Social Scientists*. London and New York: Routledge. (This contains an extensive discussion of how to code data.)

Coffey, A. and Atkinson, P. (1996) *Making Sense of Qualitative Data Analysis: Complementary Research Strategies*. London and Thousand Oaks, CA: Sage. (Using the data set they examine throughout the book, the authors work through an example of coding a passage of text.)

Miles, M.B. and Huberman, A.M. (1994) *Qualitative Data Analysis: A Sourcebook of New Methods*, 2nd edn. Beverly Hills, CA: Sage. (Contains some sage advice about coding texts, especially in a policy and programme evaluation context.)

Strauss, A.L. and Corbin, J. (1990) *Basics of Qualitative Research, Grounded Theory Procedures and Techniques*. London: Sage. (An extended discussion of many of the techniques introduced by grounded theory into the process of coding.)

Willig, C. (2001) *Introducing Qualitative Research in Psychology*. Buckingham: Open University Press. (Contains summaries of grounded theory and interpretative phenomenological analysis approaches to coding.)

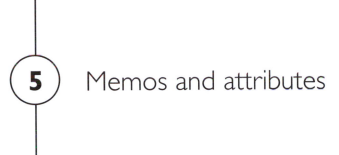

5 Memos and attributes

Qualitative analysts create much information and many documents that form part of their project yet are not original data, that is, are not transcripts of interviews, observations, primary documents and so on. One example of such information is the simple categorization of documents, events, individuals and so on in the project. This includes the attributes of the respondents in an interview study such as their name, age and location, the basic facts about the institutions featured in a case study such as their size, sector and situation, or the characteristics of the interviewers themselves. We shall look at how such information is dealt with in NVivo later in the chapter.

A different kind of information, sometimes referred to as metadata, is what is written by researchers during the life of a project about the data, how it was collected and the process of data analysis. This includes memos, annotations, draft reports, supporting documents and cover sheets. Almost all researchers find that writing about the project and its data throughout the analysis is a very important activity. Such documents not only record the development of ideas about the data and its themes but also often constitute the very process of analytic thinking itself – a theme I shall return to in Chapter 10. NVivo has a variety of ways of handling such information, and the program maintains flexibility in how the documents can be stored and dealt with. In most respects they remain modifiable at any time during the project.

Memos

Writers about grounded theory have popularized the use of memos as a way of prosecuting qualitative analysis. Memos are seen as a way of theorizing and commenting as you go about coding and about the general development of the analytical framework. They are essentially notes to yourself (or to others in the research team) about the data set. Glaser, one of the originators of grounded theory defines memos as

> the theorizing write-up of ideas about codes and their relationships as they strike the analyst while coding . . . it can be a sentence, a paragraph or a few pages . . . it exhausts the analyst's momentary ideation based on data with perhaps a little conceptual elaboration.
>
> (Glaser 1978: 83–4)

In their original conception by the grounded theorists, memos should be about nodes or coding and be kept strictly separate from the primary documents. Then by sorting and searching through memos the researcher could create categories and in an inductive fashion build a theoretical explanation of the setting being researched. Reflecting this view, in NVivo there is a special category of document called a memo that can be separated from other documents. However, other analysts are more flexible in the way they use memos, and NVivo can support this approach too. Thus in NVivo memos are documents like all others, and as well as being linked to a node, text passage or document, memos can also be coded, searched, sorted into sets and linked to other media just as any primary document can. It is up to you, the researcher, to decide how strict you want to be in preserving the divide between primary data on the one hand and your memos, notes and analytic scheme on the other. Table 5.1 summarizes some guidelines for memo writing.

To create a memo document

1 From the Project Pad click on the **Documents** tab and click on the **Make a Project Document** button.
2 This opens the New Document Wizard.
3 Click the tick box at the bottom to **Create document as a memo**.
4 Either:
   (a) if you have already written the document and have saved it in rich text format (RTF), then click the top radio button, **Locate and import readable external text files**, click on **Next>**, choose a file from the file selector dialog and then choose the appropriate option (as for other project documents); or
   (b) if you want to create a new document click on the **Make a new blank document** radio button and then click on **Next>**, give the memo a name and an optional description.

Table 5.1 Guidelines for memos

1 Always give priority to writing memos *while the flash of insight remains*. Jot down memos as the idea occurs.
2 Begin when your first field data come in and continue till the report is written.
3 Keep separate from data. Whether you do this will depend on your analytic style.
4 Keep discussion of people/cases out of document memos – they're about the nodes/concepts/ideas. Try to keep memos at a conceptual level and avoid talking about the features of individuals except as examples of the general concepts. The exception is if you are doing a case analysis. Still try to keep your comments about cases at a conceptual level.
5 Indicate what's just a hunch or conjecture and what is supported by evidence in the data. Otherwise you'll come back later and think that a mere hunch is actually supported by the evidence. (It may or may not be.)
6 Modify memos during analysis. They are not primary data. Keep the original text and just add extra commentary.
7 Once the flow starts, keep at it. It doesn't matter how long memos are. They can be split up later if need be.
8 Keep a list of nodes handy to help cross-referencing. In NVivo just refer to the Node Explorer.
9 Consider combining nodes if memos on them look similar. This is often an indication that the nodes are actually about the same thing.
10 Put dates on memos as a way of auditing progress. Select **Edit:Insert Date & Time** from the menu bar in the Document Browser. Use attributes to record standard information about them.
11 Don't hesitate to link memos to places in field notes, case analysis discussion etc.
12 Be flexible, don't standardize memo styles.

Source: adapted from Glaser (1978), Strauss and Corbin (1990), Dey (1993) and Miles and Huberman (1994)

5 Click on **Finish**. A new document is listed in the Document Explorer (and if you have chosen to create a new memo, the Document Browser is opened ready for you to write it). Memos and documents have different icons (see Figure 5.1).

📄 Document icon   📝 Memo icon

Figure 5.1 Icons for documents and memos

Linking documents and memos

At the moment, this memo is not linked with any node or document. You can do that either by linking the node to the memo or the memo to the node.

To link a node with the memo

1 In the Node Explorer, select the node you want to link the memo with.
2 Click on the **DocLinks** button in the toolbar at the top of the window,
   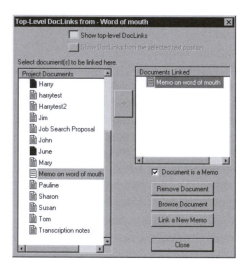.
3 This opens the **Top-Level** DocLinks window (see Figure 5.2).
4 On the left of this is a list of all the project documents. Select your memo from this list.
5 Click on the memo you want to link with and click on the add button, marked **->**. This will add the memo to the list of linked documents on the right of the window. Note that you can link ordinary documents or memos to nodes (or to other documents). The only distinctive thing about a memo is its icon.
6 When you have finished linking memos or documents with the node, click on **Close**.

Figure 5.2   The Top-Level DocLinks window

Notice that there are some other things you can do from the Top-Level DocLinks window. You can link with several documents if you want, and these can be either memos or ordinary documents or a mixture of both. You can also create a new memo from here. In fact, if you don't already have a memo document you want to import into the project, this is probably the most convenient way to make a new memo. (Click on the **Link a New Memo** button at the bottom right of the window.) You can also link with an ordinary document then convert it into a memo by adding it to the list of linked documents and ticking the **Document is a Memo** tick box. And you can browse any document or memo you have linked (see Figure 5.3). So this dialog serves the multiple functions of enabling you to add or remove links from a node to documents and memos and to browse those you have linked (e.g. if you come back to the documents linked to this node at some later time).

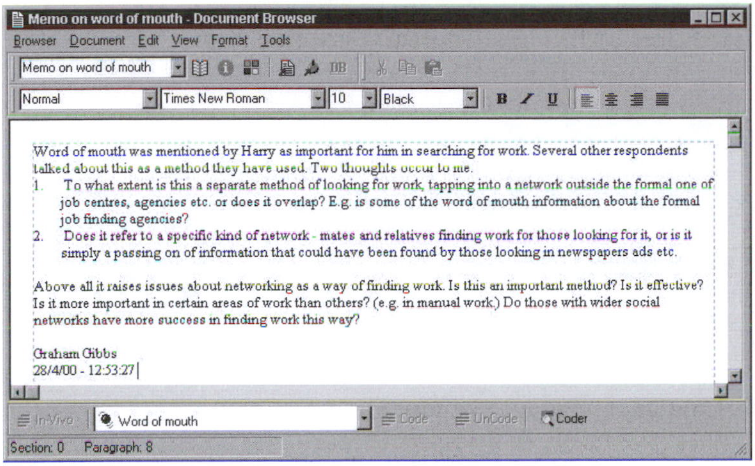

Figure 5.3   Memo in the Document Browser

Several nodes can link with the same document/memo and several documents/memos can link with the same node. Links between nodes and whole documents, between nodes and nodes and between whole documents and other documents are symmetrical. This means the links can be made, inspected and undone in either direction. Thus in the case of the memo just set up, we started from the node and linked the document (memo) with it using the Top-Level DocLinks window. We could have done this the other way round; selected the memo in the Document Explorer and linked it with the node using the Top-Level NodeLinks window (click on the NodeLinks button [NodeLinks] in the toolbar) – see Figure 5.4. This means that while reading or writing a memo you can quickly browse the text coded at the node that the memo is about.

Memo contents

What can you write in a memo? Well really anything of relevance, but it makes most sense to focus on things that will support the development of your analysis and the construction of your node system. The following are typical of the kinds of things you could memo:

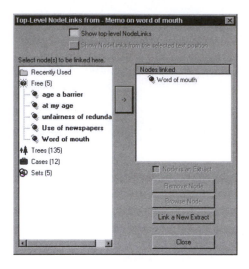

Figure 5.4 The Top-Level NodeLinks window

1 *A new idea for a node*. As in the example in Figure 5.3, this may have been sparked off by something a respondent said.
2 *'Placeholding' – just a quick hunch*. There is an example of this in the second paragraph of the memo in Figure 5.3.
3 *Integrative discussion* (e.g. of previous reflective remarks). Often this brings together one or more memos with things such as node definitions. You can cut and paste node definitions into your memo. (There is no Edit menu in the node Properties dialog, but the keyboard shortcuts Ctrl-X, Ctrl-C and Ctrl-V for cut, copy and paste still work.) That way you can use the Search Tool on the contents of node definitions.
4 *Dialogue among researchers*. Memos are a good way of sharing analytic ideas with co-workers. That's why the memo in Figure 5.3 contains the name of the person writing it.
5 *To question the quality of the data*. You may feel that the respondent was not entirely open about something or is not qualified to tell you about an issue, i.e. the story is second- or third-hand.
6 *To question the original analytic framework*. You might write a memo against an existing node in a tree you set up at the start of the project to raise questions about whether it actually makes sense or whether it should be moved elsewhere in the tree.
7 *What is puzzling or surprising about a case*. A key skill in examining qualitative documents is to be able to spot what is surprising. Sometimes we are too familiar with the context to find something surprising, or more commonly we simply fail to spot it.
8 *As alternative hypotheses to another memo*. This is a kind of internal dialogue between those involved on the project or to yourself if you are

working alone. For instance, an alternative hypothesis to the first idea in the memo in Figure 5.3 might be that respondents are using the idea of word of mouth as a kind of urban myth. Everyone knows someone who got that plum job by knowing the right person. But is that just being used as an 'excuse' or explanation by respondents as to why they can't find work?

9 *If you have no clear idea but are struggling to find one.* People often think that you can't write without a clear idea of what to say. However, the situation is often the other way round. Writing helps to clarify the ideas. You may think you are on to something, in that case trying to write it down may help sort out what the issues are. Remember you can always come back to what you have written later to see if, in the cold light of the next day, it still makes sense.

10 *To raise a general theme or metaphor.* This is a more integrative or holistic activity. At some time in your analysis you will need to start trying to bring the manifold issues together. Grounded theorists refer to this as selective coding or the identification of a core phenomenon.

Linking from places inside a document

So far we have seen examples of nodes and documents (or memos) linking with documents as a whole. But nodes and documents can also be linked with particular places in documents. Linking a document with a place in a transcript is one way you can make a note on a specific part of its contents. Used in this way, NVivo makes no distinction between such notes and other documents and memos. So if you want to keep them separate it's probably a good idea to give them a distinctive name such as putting 'N-Harry-' at the start of the name if it is a note on the document 'Harry'. As we shall see later, you can also create a set for such note documents. The advantage of using documents for notes is that the contents are still searchable and can also be coded and linked to other documents and nodes.

To link a document with a specific place in another document

1 Open the document in the Document Browser. (This procedure will also work from the text displayed in the Node Browser.)
2 Click in the text where you want the document to be linked.
3 Click on the **Make/Inspect DocLinks** button in the toolbar, 📄.
4 Unless you already have a document or memo you want to link to, click on the **Link a New Memo** button.
5 This opens the Document Browser for a new memo document with the title **DocName - Memo** where DocName is the name of the document you have linked from. You can change this later, if you want, using the document Properties dialog.

6 Write your memo or note (or cut and paste from elsewhere – and remember you can cut and paste in text from one of the primary documents).
7 Close the Document Browser.
8 If you do have a document already, click on that and move it to the Documents Linked list by clicking the add button, marked **->**.
9 You will now have a new link with a document.
10 You can make other links now if you wish, or finish by clicking on **Close**.

A small icon for a document (the same as the icon for **Make/Inspect DocLinks** in the toolbar) is inserted into the text where you indicated (see Figure 5.5). Next time you read this text in the Document Browser or the Node Browser this icon will appear and you can use its contextual menu to browse the documents it links with. Note that links into specific places in documents are not two-way. You can go from the document to those documents and nodes linked with the text, but you can't go the other way, from, say, a memo to the specific place it is linked with in a document.

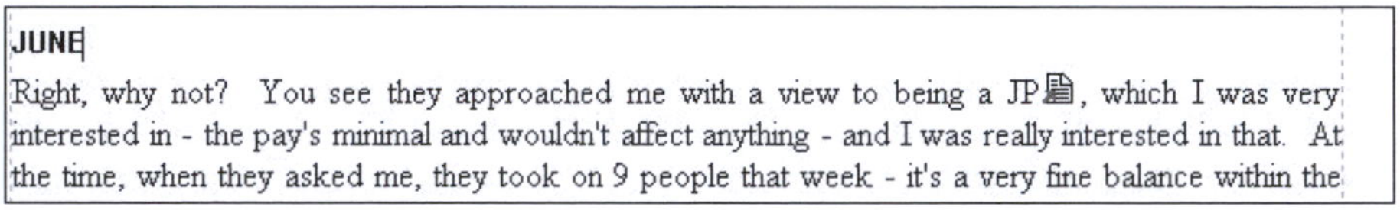

JUNE
Right, why not? You see they approached me with a view to being a JP , which I was very interested in - the pay's minimal and wouldn't affect anything - and I was really interested in that. At the time, when they asked me, they took on 9 people that week - it's a very fine balance within the

Figure 5.5   A DocLinks icon in a passage of text

You can also link with a node from a place in a document. This won't often make a lot of sense from within one of the primary documents. You can just code the text at the node. However, if, say, a respondent A mentions another respondent B for whom you have a node at which is coded everything B said, you might consider doing this. You can both code the passage in A's text at a node representing text discussing B and create a link in this passage to the node that codes what B said.

However, linking with a node from a memo can be useful. As you build up your concepts and ideas in memos you can link them together using document links (both whole memo with whole memo and with a specific place in the text) and node links. For example, in the memo in Figure 5.3 we may want to put a link in the text of the second point with a node that codes 'references to mates and relatives in work'.

To link a node with a specific place in a document

1 Open the document or memo in the Document Browser.
2 Click in the text where you want the node to be linked.
3 Click on the **Make/Inspect NodeLinks** button in the toolbar, .

4 Find the node you want to link with in the node listing on the left. Click on it and move it to the Nodes linked list by clicking the add button, marked **->**.

5 You will now have link to the node – see Figure 5.6. (Also notice at the top of the NodeLinks inspector window there are two buttons, one will look raised and be in grey and the other will appear empty or white. These allow you to toggle between a view of nodes linked with just the place in the document you are working from and a view of all the nodes linked with the document as a whole. Click on whichever is the grey, raised button to switch view.)

6 You can make links with other nodes now if you wish, or finish by clicking on **Close**. Notice that a small icon indicating a link to a node has been placed in the document at the place you indicated – see Figure 5.7.

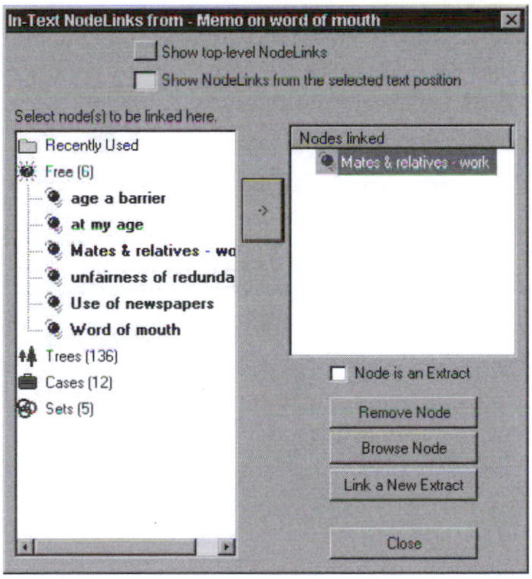

Figure 5.6   NodeLinks window to set up a link within a passage of text

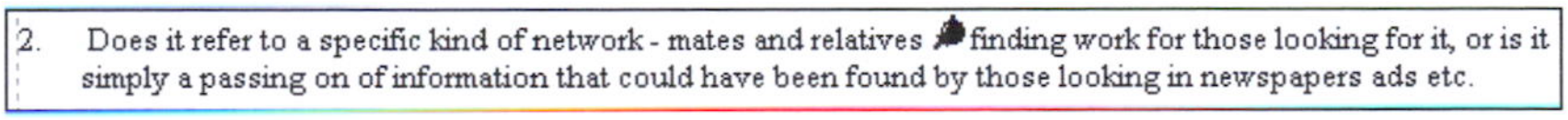

Figure 5.7   A NodeLinks icon in a passage of text

DataBites and annotations

NVivo provides one further facility for linking passages in the text of documents with other material: DataBites. These can be any kind of material stored on your computer: text files, multimedia files and so on. It is thus a way of linking your document with pictures, sound recording, digitized video, websites, spreadsheets etc. None of these items can be entered into the NVivo database but if they are stored on your computer and you have the

Quick access to linked documents and nodes from within a document

Use the contextual menu ⌂ from the DocLink or NodeLink icon in the text. This will list, at the top of the menu, the document(s) or node(s) linked with the icon at that point. Select one of these to go directly to the Document Browser or the Node Browser with the chosen document or node contents showing. This avoids having to go through the DocLinks or NodeLinks windows.

software to read the files then they can be linked with text in NVivo. The files can be opened from within NVivo using the software you would normally use to read them. For example, imagine you have been doing observations in a local school and have a map of it which you have scanned into the computer and which you can read using one of the graphics programs on your computer (e.g. Photoshop, PaintShop Pro or Paint).

To link a DataBite with a specific place in a document

1 Make sure you have the DateBite file you want to link somewhere on your computer. The External DataBites folder in the All Users folder of the project is a good place to keep it.
2 Open the document or memo in the Document Browser.
3 With the mouse, select the text you want to link the DataBite with.
4 Click on the DataBite button in the toolbar, DB .
5 Select **External File** in the Select DataBite Type dialog that appears.
6 Click **OK**.
7 In the file selector dialog that appears, locate and select the file you want to link with.
8 Click **Open**.
9 You return to the Document Browser and the text you selected is now underlined to indicate it is linked to a DataBite (see Figure 5.8).

> Above all it raises issues about <u>networking as a way of finding work</u>. Is this an important method? Is it effective? Is it more important in certain areas of work than others? (e.g. in manual work.) Do those with wider social networks have more success in finding work this way?

Figure 5.8   Underlined text showing a link to a DataBite

You can examine a DataBite or remove the link with it using the underlined text's contextual menu ⌂.

You can also use DataBites to make simple annotations to the text, although these aren't stored as documents in the project. You may find this a tidier way of keeping annotations, but the drawback is that you cannot annotate whole documents and none of the annotation itself is accessible by other NVivo tools. You can annotate this way either by linking to a text document you have already written but not imported into the project, or by selecting to make a special kind of DataBite, an annotation.

To link a DataBite annotation to a specific place in a document

1 Open the document or memo in the Document Browser.
2 With the mouse, select the text you want to link the annotation to.
3 Click on the DataBite button in the toolbar.
4 Select **Internal Annotation** in the Select DataBite Type dialog that appears.
5 Click **OK**.
6 In the DataBite annotation window that appears type the text you want as an annotation – see Figure 5.9. (Although there is no Edit menu, cut and paste using the keyboard shortcuts, Ctrl-C and Ctrl-V, will work.)
7 Click on the **Save & Close** button.

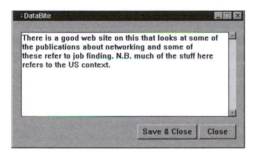

Figure 5.9   Entering a DataBite annotation

You can examine the contents of a DataBite annotation and remove the annotation in the same way as other DataBites, using the contextual menu ⌂. In addition, you can edit the contents of the annotation by opening it (use the text's contextual menu ⌂) and making the changes to the text. Making annotations to text this way is very easy, but has the one big disadvantage that the annotations do not form part of your main project database. They cannot therefore be searched or coded. It is up to you to decide whether this is a big disadvantage or not.

How to use document, node and DataBite linking

There is no question that coding texts is the most popular way of undertaking qualitative analysis. However, there are some authors who suggest that alternatives are possible and preferable. For example, Coffey *et al.* (1996) suggest that the analysis of qualitative data can be undertaken by using the kind of hyperlinks familiar to most people now through their experience of the World Wide Web – similar arguments are to be found in Lee and Fielding (1996) and Kelle (1997). The point is that links between documents can replace the need to code passages of text. The researcher can start to understand the commonalties of and differences between texts without having to resort to any kind of indexing and thus any decontextualization. However, there are disadvantages. A common experience when using the World Wide Web is 'getting lost in hyperspace': following one link after another until you have forgotten where you have come from or even what you were looking for in the first place. Multiply linked qualitative documents appears to be likely to lead to the same kind of confusion if used as a method of qualitative analysis. Moreover, when it comes to writing up the analysis, such links present the writer with a serious problem of how to tease out the ideas from the manifold links and express them in the report. That said, it is likely that in making such links, you will come to understand the data very well, and that puts you in a good position for writing. On the other hand, as Coffey *et al.* point out, hyperlinking can be a good way of preserving the connection between the qualitative analysis and the original texts. Nothing is ever decontextualized until the point of write-up, and, in fact, if high-capacity media like CD-ROMs, DVDs and the WWW are used for publishing the results, even the final analysis could preserve links to the original data by publishing them with the analysis. Of course, this raises all kinds of issues about confidentiality if the analysis is presented to a wider public, but it does at least allow the reader to see the full evidence for the conclusions that the qualitative analyst has drawn.

The linking facilities in NVivo go some way towards providing the means to do analysis in the flexible way Coffey *et al.* suggest. There are some limitations, though. On the Web, links can be in any direction and to whole pages (documents) or to specific places in pages. The latter is not easy to do in NVivo. You can link from a place in a document to another whole document, but not *into* a specific place in a document. This can be simulated, for example, by creating a new node specifically for this purpose, coding the target text at the node and then inserting a node link to it in the document. But the procedure is messy.

There is, however, one use of links that I think most researchers will find very useful: links into and out of metadata documents such as memos. In particular, I suspect that the word-processing facilities now available in NVivo will mean that you can start writing your analysis in the program as opposed to using a separate word processor. This developing analytic document is what can benefit from being linked to nodes, memos and documents from the project database. This means using a document in your NVivo project to bring together all the analytic ideas and notes that are scattered around in various documents, memos and annotations. You may find as you develop memos about the nodes, as you add ideas to them and elaborate discussions in them, that some start to constitute the bones of a possible section in your write-up. If you have made full use of the node hierarchy, these are likely to be memos on the most significant nodes in the tree. In other cases you might deliberately start memos that reflect the proposed section or chapter structure of your final report. These documents can be used as electronic versions of what Wolcott (1990: 38) refers to as 'the expanding drop file' approach. In this file (or document) you could keep all the material relating to the particular chapter. I shall look at these ideas in more detail in Chapter 10.

Attributes

Attributes are the way that NVivo treats the kind of variable-based data that is common in quantitative and statistical analysis. Variables have a set of values associated with them, and that is how attributes operate in NVivo. For example, you may want to use the attribute 'age' to indicate the age of your respondent. The name of the attribute will then be something like 'Age of respondent' and its values will be the various ages such as '21', '37' and '54'. In quantitative research, such variables are primary data, but in qualitative work (and this is reflected in NVivo) they may be primary data or data about the data, metadata. Thus the example of 'Age of respondent' I have just mentioned will be primary data, but you can also record attributes such as 'Name of interviewer', 'Date node defined' and these are more akin to metadata. In NVivo you can record attributes about documents, nodes and cases. Table 5.2 gives some examples. Note that any one document, memo, node or case will only have one of the list of possible values for each attribute. Attributes can be constructed for any variable that might influence your data, the data analysis and its validity.

Attributes provide a way of linking qualitative and quantitative data where both share respondents or cases. For example, you might have a set of data generated by a questionnaire survey linked with some interviews that were undertaken with selected individuals from those surveyed. An NVivo project could contain documents representing the interviews undertaken and attributes linked to those documents (or to cases if, for example, respondents had more than one interview) taken from the survey data. The linkage can also go the other way. Analysis of the data in NVivo might create new attributes that can then be 'exported' out into the survey data set.

There are two principal ways of creating and assigning attributes: doing

Table 5.2 Examples of possible attributes

Attribute	Applicable to	Example values	Value type
Age of person	Document, case	21, 37, 54	Number
Date of interview	Document, case	97/12/5, 97/9/26	Year, month, day
In employment	Document, case	Yes, no	Boolean*
Gender	Document, memo, node, case	Male, Female	String
Writer	Document, memo	Trevor, Mahmood, Alison	String
Date of writing	Document, memo, node	2000/4/21, 1999/8/3	Year, month, day
Interviewer name	Document, case	Helen, Sally, Shahida	String
Place of interview	Document	Home, University	String
Town of interview	Document	Leeds, London, York	String
When transcribed	Document, memo	2001/5, 2001/6, 2001/7	Year, month
Name of transcriber	Document, memo	Susan, Gill, Brit	String
Source of document	Document	Newspaper, TV, Radio, WWW	String
Archive	Document, case	Manchester, Essex, Oxford	String
Type of document	Document, memo	Interview, Committee minutes, Observation, Field notes	String
Creator of node	Node	Trevor, Wilton, Betty	String
Date of event	Node	2000/4, 1999/8	Year, month
Status of node	Node	Hunch, Defined, Agreed, Validated	String

*This refers to the idea that the values may fall logically into one of only two types, true or false, yes or no etc.

it in NVivo; and importing them from a statistical program or a spreadsheet. In NVivo attributes are created and edited using either the node attribute editor or the document attribute editor since NVivo keeps two lists of attributes: those for documents and memos and those for nodes and cases. However, if you create a new attribute in one area that already exists in the other, then the program gives you the choice of sharing that attribute name and its values across both nodes and documents, and the attribute appears in both editors.

To create a new document attribute

1 Open the document attribute editor. To do this in the Project Pad, click on the **Documents** tab and then on the **Attributes** tab. Then click on the **Make or Change a Document Attribute** button.
2 This opens the Create/Edit Attribute dialog window showing the list of document attributes (see Figure 5.10).

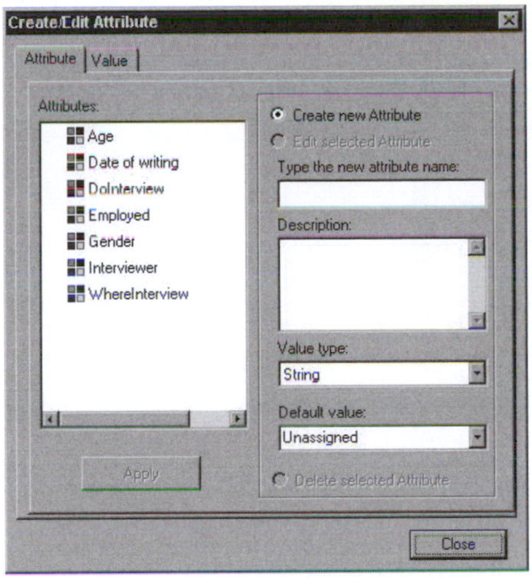

Figure 5.10   The Create/Edit Attribute dialog window for document attributes

3 Type a name for the attribute in the box at the top on the right-hand side of the window.
4 Beneath this you may enter an optional description.
5 Select an appropriate value type from the pull-down menu below this. See the explanation below.
6 Click on the **Apply** button.

Now you need to enter the values you require for this attribute.

To create further values for a document attribute

1 Select one of the attributes in the list in the Create/Edit Attribute dialog window (for example, the one you have just created).
2 Click on the **Value** tab at the top of the window.
3 If this is a new attribute then just three values will appear in the list on the

left-hand side of the window: 'Unassigned', 'Unknown' and 'Not Applicable'. These are always available for every attribute.

4 To add further values, type a name for the value in the box at the top of the right of the window. For example, if your attribute is 'Gender', type in the value, say, 'Female'.

5 Click on the **Apply** button and this value will be added to the list on the left (see Figure 5.11).

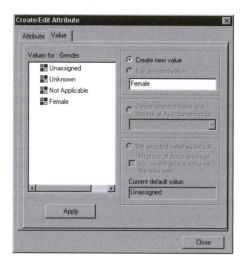

Figure 5.11   Assigning values to an attribute

6 Repeat this step until you have entered all the values you need. If you make a mistake, select the erroneous value and type in the correction on the right, then click on the **Apply** button.

7 You may now click on the **Attribute** tab to enter another attribute, and then the **Value** tab again to enter values for that attribute. Repeat this until you have set up all the attributes you need.

8 When you have finished click on the **Close** button.

You may enter as many attributes and values at one time as you like. You can always go back later to add more attributes or more values to an attribute.

Every attribute has a value type. For the examples in Table 5.2 they are indicated in the last column. Possible value types are shown in Table 5.3. If the values are ordered, this means that when you are using the Search Tool you can construct queries like 'find all the nodes that were reviewed after a certain date' or 'find all the cases older than 50'. Note that date and time formats are always expressed with the most significant figure first, for instance year/month/day or hour/minute. This makes it easy to put the values in order and hence use them in the Search Tool.

Table 5.3 Possible value types for attributes

Value type	Possible values	Ordered
String	Any sequence of letters and numbers, with a maximum of 35 including spaces	No
Boolean	True or False	No
Number	Any number, including decimals	Yes
A variety of date and time formats	For example 2000/5 or 1999/12/25 or 12/45/32	Yes

Examining and changing attributes

To inspect the attributes of a document or memo or to assign values to them, you need to use the Document Attribute Explorer.

To open the Document Attribute Explorer

1 Either:
 (a) in the Project Pad click on the **Documents** tab and then on the **Attributes** tab. Then click on the **Explore all Document Attributes** button; or
 (b) if you wish to examine just the attributes for some documents then, in the Document Explorer, select **Explore Set's Attributes** from the contextual menu ⌂ of the set you wish to examine (this includes the sets All Documents and Recently Used).
2 This opens the Document Attribute Explorer (see Figure 5.12).

The Document Attribute Explorer is a table showing (initially) on the left the documents selected and across the top, all the document attributes. Each cell in the table indicates the current value of the attribute for the particular document. Thus in Figure 5.12 the document 'Harry' has values of '47' for 'Age', 'NA' for 'Date of writing', 26 September 1997 (showing as '97/9/26') for 'DoInterview' (date of interview), 'False' for 'Employed' (i.e. unemployed), 'Male' for 'Gender' and so on. You can change or enter values from this table.

To change or enter a value in the Document Attribute Explorer

1 Right click to display the contextual menu ⌂ for the cell you wish to change. (Most likely, by default, cells where you have assigned no value will be showing just a hyphen.) See Figure 5.13.
2 Either:
 (a) select the value you want; or
 (b) select **New Value. . .** and then enter the new value as instructed in the small window that appears. Then click **OK**.

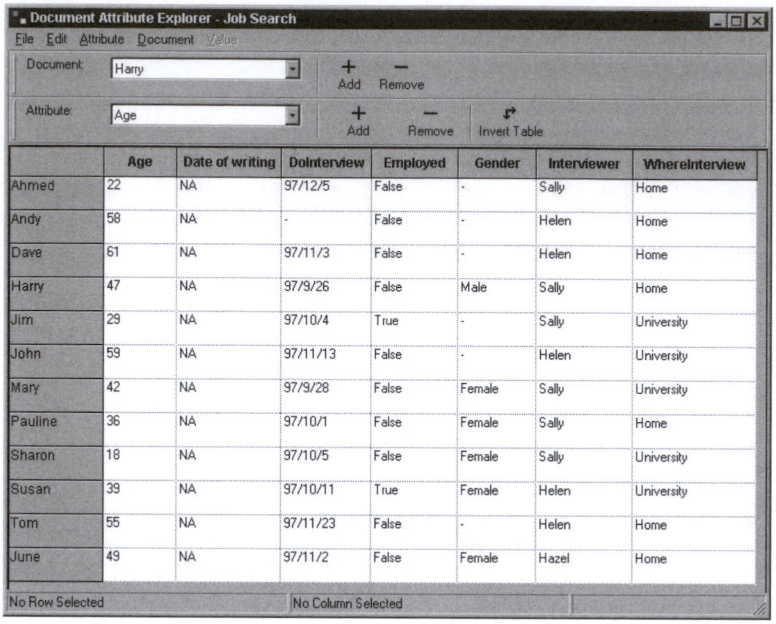

	Age	Date of writing	DoInterview	Employed	Gender	Interviewer	WhereInterview
Ahmed	22	NA	97/12/5	False	-	Sally	Home
Andy	58	NA	-	False	-	Helen	Home
Dave	61	NA	97/11/3	False	-	Helen	Home
Harry	47	NA	97/9/26	False	Male	Sally	Home
Jim	29	NA	97/10/4	True	-	Sally	University
John	59	NA	97/11/13	False	-	Helen	University
Mary	42	NA	97/9/28	False	Female	Sally	University
Pauline	36	NA	97/10/1	False	Female	Sally	Home
Sharon	18	NA	97/10/5	False	Female	Sally	University
Susan	39	NA	97/10/11	True	Female	Helen	University
Tom	55	NA	97/11/23	False	-	Helen	Home
June	49	NA	97/11/2	False	Female	Hazel	Home

Figure 5.12 The Document Attribute Explorer

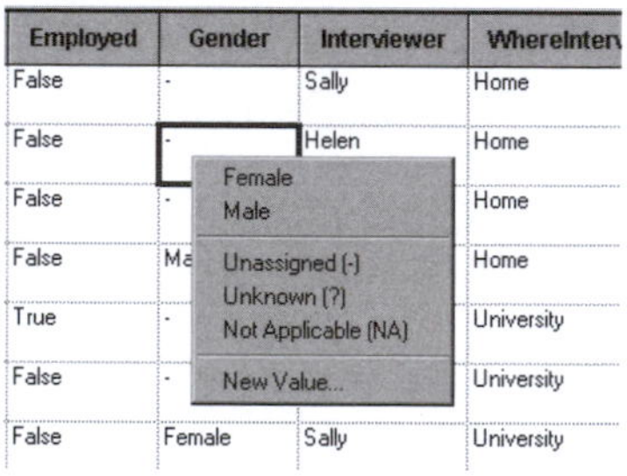

Figure 5.13 The contextual menu for attribute values in the Document Attribute Explorer

You can print the table in the Document Attribute Explorer (**File:Print. . .** from the menu) or export it as a text file or an SPSS data file (*.dat). To do the latter select **File:Export. . .** from the menu and select the appropriate file format from the pull-down menu at the bottom of the file save dialog that appears. Give the file an appropriate name and click on **Save.** In this way you can move attributes you have created in NVivo into a statistical program or a spreadsheet.

To examine just the attributes for one document

1 In the Document Explorer, select the document you wish to examine.

2 Click on the Attributes button in the toolbar, ▣ .
3 This opens the Document Attribute Explorer showing attributes for just one document.

Notice that you can add other documents (and attributes if there are any) to this table using the pull-down menus in the toolbars at the top of the window. Select another document in the menu and click on **Add** to add it to the display. (Or click on a document name in the table and click on **Remove** to remove it.) This gives a quick way to compare the attributes for two or three documents or cases.

Node attributes

As I mentioned above, attributes can also be applied to nodes and, therefore, if you use case nodes, to cases. This works in a similar fashion to document attributes, using the Node Attribute Explorer. Node attributes are created and edited using the node attribute editor. This operates just like the document attribute editor.

To open the node attribute editor

1 In the Project Pad, click on the **Nodes** tab and then on the **Attributes** tab. Then click on the **Make or Change a Node Attribute** button. This opens the Create/Edit Attribute dialog window.

Node attributes are inspected and set using the Node Attribute Explorer.

To open the Node Attribute Explorer

1 Either:
   (a) in the Project Pad click on the **Nodes** tab and then on the **Attributes** tab. Then click on the **Explore all Node Attributes** button; or
   (b) if you wish to examine just the attributes for some nodes then in the Node Explorer, select the set you wish to examine (this includes the sets Recently Used, Free and Trees) or the node you wish to examine, then click on the Attributes button in the toolbar.
2 This opens the Node Attribute Explorer.

The Node Attribute Explorer works in the same fashion as the Document Attribute Explorer. The only difference is the addition of a **Choose. . .** button in the toolbar that allows you to select a node from within the tree hierarchy to add or subtract from the display.

Counting attribute values

As you can see from Figure 5.12, attributes in NVivo look just like variables and values in a spreadsheet or a statistical program. Unless you have inverted the table, columns are variables and rows are cases, to use the terminology of statistics packages. NVivo is a qualitative analysis program and has no facilities for calculating complex statistics based on attributes. If you want to do that you should export the data to a statistics program, in the manner explained above. However, it is sometimes useful to produce some summary totals for attributes. If you just want to do a quick check of the spread of values of an attribute across a set of documents or set of nodes then the attribute profile will provide this. You might use this to get an idea of what proportion of your interviewees were male or female, or how many of the nodes you have constructed have had their definitions confirmed by your co-researchers.

To create a profile of an attribute

1 Select a set of documents or a set of nodes in the Document or Node Explorer. (We shall look at how to create sets in detail in Chapter 6.)
2 From its contextual menu △ select **Profile values of an Attribute.**
3 Then select the attribute you want to profile from the hierarchical menu.
4 The profile window opens, showing the values of that attribute for each of the documents or nodes in the set, along with totals and percentages (see Figure 5.14).

Documents	Female	Male	-	?	NA
Ahmed			1		
Andy			1		
Dave			1		
June	1				
Mary	1				
Sharon	1				
Tom			1		
Susan	1				
Pauline	1				
Harry		1			
Jim			1		
John			1		
Totals	5	1	6	0	0
Percent	41.67	8.33	50.00	0	0

Figure 5.14 The values profile for a document set

What you see may not look quite like Figure 5.14 as I have resized the columns and rows to make the display more compact. I have displayed the profile of the attribute Gender for each of the interviews in the Job Search project. As you can see, the profile makes it clear that I have not assigned attribute values to all the interview documents. Ahmed, Andy and Dave, for example, are still unassigned (the column headed by a hyphen). To assign those values you will need to go back to the Document (or Node) Attribute Explorer.

What to use attributes for

As is clear from Table 5.2, attributes can be used in a variety of ways. In some cases they can be used to give simple biographical information (in the broadest sense of 'biographical'). They can be a way of dividing coded passages by gender or age, for instance, to look for patterns affected by such attributes – for example, you may wish to compare the views on the problem of finding work of men aged over 40 with women aged over 40. Alternatively, attribute information about, for example, the place where interviews were carried out can be used to investigate the impact of this variable. Attributes can thus be a useful form of analysis whenever we want to make some comparison. However, you should be cautious about what conclusions you draw from the results obtained. For instance in a quantitative survey, based on a proper random sampling strategy, you may be able to say that, for instance, 20 per cent of women over 40 were positive about job searching compared with only 14 per cent of men over 40. As the sample was a proper random sample, you would then generalize from it to the whole population and claim that women over 40 are, generally, more positive about looking for work than men over 40. However, in the case of qualitative research we can rarely do this because sampling is not usually random. More commonly, qualitative sampling is done on a theoretical basis, that is to say, distinct subtypes of individuals are included as representatives of that subtype (e.g. older Asian women) without taking into account the proportion such individuals make up in the general population being studied. They are included because you have reason to believe they may demonstrate some interesting and varied responses. Differences found using attributes in qualitative data tell you something about the differences such attributes make, but you should not use the proportions of respondents to generalize to the wider population.

As can be seen from Table 5.2, attributes can also be used as a way of managing the process of analysis itself. Thus you may have attributes that record who coded the text, who defined the node, when the node was last modified, whether the definition has been checked and so on. You might also record information about documents, when they were transcribed and added to the project database, when interviews were undertaken and by whom, who wrote the first version of memos etc. In these cases the use of attributes is more to do with ensuring the quality, reliability and validity of the analysis than with shaping the nature of what you are discovering.

Conclusion

In this chapter we have looked in some detail at the variety of documents and links that NVivo can handle. This both provides a very flexible way of using memos in a style, which, as we will see in Chapter 8, is at the core of grounded theory, but also enables much of the thinking about projects and the development of final reports to be undertaken in NVivo itself (see Chapter 10). This means that your emerging ideas as expressed in the developing write-up can always stay linked to the nodes, documents and text that they are about. As well as supporting what might be called the more traditional forms of qualitative analysis, the forms of linking in NVivo also support some of the more recent proposals about how analysis should be done.

Attributes bring into the picture various kinds of quantitative data that can be linked to the growing qualitative analysis. Introducing such variables is anathema to some qualitative researchers, and nothing says you have to use them. However, they can be useful as ways of linking qualitative data sets with survey data and other quantitative data as well as providing ways of managing and ensuring the validity and reliability of the analysis.

Further reading

Coffey, A. and Atkinson, P. (1996) C . London and Thousand Oaks, CA: Sage. (Contains a discussion of some of the flexible ways in which linking data can be used in qualitative analysis.)
Dey, I. (1993) F . London and New York: Routledge. (Contains discussion and examples of memos and also argues that data linking can be a useful form of analysis.)
Miles, M.B. and Huberman, A.M. (1994) , 2nd edn. Beverly Hills, CA: Sage. (Contains some good advice on creating and using metadocuments of various kinds and on writing and using memos.)
Strauss, A.L. (1987) . Cambridge: Cambridge University Press. (The original discussion of the analytic use of memos as a way of developing a theoretical understanding of the data.)

6 Searching for text

Much of the activity in qualitative analysis consists of looking for things in the text. A lot of the time there is no substitute for reading and thinking. No computer can interpret the text, only people can do that. However, humans have their limits too. We can quickly get bored and sloppy with repetitive tasks, such as looking for the occurrences of specific words or phrases. The chances are that this will result in biases in the way that we code text and hence biases in the conclusions we draw from the analysis. Fortunately, computers, dumb though they are, do not suffer from boredom. When asked to find some text or a particular combination of coded text, they will find every occurrence exactly as specified. Computer searching is no substitute for reading and thinking, but it can help with completeness and reliability, both in examining the text and in the analysis.

What to search the text for

Most of the use of text searching comes down to two things: coding and checking for completeness. In Chapter 4 we saw how coding can be done by reading the documents and marking or coding sections of text. One common approach here is simply to start reading the documents and try to tease out coding and analytic ideas. As each occurs, you can create a new node (perhaps as an in vivo one, based on the respondent's terms) or code the text at an existing node if it is another example of something you have already coded. Thus a key action is the search for similar passages of text that can be coded at established nodes. This is where computer searching can help. Often the passages already coded will contain terms, words or passages that might occur elsewhere. Put these terms into the text search facility and the software will quickly find all the further occurrences. Clearly this does not mean you have now found all the passages that can be coded at that node. There may be relevant passages that do not contain the terms you have searched for or the respondent might be using equivalent terms, synonyms of the terms you have searched for. Some of these you might pick up in the new passages found in the initial search operation, and these can then in turn be used as new search terms.

As well as failing to find some relevant passages, the search may find passages that aren't in fact relevant at all. These contain the search terms but are not in fact relevant to the node in question. Sometimes this is because they are about the same subject but express a different or opposite view. In that case you might consider creating some new nodes for them. In other cases, there is no link at all with the original node idea and you will have to uncode these passages. Thus each result of a search operation needs you, the human, to read through what is found and assess its meaning and relevance to the concepts you are working on. The computer will help you find all the relevant passages, but it can't ensure that it finds *only* relevant material.

Although, by default, searching in NVivo will create a new node with all the found text passages coded at that node, you don't have to keep it. At any time you can delete nodes. You can therefore use searching simply as a way of getting to know your data. Search for terms that arise out of your theoretical hunches and then inspect the passages found in the original documents. Code the text from the documents just as described in Chapter 4.

A second important use for text searching is as a way of checking the completeness and validity of coding. As we shall see in the next chapter, searching on nodes is a particularly important way of checking hypotheses in qualitative research. This often amounts to searching for what are known as negative cases: occurrences, patterns or phenomena that don't fit the pattern or theory we think we have discovered. If after exhaustive examination of the data we can only find a few (or better, no) negative cases then we can be more confident that our hypothesis has some validity and some grounding in the data. (However, note that in qualitative analysis the discovery of negative cases does not mean we simply reject the hypothesis. We are more likely to modify it to take into account the negative case.) Using nodes to search for negative cases means relying on the fact that no significant examples have been missed in the coding at that node. Again the fallibility of the human researcher is a limitation. Qualitative texts tend to be voluminous – and reading them, looking for examples to code and all the time remaining unbiased is hard work. It is easy to miss key examples of text that should be coded at your developing node because you are not expecting to find it in this case or because it does not take the form you are looking for. It is just these examples that are likely to constitute the negative cases that are so important in validity checking. Computers are not affected by these problems. A computer search can therefore be a way of ensuring that there are no obvious examples of text (using terms and passages you know about or can think of) that should be coded at the node in question. Useful though this is, it is important not to get carried away here. The computer can never do all the work for you. There will always be examples of text that won't fit any text search pattern and will only be discovered by a careful reading of the documents.

Simple searching

Most people are now familiar with the search and replace function found in word processors. This makes it very easy, for instance, as one of my colleagues' PhD examiners insisted, to replace every occurrence of 'N. Ireland' with 'Northern Ireland' – though that didn't stop him grumbling at having to reprint his thesis. The standard word-processor search also allows for some variation of what is being looked for. For instance, you can ignore case in the search, so that if searching for 'career' the program will also find 'Career', 'CAREER' and even 'cAReEr'. You may constrain your search to whole words. If you don't, then searching for 'care' will find 'care', 'carer', 'cared' and 'cares' as well as 'scared', 'career', 'careering' and so on. However, restricting the search to whole words only will, in the case of searching for 'care', fail to find 'cares' and 'cared'. There is such a simple search facility in the Document Browser in NVivo. It can be found under the **Edit** menu, along with a replace facility. These are useful for the usual word-processing functions of text editing.

The limitations of such searching in qualitative research are quite important. Although most word processors now allow you to search repeatedly for the same text, there are two disadvantages. First, it is hard to mark the place where you have found the text. The normal assumption is that you will make a quick change to the text and move on. Second, you can only search for one string of text at a time. It is not possible to search for any one of a list of alternatives. Fortunately, in NVivo there is another search tool that is much more powerful and flexible and overcomes these problems.

The NVivo Search Tool

With the Search Tool you can search for several things at once and also retrieve all the 'finds' together. Searching lies at the heart of the analytic process supported by NVivo, and this flexible tool gives the analyst an enormous advantage both in efficiency and in accuracy and completeness over someone analysing data 'by hand'.

The Search Tool dialog can be opened by clicking on the **Search Project Database** button on the Project Pad but can also be accessed from a variety of other convenient places such as the Document menu in the Document Browser and the Node menu of the Node Browser. In most places the keyboard shortcut Ctrl-T will open the Search Tool. The tool brings together most of the searching functions in NVivo. This includes all kinds of text and string searching, along with searching nodes and attributes. The scope of searches can also be limited so that only certain documents or nodes are examined and the results of the search can be handled in a variety of ways. The key point to remember is that almost all searches in NVivo produce a collection of words or passages of text that are usually coded at a new node. This node, and the text coded at it, can then be treated just like any other node and refined, added to, renamed, merged with other nodes and moved around the node tree, a process that we noted earlier is called 'coding on'.

We looked briefly at searching in Chapter 2. We shall now examine the parts of the search tool and then look in more detail at how to do text searches and how to use sets to control searches. We shall return to look at other search operations in more detail in Chapters 7 and 9.

Searches in NVivo can be divided into three parts, and this is reflected in the three main sections of the Search Tool dialog window (see Figure 6.1).

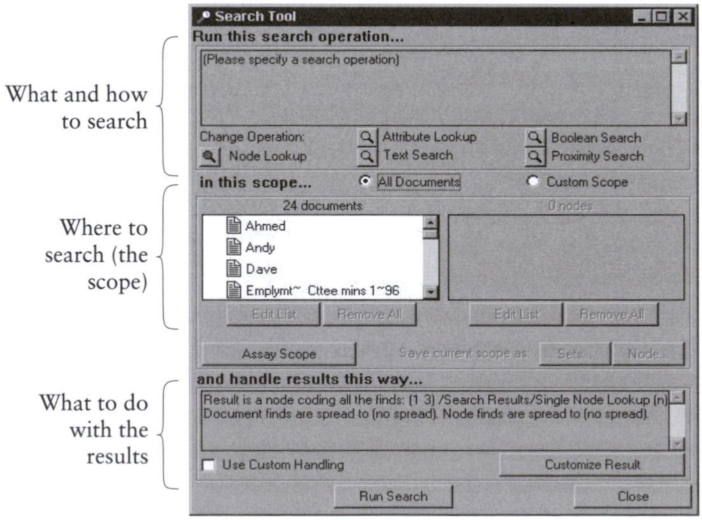

Figure 6.1 The Search Tool

The search operation

There are five options, represented by the five buttons with magnifying glass icons. After you select and set up the specification of your search, the box above the buttons will display in plain text what you have chosen to do.

Node Lookup

This allows you to search for all the text coded at just one node. You can, of course, do that in the Node Browser, but with the Search Tool you can limit the search in certain ways. For instance, you can find only the coded text in certain documents or sets. Clicking on the Node Lookup button brings up the Single Node Lookup dialog window (see Figure 6.2). Click on the **Choose** button to open a selector dialog and choose the node to search. At the bottom of the Single Node Lookup dialog window is a pull-down menu that allows you to choose how you want the results returned. This option is available in all searches. The default is to create a new node that is placed in the node tree under the root node 'Search Results', and coded at this new node is all the text that the Search Tool has found.

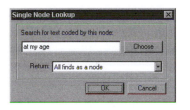

Figure 6.2   The Single Node Lookup dialog

Attribute Value Lookup

This does the same as the Single Node Lookup but finds text in documents or nodes that have been given the specified attribute. The Attribute Value Lookup dialog is shown in Figure 6.3.

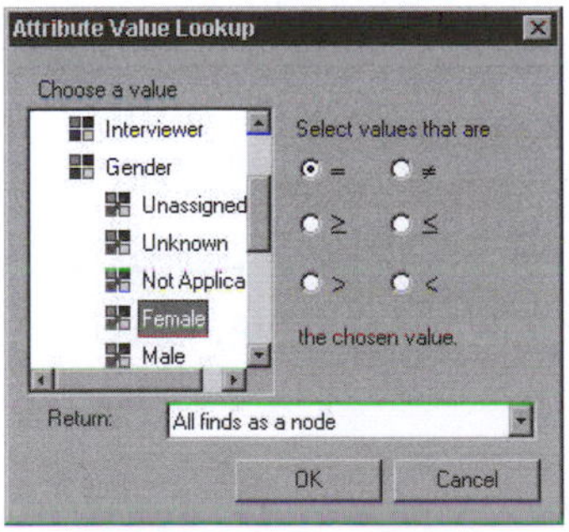

Figure 6.3   The Attribute Value Lookup dialog

Text Search

This enables you to search text for specified words, phrases or combinations of terms (see Figure 6.4). You can search for more than one word or phrase at once, and can use wildcards to look for alternative spellings or terms. An advanced option is to select **Approximation Search** from the pull-down menu in the middle of the dialog. This will find words that match the one(s) you specify to within one or more characters (depending how many you specify).

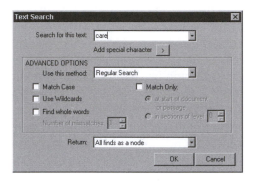

Figure 6.4   The Text Search dialog

Boolean search and Proximity search

These last two searches allow much more complex combinations. Boolean search allows the use of Boolean operators such as 'and', 'or' and 'not'. These logical connectives, named after George Boole, the mathematician who first codified them, allow you to combine searches for nodes, attributes and text together into one operation. Thus, for example, you can search for all the occurrences of the words 'search', 'find' and 'look' in the text coded at the node 'Job Search Strategy' and located in a document with the attribute 'Gender = Female'. A powerful option here, which we shall look at in Chapter 9, is matrix searching. The Boolean Search dialog is shown in Figure 6.5. At the top is a pull-down menu where you can choose the Boolean operator to work with. Below this are three buttons each of which brings up dialog window that allow you to select the node(s), attribute(s) and text to search for. You can chose one or more nodes, attributes and passages of text.

Boolean connectives do not, however, cover all the ways in which passages of text can relate to each other, and the last search option, proximity search, adds a variety of other ways in which search terms can be combined. These include 'nearness' and 'sequence' where you can specify that one identified passage of text is near or follows another passage. We shall look at the use of Boolean and proximity searches in more detail in Chapters 7 and 9.

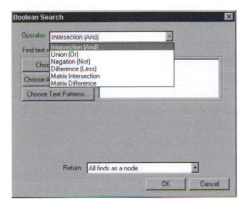

Figure 6.5   The Boolean Search dialog

 The type of search you have selected is indicated by a cyan filling to the magnifying glass icon.

Whenever you have specified or undertaken a search the configuration is remembered by the program. Next time you choose this search it is shown again as already set up. In many cases this is a very useful thing to do since after doing one search and having inspected the results, you often want to carry out a slight modification. If you are doing a complicated search, it is easier to modify one or two elements of the search you have just done rather than set the whole thing up again from scratch. For instance, if your search included the term attribute 'Gender = Female', it is easy to change the search to look for attribute 'Gender = Male' just by changing this one element in the search definition preserved from the last one you did.

Scope

This is where you can specify exactly what subset of all the text in your project the Search Tool should operate on. The default is to search all documents, but you can specify that the search should be restricted to certain documents, nodes or cases. This is done using a set, which can be one you have already created or one that you construct at the moment you need it in the search. The use of the Document or Node Set Editor to create sets will be examined in the last part of this chapter. For example, assuming you have a document set Male that includes all documents from male respondents, then you can restrict a search to these documents as follows.

To limit a search to a document set

1 In the Search Tool, click on the **Custom Scope** radio button.
2 Click on the Edit list button under the left-hand scope list (the list of documents). This opens the Document Set Editor (see Figure 6.6).

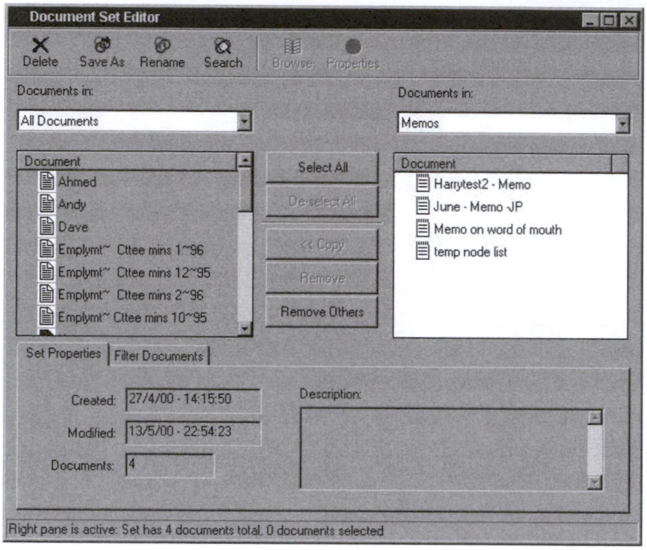

Figure 6.6   The Document Set Editor

3 Use the pull-down menu at the top of the left-hand list to select the set Male. (In the example this has already been set up. We shall see later how to set up new sets of documents and nodes.)
4 The scrolling list on the left of the dialog now displays all the documents in that set, i.e. only those by male respondents.
5 Click on the **Search** button in the button bar at the top of the dialog window to return to the Search Tool. You may find this counter-intuitive and expect an OK button to accept the set of documents and take you back to the Search Tool. However, the advantage of having the Set Editor at this point is that you can use it for further actions, such as saving the set you have created or making another by filtering and using that to search on. So if you have actually come from the Search Tool you will just need to get used to using the **Search** button to return there.
6 You will notice that the set of documents you have selected now appears in the scrolling list on the left-hand side of the scope section of the Search Tool window.

How the results are handled

As we saw above, when specifying the search, you can choose how the results are to be returned. The default is to create a new node. That means that all the text passages found that match the criteria are coded at the new node. Alternatives are to create a node for each member of the scope for which there are finds. Thus if the scope is a set of documents, a node will be created for each document in that set where any text in the document matches the search criteria (and that text will be coded at the node). If no text in that document matches, no node will be created. A third possibility is that a new set of documents (or set of nodes, depending on how you have specified the scope of the search) is created which includes all those in the scope set which contain text passages that match the search criteria. This last option is a quick way of creating new sets that can be used to restrict the scope of further searches.

An example to illustrate this can be seen in Figure 6.7, which shows the result of searching in a project containing six documents, four interviews, a memo and the minutes of a committee meeting. The four interviews have been made into a set and some text has been coded at the node 'Used contacts network'. To find out what the older interviewees had said about using a contacts network you might carry out a Boolean search to find all the text coded at the node 'Used contacts network' in interviews with the older respondents – that is to say, a Boolean search for the node 'Used contacts network' and the attribute 'Age ≥ 45' with scope the set of all interview documents. The text found would be just that coded at the node in the documents John, Harry and June. Coded text in the document Cttee. Mins. would be omitted as the document is not in the search scope, and coded text in the interview with Pauline would be omitted because she is less than 45 years old (the document has the attribute 'Age = 36'). If you had selected the option to handle the results by creating a new node then just the four passages marked in grey (= coded at the node 'Used contacts network') in the documents John, Harry and June would be coded at the new node created. If you opted to create a new set with the finds then a set consisting of the three documents John, Harry and June would be created.

If you choose to create a new node with the finds then you should rename the new node and give it a definition as soon as possible. The created nodes are given names like 'Single Node Lookup' and 'Single Node Lookup 2' that aren't very indicative of their meaning. The node Properties window contains a copy of the text from the search description and results handling description boxes in the Search Tool window so at least you know what you were searching for. But it is a good idea to add to this an explanation of why you did the search. Best of all, you should create a new memo attached to this node that keeps a copy of what the search was doing and why, along with any analytic ideas you have as a result of reading the text that was

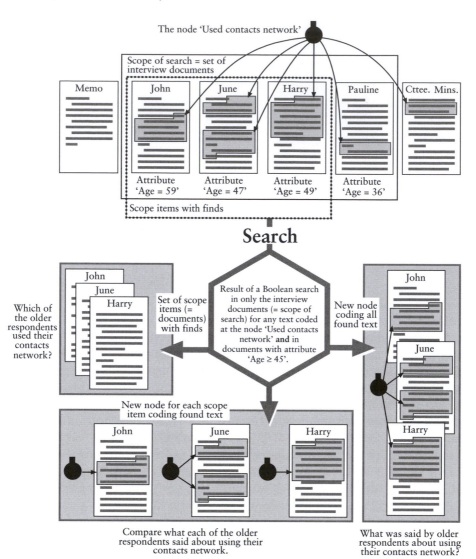

Figure 6.7   Example of the ways results can be handled in an NVivo search

found. For example, in the search illustrated in Figure 6.7, you might want to note in the memo that all the passages returned discussed using networks of work colleagues and former work colleagues. You might have a hunch that this was different for younger people looking for work, who might tend to use networks of friends, neighbours and relatives more often.

An example using the Job Search project

In the previous chapter we saw an example of a memo that recorded the hunch that the use of informal networks might be important as a way of finding work (Figure 5.3). This was sparked off by a comment by the respondent Harry who mentioned the role of 'word of mouth' in finding out about vacancies. The next stage might be to do a text search on some relevant words to see if anyone else mentioned this. We might try the words 'mates', 'relatives' and 'friends'.

To search for several words at the same time

1   Open the Search Tool window.
2   Click on the **Text Search** button.
3   Click on the **Use Wildcards** tick box to select it.
4   Enter the first word, e.g. 'mate', into the text box at the top of the Text Lookup dialog.
5   Then select the alternation character from the bottom of the pull-down menu from the **Add special character** button (marked with a **>** sign). You can also get this character from the keyboard using Shift-\. This tells the program to look for occurrences of any of the words entered.
6   Type in the next word, e.g. 'relative', another alternation character and then the third word, e.g. 'friend'. Click on **OK**. You should now see the string or pattern 'mate|relative|friend' in the search operation box at the top of the Search Tool window.
7   If you have a set of documents you want to use select that as the scope. If not use the default – **All Documents**.
8   If you now click on the **Run Search** button at the bottom of the Search Tool, the search will run but what will be coded at the new node are just the words that match the criteria. None of the surrounding text will show. You could correct that in the Node Browser by selecting all the coded text and spreading it to the surrounding paragraph, for example. But it is usually more convenient to do it in the Search Tool. To do this click on the **Customize Result** button near the bottom of the window. This opens the Specify Search Results dialog (see Figure 6.8).
9   The pull-down menu at the top of this dialog allows you to spread the resulting finds to a specified number of characters either side of the find, to the enclosing paragraph, the enclosing section or to the whole document. The paragraphs option is usually the most useful, so select this. Click **OK**.
10 Back in the Search Tool window, click **Run Search**.
11 When search finishes, a dialog displays giving you the option of directly browsing the node that codes the text you have found and, if you want,

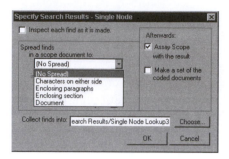

Figure 6.8   The Specify Search Results dialog

of seeing the node in the Node Explorer (see Figure 6.9). The default is just to browse the node. Click **OK** to accept this default.

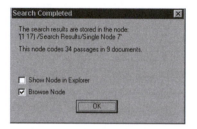

Figure 6.9   The Search Completed dialog

12   The Node Browser is opened showing the text you have just found and now coded at the new node. (You might also find that another window showing the assay of the finds is opened. This is the default when you choose to customize your results. We shall discuss assays later. For now just close the assay window.)

When you do a search like this the text you code is a mixture of relevant material, relevant material with some bits missing, spurious finds, and appropriate finds but not relevant. For instance, the search above for 'mate', 'relative' and 'friend' gave the following text passages. (The words found are underlined so you can spot them. They are not underlined in NVivo.)

The first of these is not really relevant. The word 'mate' is used but actually the extract is about the experience of ageism. The second is a spurious find. It happened because the letters 'mate' were found at the start of the word 'material'. This can be avoided by using the option in the Search Tool (under Text Search) to search for whole words only or by inserting the white space character (\w, or select it from the pull-down menu) after the word in the search string. The third passage might be relevant but further checking is needed. In this case you would want to browse the original document to see more of the surrounding text. The last passage is relevant, though even here

Document 'Andy', 4 passages, 1220 characters.
Section 3.3, Paragraph 61, 332 characters.
Well, yes. Actually, my <u>mate</u> got blown out at same time, October, and he's about 51, and he's said several times, "It's all you ever get." But they don't tell you straight out. I went after one job as a warehouse man and they were saying, "Oh, yes, yes, it'll be alright. How old are you?" I told him and he went like that . . .

Document 'Dave', 8 passages, 2187 characters.
Section 4.1, Paragraph 240, 351 characters.
Yes. There's one at Dunford, there. But you see you've got to get all your <u>material</u>, all your tackle . . . you've got to buy it - what do you buy it with? You see, I'd have to consider this - my redundancy money, which I got - if I don't get a job, that money's got to work for us, hasn't it? If I have to lay money out, then I've got nothing.

Document 'June', 6 passages, 2890 characters.
Section 2.5, Paragraph 19, 244 characters.
Well, it would've been, and I would've had to have relocated, but that's not a problem, really. It's a <u>friend</u> of mine who's a solicitor in Hull. That was the last job. Prior to that, somebody wrote me on spec, from a company called PER.

Section 2.13, Paragraph 35, 276 characters.
Just through speaking to this <u>friend</u> of mine who's a solicitor and has her own business. I went across and we had an informal interview, but when she told me how much they were paying - I didn't really think that it was . . . it would be like going back to square one, really.

you might want to browse the original document just to check all the discussion of this point is relevant. What these examples illustrate is that the text coded at a node as a result of a text search needs checking through. Just as we saw in Chapter 2, you may need to code extra text and uncode some text that has been coded by the search. Typically, the procedure would be as follows:

To review and refine the text coded after a search operation

1 Open the node created by the search in the Node Browser (this happens by default immediately after a search).
2 Inspect each found passage in turn.
3 To see the surrounding text in the document, select **Browse/Edit/Code Document** from the passage's contextual menu 🔖.

4 The Document Browser is opened and scrolled to show the text coded at the node and the actual text is highlighted. Read the text and select text to add or subtract from that coded. Click on the **Code** and **UnCode** buttons respectively to do this. The node you are working on should be showing by default in the speed coding bar at the bottom of the Document Browser. You can also use the Coder to do the same thing.

5 In some cases you may want to uncode irrelevant passages altogether.

6 If you haven't already done so, rename the node and add any relevant ideas about its meaning either in the node Properties window or in a memo linked to the node.

It is clear that a search based just on the terms 'mate', 'friend' and 'relative' will not find every discussion of using informal networks to find work. There are a couple of strategies you can adopt here to move forward.

1 In the text you have found, there may be other terms used that you can do further searches on that might find other relevant passages. For example, on reading through the text (spread to the paragraph) found by the search using the terms 'friend', 'mate' and 'relative' the following additional words to search for occurred: 'informal', 'in trade', 'in the trade', 'contacts', 'family'. Although 'relative' was in the original search, it was also clear that in a few cases people referred directly to the particular relative, so searching for 'father', 'mother', 'daughter', 'son', 'uncle', 'aunt' (at least) would also be useful.

2 Keep a glossary of these terms and others you can add either by using a thesaurus or from your own knowledge. Search on these terms too, and add any further relevant finds to the original node. For example, looking up 'informal' in a thesaurus identified 'casual' and 'unofficial' as further terms that could be searched for. Keep this glossary and any strings you want to search for in a memo attached to the node you create in the search. You can cut and paste to and from the memo and the text specification field in the Search Tool. Note that even though there is no Edit menu in the Search Tool and its dialogs, the keyboard shortcuts Ctrl-C and Ctrl-V for copy and paste do work.

This approach to searching is referred to as lexical searching. It is a very useful approach not only for finding the occurrences of key terms, but also for examining the contexts in which they occur. This will enable you to discover the range of connotations of the terms and the kinds of imagery and metaphors associated with them. But, as Weaver and Atkinson (1994) point out, you need to be aware that the resultant coding may differ in significant ways from what you might produce using other strategies (e.g. close reading of the text). However, this can be an advantage. Other approaches tend to reflect the analyst's conceptions, whereas lexical searching is much more open-ended.

If you do undertake further searches on different words you will want to merge what you have found with the node you started with. You can do that by choosing to merge the found text with the original node using the option in the Specify Search Results dialog (Figure 6.8). At the bottom of this dialog you can choose the node you created in the first search and all the new finds will be added there. (The program will ask if you want this merge or if it should create a new node. Say no.) This does the merging in one go, but the disadvantage is that if you need to check through the text in the manner described above, then you will have trouble finding the new text as this will be mixed in with the original that you will probably already have checked. A better alternative is to create a new node for the new search and, after checking, merge it with the original one. Do this in the Node Browser using **Cut** and **Merge Node** from the node's contextual menu △, to cut it (and its contents) and merge it with an existing node.

Don't feel constrained, when doing text searches, to keep exclusively to the terms and theme in question. Such searching and the required reading and checking is a very good way to get to know your data. While checking through one passage of text, you may well come across other ideas, themes or issues that are also worthy of coding. For example, in the first passage in the examples above, Andy begins to talk about the experience of failing to get a job because of his age. You might wonder if this is a common problem for older people and want to establish a new node for it. Fortunately, in NVivo you can quickly create new nodes and code text from either the Node or Document Browser using the speed coding bar and the method introduced in Chapter 2. Select the text you want to code and then just type the name of the new node. This will appear in the speed coding bar. Click on the **Code** button to link the text to this new free node. Don't forget to put some short notes in the node Properties window to indicate why you thought this text worthy of coding. Then return to your search.

So far I have treated text search as a way of creating and adding to the coding of nodes about thematic content, but you can also use it to examine the actual use of language, including the use of simile and metaphor. For instance, we can use searching in the Job Search project to discover evidence of fatalism in those looking for work. This might be done by searching for the specific use of words and phrases that express a fatalistic view. In other words, we might want to investigate the respondents' discourse. A quick read through one or two documents in the project produced the following terms that seem associated with fatalism: 'give up', 'pointless', 'in the trap', 'trapped', 'plodding on', 'can't handle any more', 'desperation', 'just luck', 'way it goes on the day'. You could use the approach explained above with Text Search in the Search Tool to find all the occurrences of these words and terms. However, the text entry box in the Text Search dialog is too small to take all these terms at once. You can get round this by searching for a few words at a time and then merging the nodes created (or do this by custom handling of the results in the Search Tool). Alternatively, you can do a Boolean search. What you do is build up a union or 'or' search on each of the words or terms, and perhaps combine this with a search for nodes or attributes as well.

To search for text using the Boolean Search tool

1   In the Search Tool click on the **Boolean Search** button.
2   This opens the Boolean Search window (Figure 6.5).
3   Select **Union (Or)** from the Operator pull-down menu at the top of the dialog.
4   Click on the **Choose Text Patterns. . .** button.
5   This opens the Choose Text Patterns dialog window (see Figure 6.10). Here you can build up a list of terms to search for in the list box on the right of the dialog. The terms you build up can be the same as the string of search items you have set up in the Text Search tool. In fact the text string entry box at the top of the dialog may well contain the last text string you searched for and the pull-down menu here will contain the last few combinations you searched for.

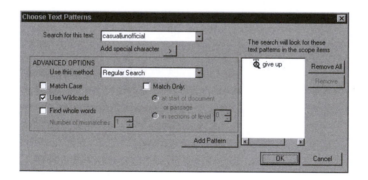

Figure 6.10   The Choose Text Patterns dialog window

6   Type the first word or phrase, e.g. 'give up' into the search for entry box. You can use wildcards and special characters if you wish, just as before.
7   Click on the **Add Pattern** button to add the term to the list on the right.
8   Repeat the last two steps for each of the further phrases, e.g. 'pointless', 'in the trap', 'plodding on', until you have built up a complete list of the terms you want to search for.
9   Click on **OK.**
10   Click on **OK** in the Boolean Search window.
11   Select the scope you want (if you don't want the default, **All Documents**).

12 Choose custom handling, click on the **Customize Result** button and
    select **Enclosing paragraphs** (or whatever choice of spread you think
    is most appropriate) from the Spread finds. . . pull-down menu.
13 Click on **Run Search**.

Keep your eyes open for new ideas

As I ran the search above trying to find evidence for fatalistic
discourse, I discovered just how much the respondents had
talked about 'luck'. This seemed like an interesting point, and
complementary to the idea of fatalism. The words I had
searched for mainly gave the impression of a kind of fatalistic
resignation to unemployment. However, the term 'luck'
suggested one of the ways in which the respondents explained
who got jobs (and by implication why they didn't). That raised a
whole new set of questions about how the respondents, in
general, explained their joblessness.

Metaphors and accounts

There has been a great expansion in recent decades in analysis of the use of
language and what it can tell us about respondents and the society and culture they inhabit. This exploration of narrative focuses not just on what
people say, but how they say it. Shared expressions and shared vocabulary
can tell us a lot about how social groups see themselves and how they account
for their experiences. Two good examples of this, where the text search facility might help, are the use of metaphor and the giving of accounts.

Metaphor is the use of imagery as a kind of rhetorical device. Very few
people have the ability and imagination of Shakespeare to create new
metaphors. Most of us, most of the time, use standard metaphors that reflect
the milieux and culture we live in. As analysts, we can investigate how the
metaphors are structured, how they are used and how others understand
them. Sometimes metaphor is used because people find it difficult to express
themselves without their use or because there is an emotional content to
what they are saying that is easier to convey metaphorically – for example,
'getting hitched' instead of getting married and 'passing away' instead of
dying. In other cases it is just an example of a shared common term.
Examples of this in the Job Search project were when a respondent referred
to looking for work as 'shopping' for jobs or when another referred to the
unemployed as being 'in a mess'. On the other hand, in some cases the use
of specific metaphors reflects shared ideas and concepts among the narrower

group to which the respondents belong and is characteristic of the specific cultural domain. There wasn't much evidence of this among the interviewees in the Job Search project, perhaps because they could not really be considered a community or social group. Being unemployed is a very individual and isolating experience for most people.

In contrast, there were some good examples of account giving. As you might expect in the unemployed, explaining why they were without a job was a major concern of many of the respondents. The examination of accounts can be traced back at least to the work of Mills (1940) who described them as containing vocabularies of motive, and they are also examples of what Austin referred to as 'doing things with words' (Austin 1962). Account giving is the specific use of narrative where people try to account for, justify, excuse, legitimate and so on their actions or their situation. There are two principal types of account: excuses, where people try to mitigate or relieve questionable action or conduct perhaps by appeal to accident, forces outside their control or lack of information; and justifications, where people try to neutralize or attach positive value to questionable actions or conduct. Account giving is exactly what I had noticed when I spotted the frequent use of the term 'luck' by the Job Search respondents to explain who did and did not get jobs.

In both the case of metaphors and accounts the text search facility can both alert you to the use of certain terms and give a good indication of how common the usage is. I put the string 'luck|lucky|unlucky' in the Text Search dialog window and customized the result to produce not just a new node with finds but also an assay report. The assay report can be seen in Figure 6.11. It

Scope Items	(1 13)	Totals	Percent
Andy		0	0
Dave	1	1	100.00
Harry	1	1	100.00
Jim	1	1	100.00
June	1	1	100.00
Mary	1	1	100.00
Pauline		0	0
Susan		0	0
Tom		0	0
Totals	5	5	
Percent	55.56		

Figure 6.11 Assay report of the documents with finds after the search for 'luck|lucky|unlucky'

Table 6.1   Using the text search facility creatively and to enhance validity

 1 Spread finds to paragraphs (or many characters either side of find) and review finds, adding and subtracting from the coding as appropriate.
 2 Carry out a search and then read the finds to become familiar with the data.
 3 Look for further relevant words and terms in the passages that are found.
 4 Merge the results of new searches with relevant previous nodes created from searches.
 5 Construct a glossary of terms to search for. Add to these using a thesaurus or your own knowledge. Keep the glossary in a memo.
 6 Look for certain types of language use such as metaphor, and investigate contrasts between different subsets of the project data such as young and old respondents. Use change of scope to do this.
 7 Use searching to look for negative cases, those that don't fit your assumed hypothesis.
 8 Check by searching to see if a theme you think is dominant really is. It may occur less often than you imagined.
 9 Use searching to try and achieve completeness in your coding, to ensure that all occurrences of the theme have actually been coded.
10 Use search on your memos to help keep control of your analysis.

suggests that five out of the nine respondents used the terms – a significant proportion of the interviewees. On reading the paragraphs in which the terms occurred, I could see that respondents were mainly trying to account for why they were unemployed or how others managed to get jobs. However, this is just the start of an investigation of account giving by unemployed people. It is necessary to check what other kind of accounts people were giving. Again, some reading is required, but this can be complemented by searching when some new terms are discovered. For example, some respondents used the term 'fortunate' in their speeches picked up by the search for 'luck'. This could be added to the search string. It would also be interesting to know if anything distinguished the five respondents who used the term 'luck'. As you can see from the assay, they weren't distinguished by gender. However, there is a hint that maybe the older people were more likely to use the term 'luck'.

The use of the text search facility is summarized in Table 6.1.

Sets

I mentioned sets above as one of the ways of restricting the scope of searches. A set is simply a collection of some of the nodes or documents in the project. You can have a set of documents or a set of nodes, but documents and nodes cannot be mixed in the same set. Sets are a way of organizing the large number of nodes and documents that projects typically involve. Thus, for example, in the Job Search project, I created document sets for all respondent interviews, male interviews, female interviews, memos, and all prepared documents. In the case of the prepared documents I used this to indicate that I had properly formatted the interview with styles to indicate sections. Similarly, I had some node sets too. The program automatically creates one combining any in vivo nodes you create, but I also had one for older respondents containing cases referring to people over 45. You might also consider making sets of nodes that relate closely to each other or that you are likely to be coding together as it is easy to display them in the Coder if they are gathered together into a set.

 A quick way to search using a set as scope in a search is to select the set in the Document Explorer (or the Node Explorer) and then search (use Ctrl-T). The same works for individual documents and nodes.

The most frequent use for sets is to restrict the scope in searches. But they can also help you keep things tidy, especially in big projects. You can use sets rather like attributes to keep collections of different kinds of documents such as those interviewed by different interviewers or those nodes created by each of your co-researchers. Also, as we saw above, sets of nodes make it easier to manage the list of nodes you want to work with in the Coder. You can use the provided set called Working Set for this or you can create your own. Either way you might start with a number of nodes you need to work on – you might be reading through the documents looking for text to code at these related nodes. Then you can add to the set in the Coder by just dragging any new nodes you need to work on from their place in the node tree (or in free nodes) into the set. This creates a shortcut or alias to the original node. If the nodes in this set are very closely related you might find that there is a passage that you want to code at   the nodes in the set. You can do this in one action by selecting the text and then the set name in the Coder and clicking on the **Code** button. You can uncode a whole set of nodes in the same way.

There are essentially three ways of creating and editing sets: from the Node or Document Explorer; from the Node or Document Set Editor; or, as we saw earlier, using results handling in the Search Tool. The first of these is the simplest and works well if you already know what documents or nodes should be in the set. I shall describe the features for document sets, but the tools for node sets are almost identical.

To create a document set from the Document Explorer

1 If you don't already have a set to which you wish to add documents then create one using **Tools: New Document Set** from the menu bar. To

rename the set, click once to select it (a newly created set is already selected) and click again to edit the title. Type the new name and press ↵ or **Enter** on the keyboard to save the name.

2 Click on the folder icon for all documents so that the list of all documents is showing in the right-hand pane.

3 Scroll down the left-hand pane until you can see the folder icon for your new set.

4 Drag one of the documents you want to include from the right-hand pane onto the new set folder icon. This puts a shortcut or alias of the document into the set.

5 Repeat stage 4 for all the other documents you want to include.

If you make a mistake or want to delete a document from a set then use **Document: Remove from Set** from the menu bar. You can delete the whole set using its contextual menu 🖰. You can create and edit sets of nodes from the Node Explorer in exactly the same way.

This approach works if you know what documents or nodes you wish to include, but if you want to use various criteria such as the document has a certain attribute, contains a text coded at a specific node, has certain links or some other feature, then you will need to use a set editor.

To create a document set from the Document Set Editor

1 Open the Document Set Editor. From the Project Pad, click on the **Documents** tab then on the **Sets** tab. Click on the **Make or Change Document Set** button.

2 The Document Set Editor is opened.

3 This dialog contains two pull-down menus of all the sets of documents and below each a scrolling pane showing all the documents in the selected set. Below this are two tabs for using criteria to select documents that are to go into a set. The basic procedure is to use criteria to select documents from sets in the left-hand pane and add them to a set in the right-hand pane. Notice that the pull-down list of sets includes **All Documents** and **Recently Used Documents** that confusingly appear in the Document Explorer as document folders rather than sets, and two sets, **All Memo Documents** and **All Non Memo Documents,** that do not appear in the list of sets in the Document Explorer. These are all created by the program automatically and cannot be changed by the user.

4 If you haven't already created an empty set in the Document Explorer do that now. In the Document Set Editor, select any set in the right-hand pane. Click on the **Save As** button at the top of the window and give the new set a name and, optionally, a description. Now remove all the existing

documents from the new set by clicking on the **Select All** button between the two set lists then on the **Remove** button below it.

5 Now add documents to this empty set from those in the left-hand pane. Either,

(a) choose a set and select documents from it by clicking on them (use Ctrl-click to select more than one document at a time). Then click on the **Copy>>** button to move them to the empty set. Or

(b) use the Filter Documents tab at the bottom of the dialog to select documents to copy across (see below).

6 When you have finished creating your set, then either close the window or, if you came from the Search Tool, click on the **Search** button in the button bar to return there.

The filters can be used to select documents for a set using quite complex combinations of coding, attributes, links and other features such as date of creation and icon colour.

There is a Node Set Editor that looks identical to the Document Set Editor and works in almost exactly the same way. This can also be accessed from the Project Pad, Search Tool or Node Explorer in the same fashion as the Document Set Editor.

The third way of creating a set is to use the Search Tool. As I discussed earlier in this chapter, you can choose to save the results of a search as a set of the scope items in which there have been finds. If the scope is a set of documents (e.g. all documents) then this is a document set. If the scope is a set of nodes (e.g. all nodes) then this is a node set. For most sets you might want to create, either the relevant set editor or the Search Tool will do the job. Use whichever you find easier and more convenient. However, there are some sets that are easier to create in the Search Tool. For instance, the set of all documents containing a reference to the text 'children' or 'kids' is best created using the Search Tool and saving the results as a set of documents. This is because you cannot use filters in the Document Set Editor to select words or passages. On the other hand, if you want to create a set of all the documents with green icons (perhaps used to indicate that you have thoroughly coded them) or that have top-level links to a particular document then you will have to use the Document Set Editor.

Conclusion

I hope it is clear by now that by judicious and imaginative use of the Search Tool and sets you can achieve some very creative ways of examining and searching the documents and nodes. This is particularly powerful when searching using nodes and attributes to make comparisons and look for patterns. We shall examine this in more detail in the next chapter.

Further reading

Gilbert, G.N. and Mulkay, M. (1980) *Opening Pandora's Box: A Sociological Analysis of Scientists' Discourse*. Cambridge: Cambridge University Press. (An analysis of scientists' accounts of scientific discoveries. The authors argued that interviews should be regarded as accounts rather than be taken at face value.)

Lakoff, G. and Johnson, M. (1980) *Metaphors We Live By*. Chicago: University of Chicago Press. (The standard text on the ubiquity of use of metaphors in everyday thought and language.)

Potter, J. and Wetherell, M. (1987) *Discourse and Social Psychology*. London: Sage. (The original text on discourse analysis. Suggested a key role for discourse and rhetorical devices in how people talk about their world.)

7 Developing an analytic scheme

The forms of analysis examined so far can be seen as aspects of data reduction. Essentially the data have been categorized and reordered so that you can begin to see patterns. The next stage of analysis is to clarify those patterns and to use the categorization and coding of the data to test out ideas you have about what is going on in the study. This stage, sometimes referred to as theoretical elaboration, involves the creation of a framework for the data as well as the exploration and examination of explicit hypotheses about the data. In NVivo these activities revolve around the manipulation of the node tree and using the Search Tool on attributes and nodes.

Ways of coding at nodes

Superficially the links between a text and the nodes it is coded at seem fairly simple, but on closer reflection there are, in fact, several ways passages of text may be coded at nodes. One node can code more than one piece of text. This is not required. There may be good reasons why a node only codes one single passage. However, normally nodes code several, if not many, separate passages of text and commonly passages in different documents. At the same time, one document may be coded at several different nodes. The way this is done is important for developing a clear idea of what the nodes are about and how they relate to each other.

Variables

Some qualitative researchers avoid the term 'variable' altogether. For them, the language and logic of variables belongs to quantitative research. Others, such as Miles and Huberman (1994), make no distinction between codes and variables and seem to use the terms interchangeably. In his discussion of types of coding in qualitative research, Kelle (1995) distinguishes 'facts' and 'signposts'. This is a useful distinction here. Most of the nodes used in qualitative research are signposts, that is to say, the node is just a pointer or signpost indicating an idea, concept or notion. For example, the node titled 'Guilt' will be a signpost pointing to the concept of 'feeling guilty about using government employment services', and it will be linked with any passages of text that express or exemplify this idea.

On the other hand, we may want to record facts, that is to say, an attribute or characteristic of some individual, case, institution, passage of text or other entity in the data. This is almost exactly what a variable does in quantitative analysis. For example, in a study it mighty be important to record the town each individual came from. The variable 'Home town' might take the values 'Bradford', 'Leeds', 'Manchester' and 'Bolton'. Each person would be assigned one, and only one, of the values from this list (assuming there were no people from any other towns in the study).

NVivo can handle variables in one of two ways, with attributes or serial coding. If the facts can be applied to documents or nodes, then you can use attributes. As we saw in Chapter 5, in NVivo attributes have values in the same way as variables do. The attributes of a document might include, for example, the names of the interviewer and interviewee, the date of interview or creation of the document, the name of the transcriber and the setting. The attributes of a node might include gender, age, length of time unemployed etc. (if the node codes all the text from one respondent) and name of the researcher who created the node (e.g. if working in a team). Thus attribute values do not directly code text, but do so indirectly, through the documents or nodes they are values of.

Serial coding

Not all variables can be dealt with using attributes, and in these cases the text must be coded at nodes. For example, we may want to categorize the content of a series of focus group interviews by the simple fact of who was speaking. In this case the variable would be 'Speaker' and its values the names of the various speakers, say 'Art', 'Beth', 'Cath' and 'Del'. Attributes cannot be used because the facts are not about documents or nodes but rather about passages of text. Therefore new nodes, one for each of the speakers, would need to be created. All the text spoken by Art in any interview could then be coded at a node called 'Art' and all that spoken by Beth at a node called 'Beth' and so on. (Note that once nodes for 'Art', 'Beth' and so on have been created, you can assign each of them attribute values such as their age, gender and educational level.) As we shall see later in this chapter, nodes representing values can be neatly arranged in a node hierarchy.

Such coding breaks the document up into sections rather in the same way that chapters divide up a book and is referred to as serial coding. A common use for serial coding is on text from semi-structured interviews where each part is about a different topic determined by the question list used by the interviewer. The interviews in the Job Search project are like this. They were divided into sections about issues such as 'Current job', 'Application experience', 'Career advice formal and informal', 'Check list of services used', and so on. Each section of the text can thus be coded at a node representing each particular section of the interview.

With some interviews serial coding will work well. Interviewers and interviewees keep to the topic in hand and do not wander on to other issues, so each section of text will focus on one thing and can be coded at the appropriate node. However, in many cases respondents will wander off the topic and start to discuss some issue that is due to come up later, or was dealt with partly in an earlier section, or interviewers ask about issues in a different section (perhaps prompted by what the respondent has said). Simple serial coding of the document may well code inappropriate passages at each node. You will need to go through the document refining what is coded, taking out the passages that are inappropriate, and adding others from elsewhere that should be included under that node. We shall look at this process a little later.

Non-serial, signpost coding

Perhaps the most common use of nodes is to connect together material from different documents and different cases that all seem to exemplify the same idea, concept or notion – signpost coding, to use Kelle's term. Anything can be coded at a non-serial node: one character in one document, a passage from one document, passages from several documents and whole documents. Moreover, a passage of text may be coded, in part or in full, at one or more other nodes. Unlike serial coding, there is no requirement that every part of a text should be coded at one of a set of nodes.

The non-serial coding of groups of nodes can be exclusive or inclusive. If the coding is exclusive, then, like serial coding, it will not make sense to code the same passage of text at more than one of the exclusive nodes. A simple example of this is the nodes 'age a barrier' and 'age not a barrier' used to code just those passages respectively where respondents talked about their experiences of interviews where they found their age was an impediment or those interviews where they did not. The coding is exclusive as it makes no sense to code the same passage at both nodes. The coding of text at a group of nodes is inclusive when the same passage can be coded at one, two or more of the nodes. For example, the same passage in an interview could be about 'Using personal contacts', 'Uses newspapers', 'Use of Job Shop' and so on as ways of finding jobs.

At the early stage of analysis it is usually more important to generate nodes and code text at them rather than worry too much about what type of coding you are using. However, as your analysis proceeds, you will start to refine your nodes and their definitions. As we shall see later, it is then that these distinctions become important.

Placeholders

Some nodes are created not to have text coded at them but merely to organize other nodes in a tree or a hierarchy of nodes (see below). Such a place-holder node is simply a name for a group of other nodes. Although no text may be coded at it, the node still plays an important analytic role, and for that reason you may find it useful to link it to memos and to other nodes. As your analysis progresses you may find it useful to code material about the more general category at the node.

Creating and manipulating a node tree

In Chapter 5 I explained the central importance in qualitative research of using memos to record your developing ideas about nodes and their relationships. The creation and manipulation of a node tree is one of the ways in which, using those ideas, you can come to a clearer understanding of the structure of your analysis.

As we have seen, NVivo has two ways of storing nodes, as free nodes and in a node tree or hierarchy. The easiest way to create nodes is as free nodes (especially if they are in vivo nodes). Eventually, as you do this, two things will happen. You will start to realize that your list of free nodes is getting too long and is unwieldy. It becomes progressively harder to spot the node you want to code some text at and you start to notice that you seem to have some duplicate nodes – not least because you've created new ones, forgetting that you already had a suitable node. Second, you will start to notice that some of the free nodes are related to each other. They are about similar kinds of things or they are examples of types of other nodes. The time has come to move free nodes into a node tree and to tidy up the list of nodes and their definitions.

This makes it sound as if you should start with just free nodes and then at a later stage rearrange them into a node tree. That is often what researchers do, but it is not the only way to proceed. As I noted earlier, sometimes it is possible to establish a node tree from the very start of a project. This may be because you are testing out a particular theory about the data or because the data collection was such that certain nodes and their relationships are useful devices for coding (such as in a semi-structured interview). In fact these are not mutually exclusive strategies. Most researchers do a bit of both. Some, especially those following the prescriptions of grounded theory, tend not to start with a tree and try to delay its construction till later in the analysis, so they are not overly influenced by pre-existing theory. On the other hand, if your research is testing out an existing theory or notion then establishing a node hierarchy from the start of coding will be a useful strategy. Even here, though, don't let the tree dominate your thinking. Add new branches and nodes to the tree as you need to and regularly review the tree's structure to make sure it still adequately reflects the coding and the state of your thinking. Whether you start with a node tree or develop one in the process of analysis, the key is to remain flexible and fluid. Never feel that you cannot rearrange and modify the tree. The node tree is an important representation of at least one aspect of your analysis, and thus modifying the tree   analysis.

The one aspect of your data you will almost certainly have prior ideas about is the attributes. You may have derived these from a quantitative study and imported them as a tab separated file. (For details of how to do this see the NVivo Reference Guide.) But even if not, it is very likely that as you start the analysis you have some good ideas about the kinds of attribute that may be significant in creating patterns in your data or you'll know the kinds of hypotheses about differences by gender, age etc. that need examining.

Rearranging nodes in NVivo

In Chapter 4 we looked at how to create new nodes in the tree as parents, children or siblings, how to move a node by dragging and how to delete it. There are one or two further operations on nodes that are useful when building and modifying a node tree.

You can move a node by dragging it, but sometimes it is more convenient to cut and paste or copy and paste it.

To cut and paste a node

1 In the Node Explorer, select **Cut** from the contextual menu 🔒 of the node you want to move.
2 The node is removed from its current position.
3 Select **Paste** from the contextual menu 🔒 of the node under which you want to paste your node.
4 The node is inserted as a *child* of the node selected.

This process is called attaching, and it happens whenever you move or cut and paste a node. Note that both dragging to move a node and copy and paste leave a copy of the node in its original place. Cut and paste, however, removes the original.

In many cases you do not want to attach a node, you want to merge its contents with another node. In other words, you want to combine the text coded at each node under just one.

To merge a node with another

1 Copy or cut the node you want to merge. This is called the source node.
2 Select **Merge Node** from the contextual menu ⌂ of the node you want to merge it into. This is called the target node.
3 The Merge Nodes dialog window is displayed (see Figure 7.1).
4 When you have chosen the options (see below), click on **OK** and the nodes will be merged. Note that if you copy (rather than cut) the source node before merging, it is left unchanged by the process.

In the example shown in Figure 7.1 I was merging the text coded at the free node 'Company internal bulletins' with the tree node 'Company internal bulletins'. The numbers 12 2 1 in brackets after the target node's name indicate it is a tree node and give its position in the tree. It is the first child of the second child of the twelfth root node. Note that the numbers indicate the order in which the nodes were created and not necessarily the order they appear in the Node Explorer.

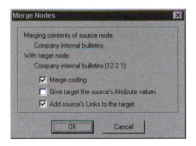

Figure 7.1 The Merge Nodes dialog window

There are three options in the dialog. Each can be chosen or not independently of the others.

- **Merge coding** merges all the text coded at the source node with that coded at the target node. This means the target node has coded at it all the text coded at the source node, as well as retaining all previously coded text.
- **Give target the source's Attribute values** gives you a way to move attribute values,   , from one node to another, and by deselecting the first and last options you can do this without changing the node's coding or links.

- **Add source's Links to the target** does the same for any links to the source node. The first and third options are the default and the most commonly used.

Moving a node and its descendants

When you cut/copy and paste or move a node with descendants (children) you would normally want to take its children with it, so that branch of the tree is moved complete from one place in the tree to another. You have the option of doing this or just pasting the parent node itself. The program will ask if you want to do this. Beware: if you have cut the original parent and descendants then pasting just the parent or merging the parent may lead you to loose its descendants. Note that pasting or merging only the parent leaves the full branch in the clipboard. So immediately afterwards you can still paste the parent node and its descendants somewhere else in the tree.

For example, in the Job Search node tree I had a node called 'Career Advice' where I wanted to collect together all the nodes about getting advice and people's evaluation of it. I already had a node in the main tree called 'Evaluation of advice given', with two children, 'Positive views' and 'Negative views' (see the tree fragment in Figure 7.2a). Moving the parent node, 'Evaluation of advice given' (or cutting and pasting it) to attach it to the node, 'Career Advice' produces the warning dialog shown in Figure 7.3. The default is **Yes**, which keeps all the children with the parent when it is attached to the new node. This will then produce the tree fragment shown in Figure 7.2b.

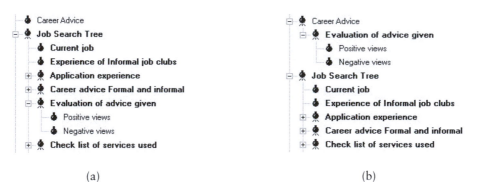

(a)   (b)

Figure 7.2   Moving a node and its descendants

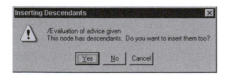

Figure 7.3   Warning that a node has descendants

Grouping nodes into the node tree

In Chapter 4 I suggested some reasons for having a node tree. These were: to keep things tidy; to represent a taxonomy; to gain an overall view of the growing conceptual framework; to prevent node duplication; and to form the basis for using matrix searching. I'll return to the issue of node duplication and searching later in this chapter. For now let us examine some heuristics for keeping nodes tidy and producing a taxonomy. As you will see, doing this helps you to think about your data, and lets you see other feasible analyses and logical possibilities in a way that will deepen your conceptual scheme.

At its most basic the node tree can be used for keeping similar nodes together under a shared parent. This requires two things: an appreciation of what the nodes have in common and the recognition of what node might be their parent. The key to both these is understanding what the relationship between the group of nodes and their common parent might be. This relationship, assuming it is shared by the sibling nodes, tells us what they have in common and at the same time suggests what the parent could be. A simple example of this is a group of nodes that are all about the same type of thing. The important point to remember is that the relationship between the nodes is about the concepts represented by the nodes not a relationship of the text linked to the node. In other words, it is not about one passage of text containing another lower in the tree. Rather it is about the relationships between the concepts the nodes represent which are summarized by the node label and its definition.

An example from the Job Search project

In the Job Search project there is a group of free nodes about different ways in which respondents looked for work. They are therefore all types or dimensions of job search strategy, and that suggests a title for a parent node for all of them. They could be moved into the node tree by creating a new node called 'Job search strategies' and then moving each in turn to be a child of this node. Thus we would move them from the free nodes in Figure 7.4a to the tree fragment in Figure 7.4b. Notice that the free nodes on the left are in no special order and are mixed up with other node topics. That's just the way they got created. You might copy the nodes from the free area into a tree and then later, when you want to, delete them in the free nodes. Alternatively, cut and paste them from the free nodes into the tree. The latter is probably the better option as having two identical nodes with the same name is confusing, especially if you start to code more text at one of them.

One or two other possible job search strategies now come to mind, and these can be added in as nodes at the bottom of the tree ('Routine' and 'Job Centre'). At the moment no text is coded at them (that's why their names are

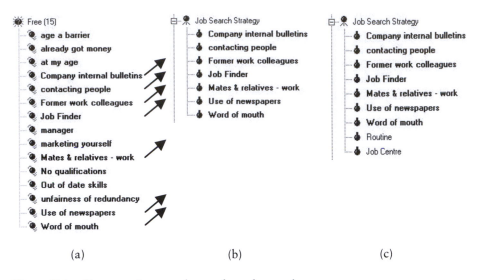

Figure 7.4   Constructing a node tree from free nodes

not in bold), but they will remind you to look for these possible strategies later. This gives the tree in Figure 7.4c.

This is a typical example of tidying up free nodes into a tree. Now when you want to code an example of a job search strategy you know where to look since the nodes for strategies are all grouped together. You will also know quickly if you haven't yet got a node for the strategy mentioned in the text and you can add it directly to the node tree as another child of 'Job Search Strategy'. You can also see immediately if you don't have a node that should logically represent something you expect to find. You may not want to rearrange nodes like this immediately. In that case you can preserve the hunch about the grouping of the nodes by creating a set of nodes (see the previous chapter). Then later you can return to the set to consider if making a new tree branch is the right thing to do. You can use sets of nodes as putative branches in a variety of ways. For example, you can cluster into sets all those nodes that are about issues that have arisen or that are contexts in which events or activities have occurred. Later move them into the node tree.

Comparing nodes

There is some further tidying you can do that begins to be more analytical. For example, looking at the nodes in the tree in Figure 7.4c, you might think that the nodes 'contacting people' and 'Former work colleagues' could be coding the same kinds of things. That needs checking since you might want to merge the nodes. There are several things you can do to check. First, have a look at the description of each node in the node Properties window – assuming you have written them. If they seem similar then the nodes are candidates for merging. Second, you can look at the text that is coded. Browse each node in turn and look at the kind of passages linked to the node. You will need to do this if you haven't got node definitions to work with. To see what passages are shared use the Coder or show coding stripes.

To compare text coded at two nodes using the Coder

1 Open the Browser on one node and then open the Coder.
2 Select the other node in the Coder. This will highlight all the text coded at the node being browsed that is also coded at the other.
3 Repeat steps 1 and 2 with the nodes reversed in case there is text coded at the second node that is not coded at the first. This will help you spot any differences in what is coded at each node.

To compare text coded at two or more nodes using coding stripes

1 Create a set of the nodes you want to inspect.
2 Open the Browser on one of the nodes and then show coding stripes.
3 From the menu bar select **View:Select Coding Stripes. . . .** In the dialog select the node set you have just created.
4 Click **OK**. Only the coding stripes for those nodes in the node set now show.

If you decide the nodes are about the same things then merge the nodes. If you decide they aren't then leave them as they are but consider changing the node name(s) to make the difference more obvious and put some notes in the node definition to indicate now what you think the differences are. It might even be worth putting your thoughts into a memo attached either to one of the nodes or to their parent node.

Clarifying node groups

Another thing to notice about the tree in Figure 7.4c is the node 'Routine'. The name of this node does not seem to indicate a strategy in the same sense as its siblings. Again, inspect the node definition to see if this sheds any light and consider renaming the node if it will make things clearer. On the other hand, the title, 'Routine', suggests something else, namely not a strategy so much as a way of carrying out a strategy. Some respondents did have a routine of reading newspapers, going to the Job Centre and so on. Others were more haphazard in their approach. So maybe what we have here is not an example of a job strategy in the same sense as the other children of 'Job Search Strategy' but an example of a manner of searching. In that case we need another parent node (as a sibling of 'Job Search Strategy'), with

'Routine' and perhaps 'Haphazard' as children. This would give the tree fragment in Figure 7.5. Such clarification might also set you thinking further about the data. For example, you might wonder whether alongside 'Haphazard' and 'Routine' you might need nodes for 'Rational/instrumental' or 'Long term planning'. If you couldn't find any text to code at these two nodes, that very fact might be analytically significant.

Figure 7.5   A tree fragment with two parents

Alternatively, and after further thought, you might decide that the children of the node 'Job Search Strategy' are in fact actions and not strategies and that 'Routine' and 'Haphazard' are really strategies. In that case rename the parent nodes to reflect this. It might then make sense to put both these branches under a single parent node called 'Job Searching'. This gives the tree fragment shown in Figure 7.6. One branch is strategies of . . . and one branch is activities of . . . . This may still not be the best way of structuring the tree, but it is a start in the process of analysing the ways in which respondents looked for work and it also supports some of the uses of the Search

Figure 7.6   A tree fragment with two branches

Tool we shall look at later. Notice that 'Strategy' and 'Activities' are place-holder nodes in the sense I discussed earlier in this chapter.

The example just discussed is an instance where the relationship between parent and children in the node tree is one of being types of or dimensions of. This is a very common relationship and is characteristic of a taxonomy, but it is not the only possible one. Some other possibilities are listed in Table 7.1. Notice that in general these seem to answer the questions (of the parent node) what, when, where, how, why and who. It is not a bad idea, when trying to group nodes and assemble them into a tree, to ask yourself these questions about each node or group.

Are groups of nodes exclusive or inclusive?

It is at this stage that it becomes useful to think about whether the nodes you are rearranging into groups are exclusive or inclusive. Sibling nodes should, in most cases, either all be exclusive or all be inclusive. In the example in Figure 7.6 the node 'Strategy' might group exclusive nodes. It has two children, 'Routine' and 'Haphazard'. A passage about looking for work can be coded at either one or the other, but not both. On the other hand, a passage about job searching might contain text about a variety of activities and so the same passage could be coded at more than one job search activity. 'Activity' in the example in Figure 7.6 groups together inclusive nodes. The mixing of exclusive and inclusive nodes under one parent is not necessarily impossible, but it is a sign that you should consider splitting up the group and putting them under different parent nodes.

The example of 'Strategy' in Figure 7.6 might even be acting like a variable. That would be the case, say, if the characteristic 'Routine' applied to

Table 7.1 Possible types of conceptual relationship in a tree

---

 1 Are types or dimensions of . . .
 2 Are caused by . . .
 3 Affect or constrain . . .
 4 Happen in these places/locations . . .
 5 Happen at these times/stages . . .
 6 Precede (succeed) these . . .
 7 Are explanations of . . .
 8 Are consequences of . . .
 9 Are done by/to these types of person . . .
10 Reasons given for . . .
11 Duration
12 Are attitudes towards . . .
13 Are strategies for . . .
14 Are examples of the concept of . . .

---

the respondent and not just to the text coded at that node and if every respondent in the project is coded at one and only one strategy. Then you might consider making a node like this into an attribute. However, think carefully before doing so. Does this characteristic apply to the respondents in all circumstances? In other words, are particular respondents routine job searchers in all situations? By making something an attribute you are in effect saying that all the text contributed by that person (the interview document in the Job Search project) has that characteristic. If that makes sense then go ahead and create a new attribute. (You can still keep the nodes so you can refer to the text that is the evidence for the attribute value.) If not then you probably just have an exclusive node group. In the example of 'Strategy' in the Job Search project, my preference is to keep it as a node. This is because it seems to me that how a person looks for work is not necessarily (or at least not yet proved to be) a core characteristic of that person. It is more likely to reflect the particularities of the situation they find themselves in. I want to retain the possibility that a passage at one place in a person's interview is coded at, say, 'Routine' and another passage somewhere else in the same person's interview is coded at 'Haphazard'.

Splitting nodes

As you code more text you may find that your original assumptions about the scope of terms or labels used for a node (i.e. the concept that lies behind the node) change. As new events or views are coded, you might feel you need to split the node into two, one for the original use and one for the new idea.

To split a node

1 In the Node Explorer, copy the node you wish to split and give the copy a name related to the new idea it represents.
2 Browse the original node and uncode all text not relevant to the original definition.
3 Now browse the new node.
4 Open the Coder and select the original node. Text still coded at it is now shown with a coloured background in the Browser. It is likely that you will want to uncode most if not all of this text from the new node.
5 Work through the highlighted text and uncode what is not relevant. You may decide that some passages are still relevant to both nodes. In that case do not uncode them.
6 If necessary move the new node to a more suitable place in the node tree.

Another way to do this is to browse the original node and then 'code on' relevant passages at a new node. You could then revise the coding of the original in the manner just described. If you are sure the nodes created from

Table 7.2   Summary of ways to develop and tidy up a node tree

1 Group nodes as siblings and think of appropriate parent nodes for them.
2 Create new parents to accommodate siblings that don't fit.
3 Merge nodes if they seem to be about the same idea.
4 Watch out for changes in the scope of nodes. Do they now apply more generally or narrowly than originally? If so, change the definition to reflect this.
5 Move nodes and sub-branches up and down the tree to develop the hierarchy.
6 Split a node if it seems it is actually about two different things.
7 Don't try to do too much at once. You can over-code and over-organize. Let the node system develop, driven by your growing understanding of the data.
8 Use sets to group nodes temporarily if you're not sure whether to put them together in the node tree.
9 Keep note in the definition field of nodes, and especially of new nodes, what changes your rearranging of the tree have made. Keep memos attached to nodes to record the thinking that led you to rearrange the tree.

the split should be mutually exclusive then you can check this using Boolean search. Choose **Difference (Less)** with the new (copy) node as the first selected and the original node as second selected. No text should be found if the nodes are exclusive.

Pattern searching and checking hunches

The construction of node trees, which is mainly about the building of a structure for our data, can be seen as largely inductive in nature, that is, creating new ideas and understanding grounded in the data. By contrast, the use of the Search Tool can be both inductive and deductive. It can be used in an inductive fashion to look for patterns in the nodes and texts, and deductively to check ideas about the relationships between the data. As I explained in Chapter 1, in the hypothetico-deductive method, hypothesis testing usually involves the researcher in making some kind of (bold) conjecture about what is happening in the data and then collecting together the evidence from the data to see if that is true or not. If there is contrary evidence then the hypothesis is rejected. Checking ideas and hunches against the data is the analogue of this in qualitative analysis. However, there are some key differences. First, we usually collect the data before we come up with any ideas or hunches. In fact the very collection of data and its examination will throw up ideas we want to check. The kinds of taxonomic patterns produced by a node tree are typical of the kind of data examination that can suggest patterns and hunches. Second, the discovery of negative cases or counter-evidence to a hunch in qualitative analysis does not lead us to reject it immediately. We may investigate the negative cases and try to understand why they occurred and what circumstances produced them. Then we might extend the idea to include the circumstances of the negative case.

Another important result of searching nodes and attributes is often a better understanding of the dimensions of the responses. As a consequence we can construct further branches of the node tree to extend the typology. For example, imagine we have done a node search to bring together all the text about the evaluation of work-finding services. Reading through this text, we might realize that there are several different kinds of response to the services. Some respondents found them helpful, others found them inaccessible, others found them irrelevant to their needs. These can then be added as children of the node on evaluation and form a dimension of the concept of evaluation.

When using the Text Search tool it is clear that what is being *searched for* is text and what is being *searched* is text. It is important to recognize that the same is true when searching nodes and attributes. In these cases what is compared in the search is the actual text coded at or linked to the node or attribute. Thus in the simplest case, if you search for the union of two nodes, that is to say, one node *or* another, what is compared is the text coded at these nodes. The search for the union of two nodes will find all the text coded at either node, if any (including that coded at both nodes, if any). The idea is that the inspection of the text that is found will help you decide about the pattern you are looking for or the hypothesis you are testing.

If the search produces an interesting result then you will want to keep it. Rename the node, add to its definition (there will already be a record there of the search used to create it) and even write a memo on it. Move it to a place in the node tree, creating a new placeholder parent node for it if necessary.

 If you use a node or attribute in a search and then later you change the text coded at the node or the nodes or documents linked to the attribute, this will not be reflected in the text coded at the node resulting from the search. That is to say, the text coded at the node created by the search reflects the state of coding etc. at the time it was created only.

Node and attribute searching in NVivo

As we saw in the previous chapter, in NVivo you can search nodes and attributes one at a time. But a more common use for node and attribute searching is to examine the relationship between the text coded at two or more nodes or linked to two or more attributes. For example you can use an intersection (and) search to find all the text that is coded at one node and at another. The search returns a node coding just the text that was found at both nodes but not any text that was coded at only one or neither node. There are two kinds of searching we shall examine here. The first is Boolean searching, which we examined briefly in the previous chapter. This allows intersection (and), union (or), negation (not) and difference (less) combinations of nodes, attributes and text to be searched for. The second is proximity searching. This allows co-occurrence (near), sequence (preceding) and inclusion (surrounding) searches of nodes, attributes and text. There are matrix versions of both Boolean and proximity searching, and we shall examine these in Chapter 9. The non-matrix operations and their meanings are summarized in Table 7.3.

The words in italic in Table 7.3 are key to understanding how the search is carried out. For example, intersection search finds text referenced by *all*

Table 7.3   Simple Boolean and proximity searches in NVivo

Search	*Finds all the text referenced by:*
Intersection (and)	*all* of the specified items (nodes, attributes or text strings).
Union (or)	*any* of the specified items (nodes, attributes or text strings).
Negation (not)	*none* of the specified items (nodes, attributes or text strings).
Difference (less)	*any* of the specified items (nodes, attributes or text strings) in the first list but referenced by *none* in the second list.
Co-occurrence (near)	the first specified item (node, attribute or text string) that is *near* the text referenced by a second item specified. You can retrieve any combination of text referenced by the first item, text referenced by the second, and text between the two items.
Sequence (preceding)	the first specified item (nodes, attributes or text strings) that *starts before* the text referenced by a second item specified. You can retrieve any combination of text referenced by the first item, text referenced by the second, and text between the two items.
Inclusion (surrounding)	the first specified item (node, attribute or text string) that *surrounds* the text referenced by a second item specified. You can retrieve either the text referenced by the first item, or the text referenced by the second item, or both.

the nodes, attributes etc. specified. This means that if you specify three nodes then the search will only find those chunks of text that are coded at all three nodes. Text coded at just one or two of the specified nodes will not be found by the search. Hence the 'And' in brackets after its name. The search finds text coded at the first node *and* the second node *and* the third etc. In contrast, union search finds text referenced by any of the items (or by several of the items). It will find text coded at the first item and/or text coded at the second and/or text coded at the third and so on. Negation finds text referenced by none of the nodes, attributes etc. specified. Be careful, negation might find a lot of text, if the nodes etc. you specify do not code very much text! Negation is effectively all the text in your project *except* for the union of the nodes etc. specified. In the case of difference you specify two lists of nodes etc. Difference finds the union of the text coded at the nodes etc. in the first list except for any text coded at the nodes etc. specified in the second list.

The last three operations in Table 7.3 are non-Boolean operators, called proximity operators in NVivo. They rely on the fact that the text in the documents in the project is actually in an order. One sentence follows another. For proximity searches you can only specify two items, a first and a second. They need not both be the same kind, e.g. one can be a node and the other an attribute or one a node and the other text. (You can use two document attributes, but be aware that this may not make a lot of sense. Depending what you do with the results, you will get the equivalent of intersection or union.) Co-occurrence finds text coded at the first specified node etc. that is near text linked to the second specified item. 'Near' can mean the linked texts actually overlap, are just in the same paragraph or are in the same section (if you specified the scope of the search in terms of documents) or the same coded passage (if the scope is nodes). When you specify section for the meaning of 'near' you can select what level of section heading. Choosing level 0 means the texts are considered near if they are in the same document. Sequence does the same as co-occurrence, except that the text linked to the first item has to start before the text linked to the second. In both these cases you can find the text linked to the first items or that linked to the second or all the text between or any two or all three of these. Inclusion is like sequence except that there is a find only if the first item also ends after the second. Figure 7.7 gives a graphical representation of the nodes and the text coded at them that result from simple Boolean and proximity searches.

Examples of questions addressed by searching with nodes and attributes

There is a very wide range of types of searches that can be carried out using the Search Tool on nodes and attributes. Below are a few examples based on

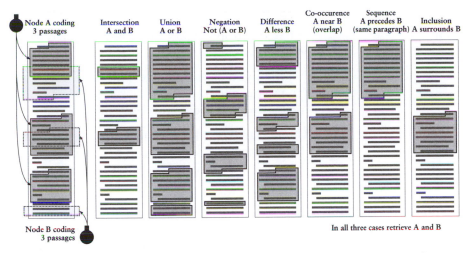

Figure 7.7 Graphical representation of the nodes created by different searches

the Job Search project. In each case I have suggested what the search might be trying to find out, what nodes etc. it will need, how the search will be done and what conclusions you might draw. Note that forward slash (/) is used to indicate the full node address. Thus 'Excuse accounts/types/Luck' means that the node 'Luck' is a child of the node 'types' which itself is a child of the node 'Excuse accounts'.

Opinions, views, attitudes

Example	What do interviewees say about the services for job searching (omitting what any government reports and committees say)?
Nodes etc. used	All the children of the node 'Work finding services/ Services/'. This is a list of all of the various services on offer, one node for each. Coded at each is what the interviewees said about the service. Set of documents for the interviews.
Search used	Union search on children of 'Work finding services/ Services/'. Scope = set of documents for interviews.
Example interpretation	Respondents said how much and when they used the services (possible data for new nodes on this) and evaluated the services in several ways: helpful, unhelpful, relevant, appropriate or not etc. (again these might be candidates for new nodes).

Example	What did respondents say about old age as an issue in looking for work?
Nodes etc. used	Nodes: 'age a barrier' (a free node) and 'at my age' (an in vivo node). Text string 'age|old|mature|ancient'.
Search used	Union search on the two nodes and the text string. The found text was coded at a new node that was renamed 'Age an issue' and moved into the node tree.
Example interpretation	The text retrieved contained some passages that weren't about age as an issue of looking for work. These were uncoded. Remaining text represented that about age being an issue in looking for work.

Example	What did those respondents who noted age as a barrier to employment say about their job application experience?
Nodes etc. used	Node 'Job Application'. This codes all the text about applying for jobs. Node 'Age an issue' created by previous search.
Search used	Co-occurrence search with 'Job Application' as first node and 'age a barrier' as second. Specify 'near' as in the same section at level 0 (= in same document). Retrieve only text coded at the first node 'Job Application'.
Example interpretation	Passages tended to be about job interviews and fell into two groups, the young who had insufficient experience, and those over 45 who were concerned that their long experience was no longer marketable.

Nuances of meaning and dimensions of nodes

Example	Does getting skills mean different things to people who have good and bad experiences of the services for the unemployed?
Nodes etc. used	Node 'Getting skills' that codes all discussions of skills, which skills were needed, how they were acquired etc.

	Children nodes of the node 'Work finding services/Evaluation' – 'Helpful', 'Inaccessible' and Irrelevant to needs'.
Search used	Node Lookup on the single node 'Getting skills'. Scope = set of documents coded anywhere at good evaluation (and repeated for those with poor evaluation). Sets created 'on the fly' using the scope filter.
Example interpretation	Two nodes were created. The text coded at them was browsed and compared. Those with good experiences of the services saw skills as something they could improve or acquire. Those with bad experiences saw skills as something they didn't have or that they had but were out of date. This raised the question of why this difference occurred. Was the different experience because of different attitudes towards changing skills, or did the different experiences produce different views about their skills?

Patterns of coding

Example	Do men consistently talk differently (or less) about the experience of looking for work than women?
Nodes etc. used	Node 'Application experience' coding all passages about the experience of looking for work. Attribute 'Gender' (values 'Male' and 'Female').
Search used	Intersection search on node and attribute, once with attribute 'Gender = Male' and repeated with attribute 'Gender = Female'.
Example interpretation	Two nodes were created, renamed and moved into the node tree. Both were browsed. Men's accounts mentioned using contacts to get work, ageism by employers, and seemed more fatalistic. Women's accounts mentioned fitting work in with childcare, the benefits trap, showed less evidence of feeling stigmatized by unemployment.

Example	Do younger respondents talk more about luck than older ones and less about skills as accounts of problems finding work?

Nodes etc. used	Nodes 'Luck' and 'Wrong skills', both children of the tree node 'Excuse accounts/types' Attribute 'Age' (values '≥ 45' and '< 45').
Search used	Intersection search on each node in turn with each range of the attribute.
Example interpretation	Search produced four nodes. Text coded at these was browsed. Most respondents used accounts referring to luck, no matter what age they were. Only one young respondent used an account referring to skills they didn't have. Several older respondents used accounts referring to skills but these were in terms of their skill being out of date.

Relationship between nodes

Example	What is the nature of excuse accounts about failure at interview in those passages where respondents were describing haphazard job searching strategies?
Nodes etc. used	Tree node 'Excuse accounts/interviews'. Tree node 'Job Searching/Strategy/Type/Haphazard'.
Search used	Node intersection on the two nodes.
Example interpretation	This only shows excuse accounts where they were part of the passage coded at 'Haphazard'. These accounts made little reference to specific qualities and issues and referred to luck, or bias or serendipity. This might be interesting, however, you should be cautious about overemphasizing the positive. Repeat this with other strategies (e.g. 'Routine') to check.

Example	Is talk about fatalism always talk about luck?
Nodes etc. used	Node 'Fatalistic talk'. Node 'Luck'.
Search used	Node intersection on the two nodes. Node union on the two nodes.
Example interpretation	The intersection search found text for many respondents. This suggests that fatalism may be

expressed in terms of luck. Beware, however: you need to examine text that was not common to both nodes. Check this by browsing the node resulting from the union search and using the Coder, select the node produced by the intersection search to highlight the text coded at it. Text not highlighted was that not common to both 'Fatalistic talk' and 'Luck'.

To carry out an intersection search on nodes, attributes etc.

1 Open the Search Tool.
2 Open the Boolean Search dialog window by clicking on the **Boolean Search** button (see Figure 6.5).
3 From the Operator pull-down menu at the top of the window choose **Intersection (And)**.
4 Click on the **Choose Nodes. . .** button This opens the Choose Nodes dialog (see Figure 7.8).

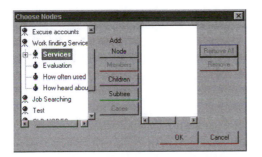

Figure 7.8   The Choose Nodes dialog window

5 From the list of nodes on the left-hand side (double-click to open the list and sublists if necessary), select the nodes you require. You can select individual nodes one at a time or all the children of a selected node or the whole branch of a node.
6 Click on the appropriate **Add:** button. You can choose to add one node at a time or all the children of a selected node or the whole branch from (and including) a selected node downwards. You can also choose all the members of a selected set and all the individual cases in a case type. Repeat as required.
7 When you have added all the nodes you need, click on **OK.**
8 Repeat steps 5–7 for any attributes you need to add. Click on the **Choose Attribute Values. . .** button to open the Choose Attribute

Values dialog (see Figure 7.9). Note that you need to double-click on either the Document Attributes folder or the Node Attributes folder to see the list of attributes and then double-click on an attribute to see its values. You must specify the value you want to include, e.g. Gender = Female. Note that two values of the same attributes will never intersect – no one is both male and female.

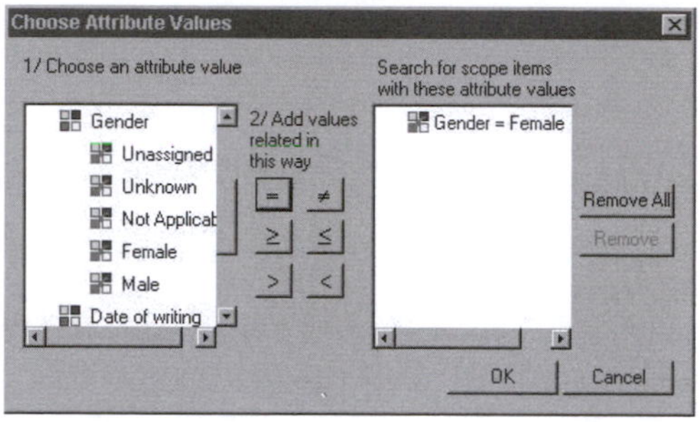

Figure 7.9   The Choose Attributes dialog window

9 You can also specify text strings to search for. This was covered in the previous chapter.
10 Click **OK** to close the Boolean Search dialog window. You have now specified the intersection search.
11 You may now specify the scope of the search and any custom handling. These were described in the previous chapter and are standard to all searches.
12 Click on **Run Search**.

Other searches are carried out in a similar way. Intersection identifies only text coded at any of the nodes selected *and* with values of any of the attributes specified *and* containing any of the string(s) you specified. This can be very selective. Compare the results of intersection and other searches in Figure 7.7. Sometimes you want to do the opposite, gather together material coded at several nodes or that contains several stings of text or that has more than one value of an attribute. You need a different search for this. For example, a union search finds everything with any of the specified characteristics.

To carry out a union search on nodes, attributes etc.

1 Follow the instructions for intersection search above, only choose **Union (Or)** from the Operator pull-down menu at the top of the Search Tool dialog window.

To carry out a negation search on nodes, attributes etc.

1 Follow the instructions for intersection search above, only choose **Negation (Not)** from the Operator pull-down menu at the top of the Search Tool dialog window.

To carry out a difference search on nodes, attributes etc.

1 Follow the instructions for intersection search above, only choose **Difference (Less)** from the Operator pull-down menu at the top of the Search Tool dialog window.
2 The Boolean Search dialog changes to show selectors for a second list of nodes, attributes and text (see Figure 7.10).

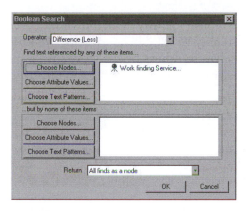

Figure 7.10   The Boolean Search dialog window for difference search

3 Choose nodes, attributes or text for the first list in the same way as in intersection search.
4 Choose nodes, attributes or text for the second list in the same way.
5 Click **OK**.
6 Continue by setting up scope and results handling in the standard way.

Proximity searches are carried out in a similar fashion, but you always need to specify a first node, attribute or text string and a second one.

To carry out a co-occurrence search on nodes, attributes etc.

1 Open the Search Tool.
2 Click on the **Proximity Search** button to open the Proximity Search dialog window (see Figure 7.11).

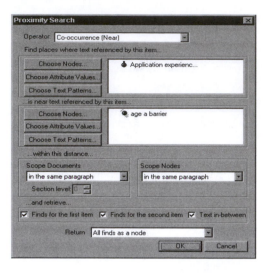

Figure 7.11 The Proximity Search dialog window

3 From the Operator pop-down menu at the top of the window choose **Co-occurrence (Near).**
4 Choose nodes, attributes or text for the first list in the standard way.
5 Choose nodes, attributes or text for the second list in the standard way.
6 Specify the distance that counts as near. There are two pull-down menus for this, one if you are using documents to specify the scope of your search and one if you are using nodes. Either:
   (a) select 'overlapping' or 'in the same paragraph' or 'in the same section level' from the pull-down menu for documents. If you select 'in the same section level' then choose what section level to use. 0 signifies that near means anywhere in the same document. Or:
   (b) select 'overlapping' or 'in the same paragraph' or 'in the same coded passage' from the pull-down menu for nodes.
7 Choose what to retrieve by clicking in the tick boxes at the bottom of the dialog window.
8 Click **OK** to close the Proximity Search dialog window. You have now specified the co-occurrence search.
9 Continue to set up scope and results handling in the standard way.
10 Click on **Run Search**.

To carry out a sequence search on nodes, attributes etc.

1 Follow the instructions for co-occurrence search above, only choose **Sequence (Preceding)** from the Operator pull-down menu at the top of the Search Tool dialog window.

To carry out an inclusion search on nodes, attributes etc.

1 Follow the instructions for co-occurrence search above, only choose **Inclusion (Surrounding)** from the Operator pull-down menu at the top of the Search Tool dialog window.
2 Choose the first and second node, attribute or text string in the standard way.
3 There is no need to define 'near' for inclusion search, so this option is not available.
4 There is no text in-between so this option is not available.
5 Otherwise continue as for co-occurrence and sequence searches.

When to use intersection and when to use co-occurrence

Intersection works well if at least some of the text coded at the nodes overlaps. Intersection search can then be used to focus in on those passages that are coded at (or have attributes for) all the items in the list. For example, if you carry out an intersection search on passages that are coded at 'Application experience' and are coded at 'Use of personal networks' you might expect at least some of the discussion of application experience to have mentioned personal networks and thus to have been coded at that node. The search would return those passages. You may discover that some of the text about personal networks is not coded at the first node. Spreading the found text to, say, the paragraph might be enough to cover those cases. In summary, intersection is most useful for splitting up nodes or for paring them down.

However, if you are not certain that all the items in the list have some text in common then intersection search will not find any text. (You know this if you carry out an intersection search and find no text.) In this case non-Boolean searching will probably be of more use. Suppose, for example, you want to recover text about use of personal networks from cases or documents where the person in question uses a specific job searching strategy, say 'Routine'. The text coded at 'Routine' may be quite short and will probably not contain that coded at 'Use of personal networks' but may, nevertheless, be a way of identifying that person. Then you will find it most convenient to use co-occurrence search. Alternatively, you could convert the nodes for job searching strategy types into attributes of the document (or case) and then use intersection search. However, there is no easy way to convert nodes into attributes. It is quicker to do a co-occurrence search defining near as 'in the same document' (section level = 0) and returning text coded at the second item only. This achieves the same result in one go.

Co-occurrence search is not very useful for dividing up text coded at nodes. However, very often that is not strictly what is needed. A co-occurrence search with nearness defined as overlapping and set to return text from the second item only will return everything that an intersection search would but without the need for a messy spread of finds in order to retrieve any text coded at the second item but not coded at the first. For this reason you will probably find yourself using co-occurrence more often than not. It can find all the text intersection search does but in addition return all text coded at the second item (or the first if that is more appropriate) and not just that coded at both the first list item and the second list item.

Conclusion

Searching is a powerful tool. However, it is only as good as your coding. As I suggested in the previous chapter, the Search Tool can help to check that your nodes are coded at all the relevant text. However, it is still up to you to ensure that nodes are clearly defined and that the text coded at them is relevant and coherent. Even with the help of text searching you will still need to keep a constant eye out for text that has been missed in your coding. But even with perfect coding, node and attribute searching is not a perfect tool for hypothesis testing and pattern searching. Finding relationships (or failing to find them) is only reliable if the text reflects the assumptions built into such searching. Among these assumptions are that the recorded text is complete (it records all the relevant things that actually happened, could have been said etc.) and that the text is well structured (all the discussion about an issue is close together in the documents). Of course, qualitative data rarely conform perfectly to these assumptions. It is therefore worth bearing in mind the caution expressed by Coffey and Atkinson:

> Given the inherently unpredictable structure of qualitative data, co-occurrence or proximity does not necessarily imply an analytically significant relationship among categories. It is as shaky an assumption as one that assumes greater significance of commonly occurring codes. Analytic significance is not guaranteed by frequency, nor is a relationship guaranteed by proximity. Nevertheless, a general heuristic value may be found for such methods for checking out ideas and data, as part of the constant interplay between the two as the research process unfolds.
>
> (Coffey and Atkinson 1996: 181)

Used judiciously, searching is a core device supporting qualitative analysis. As we shall see in the next two chapters, it can be used to carry out some of the key procedures used by a wide range of qualitative researchers.

Further reading

Coffey, A. and Atkinson, P. (1996) *Making Sense of Qualitative Data Analysis: Complementary Research Strategies.* London and Thousand Oaks, CA: Sage. (Chapter 7 discusses hypothesis testing and theory building.)

Dey, I. (1993) *Qualitative Data Analysis: A User-Friendly Guide for Social Scientists.* London and New York: Routledge. (Much discussion of coding strategies and joining and splitting nodes.)

Miles, M.B. and Huberman, A.M. (1994) *Qualitative Data Analysis: A Sourcebook of New Methods*, 2nd edn. Beverly Hills, CA: Sage. (Many good examples of comparative techniques.)

Richards, L. and Richards, T.J. (1995) Using hierarchical categories in qualitative data analysis, in U. Kelle (ed.) *Computer-Aided Qualitative Data Analysis.* London: Sage. (Argues for principles of node tree construction.)

Strauss, A.L. and Corbin, J. (1990) *Basics of Qualitative Research, Grounded Theory Procedures and Techniques.* London: Sage. (For discussion of issues of grouping nodes and constructing node dimensions.)

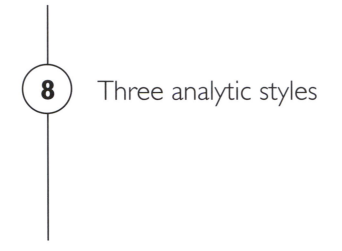

8 Three analytic styles

So far in this book I have considered various techniques for qualitative analysis as if there were just one, unified approach. Indeed, there are many techniques and approaches used by almost all qualitative researchers. Linking data, coding and pattern searching are three examples. However, there is no unanimous agreement about the wider range of techniques. Some approaches to analysis make little use of coding and linking data, for example. To others the use of quasi-quantitative data such as attributes is anathema. In this chapter I want to illustrate some of this diversity by examining three different approaches – structured analysis, grounded theory and narrative – and suggest some ways in which NVivo can be used to support them.

Structured analysis

What lies behind the thinking of most approaches that fall under this heading is the concern with causality and validity. As I discussed in Chapter 1, the origins of this lie in quantitative research where there is strong emphasis on ensuring the validity, reliability and generalizability of results so that we can be sure about the true causes of the effects we observe. However, it is now recognized that, even in quantitative research, rigorous methods to ensure such validity are not always possible. For example, researchers using experimental designs are in many cases not able to allocate participants randomly to different conditions. This is the key criterion of an experimental design and gives the design its power to correctly identify the true causes of the observed effects. It was the ground-breaking approaches of Campbell and Stanley (1966; see also Cook and Campbell 1979) which established that such research could still, in certain circumstances, produce valid results about causality. These approaches they called quasi-experiments. The point they made was that certain quasi-experimental designs, along with careful examination by the researcher to eliminate any possible threats to validity, could produce good-quality research. Most of the qualitative approaches I have grouped together under the title 'structured approaches' take a similar line with qualitative data. That is to say, they are based on the idea of collecting and analysing the data in a particular way, combined with the careful examination of the data for any potential threats to validity in order to discover the true causes of the effects recorded.

Typical threats to validity include historic threats and changes in participants. The former situation is where changes in the general background circumstances happen during a study and these, rather than any of the aspects included in the study, cause the changes being studied. An example of this might be where during the evaluation of the effectiveness of a back-to-work scheme for the unemployed a large new factory opens in the locality. Any increase in how many participants find work may have as much to do with increasing job opportunities as with the effectiveness of the scheme. Similarly, threats to validity may come from the people involved in the study. Key participants may drop out, undermining the representativeness or at least the theoretical range of the sample, and respondents may both be changed by the study and change their actions in response to being studied. Generalizability, sometimes known as external validity, may be threatened in a similar way. This may be because the setting is unusual, or events happen at an unusual time or because we are unsure of how far the variability of those in the study reflects those in the wider population. For example, we may have evaluated the operation of several different kinds of back-to-work schemes in a district, but their success (or lack of it) may not be typical of other districts if the employment opportunities in the locality are very different from other districts. Checking for threats to validity means inspecting the circumstances of the study as widely as possible, attempting to identify any such threats and if identified attempting to control or eliminate their effects.

Pattern matching

One set of approaches here can be grouped under the general title of pattern matching. The analyst compares a pattern of results found in the data collected with a pattern predicted on the basis of previous knowledge and/or theory. Ideally this predicted outcome should be grouped with several other alternatives that are feasible but should not happen if the theory is correct. The idea is to look for and try to establish causal connections between the circumstances investigated and a predicted outcome. If the pattern of circumstances and the outcome coincide with that predicted then strong support is given to the validity of the results.

One example of this is what Yin (1994) refers to as non-equivalent dependent variables as a pattern. The idea here is that we have a theory we are trying to test that predicts a variety of distinct (non-equivalent) outcomes (i.e. variables) in our research setting. In addition, there are several identifiable outcomes that are predicted not to happen by the theory. These might include outcomes resulting from circumstances that we would consider threats to validity. We then examine the data. If we can find evidence that all the predicted outcomes have occurred and none of those predicted not to, then we can infer causal influence between the original conditions and the observed outcomes. Yin provides an example of a study of office automation. In the setting, automation is carried out using a decentralized approach. According to Yin, previous decentralization theory in organizations suggests four possible, distinct outcomes: employees create new, idiosyncratic applications; traditional supervisory links are threatened; organizational conflicts increase; and productivity increases. If on inspection of our data we find all four outcomes have in fact happened then we can be very secure in drawing the conclusion that it is indeed the decentralized approach that caused these outcomes.

A similar design is one that tests rival explanations of a common outcome. In this instance we may have a variety of different starting circumstances, settings or individuals and several different theories that might explain the common outcome. In a similar fashion we examine the data to see which theory best fits all the different starting circumstances in predicting the common outcome.

Both these approaches are good examples of where it makes sense to set up a group of nodes before any coding takes place. The nodes would reflect either the non-equivalent outcomes or the different initial circumstances. A possible set of nodes for the automation example is shown in Figure 8.1. In addition to the four outcomes, I have included some sample child nodes at which different examples of the phenomena could be coded. Assuming that all the relevant text was in the same document, you would want to determine that the last three parent nodes (or their children) coded some text. Do a node search with scope restricted to the relevant document and then examine the text that is found. One of the issues with this approach is determining whether the evidence in the text is sufficient to be sure that the pattern fits. We need to balance an overly restrictive application of the pattern matching with too loose a match. Close reading of the text recovered by the node search will help. In the case of the first node, 'New applications', the

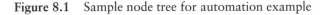

Figure 8.1 Sample node tree for automation example

theory predicted that these would be idiosyncratic. So we would expect
each one to code text that is contained in the text coded at only one
employee.

To check each node codes only one employee

1 Assuming you already have a set of nodes (with text coded at them) for
  all the passages about one employee, do this using the Coder.
2 Browse the text coded at one of the new application nodes.
3 Open the Coder and select a node referring to one of the employees.
4 Check that either no text is highlighted in the browser, or that all the
  text is.
5 Repeat this for each employee node in turn.
6 Then repeat for all the other application nodes.
(Alternatively use a proximity matrix search – see Chapter 9.)

The logic in both examples of pattern searching is that it is unlikely that
any threats to validity could have caused all the same outcomes or could
have resulted from all the different starting circumstances. In the case of
non-equivalent dependent outcomes, if we were examining only one outcome, then a rival explanation, based on some peculiar circumstances, might
be responsible. But with several, distinct outcomes all as predicted, this is
much less unlikely. Nevertheless, some replication of the analysis to different cases would make the conclusions even more secure. This could be literal
replication, that is, more cases of the same kind. This would allow you to
check against the threat to validity arising because there were particular or
unusual circumstances in the first case that produced the positive result. In
addition, you could carry out some theoretical replication. This is where the

cases are chosen on the grounds that their circumstances are such that the theory makes different predictions. A clear example of this in the automation example would be an organization where the automation was centralized. In both literal and theoretical replication what is required is a case-by-case comparison. This is supported in NVivo by the use of case nodes.

Cases in NVivo

Case nodes are found in a special type of node tree in NVivo. They have all the characteristics (attributes, coding etc.) of tree nodes except that they themselves cannot have children. The idea behind case nodes is that they should be linked to all the data on a specific case. Typically, then, you would code at a case node all the text associated with the case. Though they cannot have children, case nodes can be kept in a tree structure by the use of case type nodes. These are effectively folders holding cases or other case type nodes (see Figure 8.2). The advantage of using case nodes over ordinary tree nodes is that if you set up the case type nodes first and assign to them appropriate attributes, then any case nodes linked to them as children will inherit the attribute values of the parent. (Note that this inheritance only works if you set up the case type nodes and the attributes *before* the case nodes.)

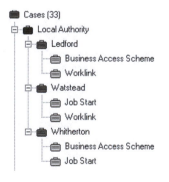

Figure 8.2   Case type and case nodes in a tree

There are two main kinds of research in which the use of case nodes makes sense. One is where you are actually carrying out a case study and where each case may be linked with several documents. For instance, in the example in Figure 8.2 I have imagined that the research is concerned to evaluate three schemes to help the unemployed (Business Access Scheme, Worklink and Job Start), operating in three different towns (Ledford, Watstead and Whitherton). Two schemes in each town form the six cases in this study. In each case interviews were carried out with people who were unemployed and with some of those running the schemes. The case also included some documents recording activities in the scheme. In the NVivo project there would therefore be several documents all relevant to a single case. All these would be coded at a single case node that would inherit all the attributes of the case type node of which it was a child. In this example the attributes might include quantitative details about the town, its size, unemployment rate and so on, as well as qualitative information such as the ruling party in the town council, their manifesto commitments and the town's dominant industries.

The other example where case nodes are useful is where some of the documents contain material that belongs with other documents. A clear example of this is where you have both individual interviews and some group interviews (e.g. focus groups). Each person could be a case, and at their case node you would code the individual interview(s) done with them as well as those sections of the group interview which they contributed.

The use of case nodes in this way has the obvious advantage of keeping things tidy. Browsing a case node immediately gives you all the text relevant to that case alone. In addition, case nodes can be used in searching to restrict the scope. Thus any analysis you want to do you can do on a case-by-case basis.

 You can have multiple case node trees. That means you can have one in which settings or organizations are case nodes and another in which the people in those settings or organizations are case nodes.

To create a case type node

1 Select **Create:Case Type Node** from the contextual menu of the root 'Cases' node or the case type node under which you wish the case type node to appear.
2 Give the new case type node an appropriate name.
3 Set up and assign any relevant attributes. Do this before setting up any cases as children of this case type node, so that they will inherit these attributes.

To create a case node

1 Select **Create:Case Node** from the contextual menu of the case type node under which you wish the case node to appear.
2 Give the new case node an appropriate name.
3 Code all appropriate text at this node.

To code text at a case node

1 If you already have some free or tree nodes with coding that is appropriate here, then copy and merge the coding into the case node.
2 Alternatively, if you need to code whole documents at this case node then
    (a) open the Document Explorer;
    (b) browse the document and select all the text;
    (c) drag the appropriate case icon on to the selected text (or use the Coder).

Explanation building (analytic induction)

A second example of a structured approach, explanation building, is actually a special case of pattern building and, not surprisingly, is most useful in research of an explanatory kind. It consists of two key elements, the building up and testing of a set of causal links among events, actions etc. in one case and an iterative extension of this to further cases. The procedure, sometimes referred to as analytic induction, because it builds up support for an explanation in an inductive way, is an old one and most often used in applied or evaluation research. One of the earliest formulations is in Robinson (1951), but a more recent discussion can be found in Robson (1993: 379–81). Yin (1994: 111) summarizes the itterative process in the following way:

1 Make an initial theoretical statement or an initial proposition about policy or social behaviour.
2 Compare this against the findings of an *initial* case.
3 Revise the statement or proposition so it fits the case.
4 Compare other details of the case against the revised statement or proposition.
5 Again revise the statement or proposition.
6 Compare revision to the details of a *second, third, or more* cases.
7 Repeat this process as many times as is needed.

At each point of comparison it is important to entertain other plausible, rival explanations and compare them with the evidence. It is also important to refer back regularly to the initial research aims, as there is a danger that the explanation being built up may drift far from the initial concerns.

The use of case nodes in NVivo is clearly important for this approach too. Any node or text searching can then be limited to a single case. Note, however, that if the cases are limited to one document only, then there is no need to create case nodes as you can use documents to limit the scope of the search tool. For example, in the Job Search project we might use explanation building to construct a theory about why some people find it easier to get work. Based on the account of, say, Dave, we might propose that people searching for jobs will have more success getting interviews if they have had experience of job searching. Do a union search on all the nodes about the experience of job searching, with scope limited to the interview with Dave. Browse the text found. This would indicate that Dave has limited success getting interviews but has experience of job searching, although it is 20 years ago. Therefore we might revise the initial proposition to state that experience should be recent (say, in the last 5 years). Looking again at Dave's account we realize that his job for nearly the last 20 years is one for which there is now little demand. We might therefore want to add a clause to the proposition to the effect that the job searcher should have skills for which there is a demand. Then we might compare this revised proposition with another case, say Ahmed, to see if it fits his case, and so on.

All the time we need to be aware of alternative, rival explanations. One example might be that people who have been on training courses run by talented trainers are better at getting work. For example, you may want to check to see if all those successful at getting work have experience of the same training schemes. This is easiest if you have set up attendance at each training scheme as an attribute. Then make a set of those successful at getting interviews and one for those unsuccessful (a set of cases or a set of documents). Now inspect the attributes for the successful set (see Chapter 5). Compare that table with the one for attributes for the unsuccessful set. Note that you will need to ensure that your attributes are document attributes if your set consists of documents or that they are case (= node) attributes if your set is one of cases.

Time series and chronologies

If you have collected data from a setting over a long period of time then you can use changes over time to determine the causal effects of changes. For example, in the Job Search project, many respondents noted that job-finding schemes did not seem relevant to them. Imagine that in a follow-up evaluation of several job search training schemes you were asked to determine whether modifications to their curriculum and their activities made them more relevant to those attending. To use a time series approach you would need to have data for some time before the modifications were made and for some time after. Then you can compare the responses from participants about relevance from before the modifications and from after them. What you look for is a distinct break or change in the pattern of responses at the moment the curriculum was modified. If you find that, then you have good evidence that the modifications did indeed cause the change in participants' views about relevance. Important points to note are that the patterns before and after should be distinctive and different. If there is a gradual shift in the pattern over the whole period investigated – in other words, if there is no clear time at which the pattern changed – then you do not have good evidence for the causal efficacy of the curriculum modifications. Moreover, the change, even if it is abrupt, must happen at the time of the modifications. Both the case of a gradual change in the pattern and that of a change at the wrong moment suggest some other factor is at work over the time period.

						Month of course				
Nodes	Oct.	Nov.	Dec.	Jan.	Feb.	Mar.	Apr.	May	Jun.	Jul.
Addressed personal needs						O	O		O	O
Used my skills							O	O	O	O
Good for people my age						O	O			O
Felt positive at end of course								O	O	O
Not relevant	O		O	O	O					
"Not for me"	O	O		O				O		
Reinforced problems finding work			O	O	O					

Curriculum changed

Figure 8.3   Data from evaluation of job search training schemes using the time series approach

Figure 8.3 shows the data we might obtain for 10 cohorts (one per month) of the training course. Circles are used to indicate where there is some coding at the node. The curriculum was modified between the February and March sessions. In this case there is generally good evidence for the positive effects of the modifications in curriculum. The one oddity is the coding at the node 'Not for me' in the May cohort. You would need to inspect the coded text and then the data about whoever said that (it may only be one person) to see if there are special reasons for their response. For instance, the explanation may be unrelated to the issues addressed by the curriculum change.

To create a chart like Figure 8.3 you will need not only the nodes but also some way of telling which cohort respondents were in. The obvious way to do this is using attributes.

To use attributes to create a time series

1 This assumes you have one document for each respondent/attender at the training scheme and that there was one scheme a month only.
2 Assign each respondent's document an appropriate value of a document attribute for 'Month of course'.
3 With the Document Set Editor create sets of the documents, one set for each month cohort, using the filter operating on attributes.
4 Use union node search on the 'positive' nodes, with the scope restricted to each cohort document set in turn.

5 Repeat this on the 'negative' nodes.
6 Browse the found text to check that the positive or negative interpretation makes sense and to investigate any alternative explanations.

This approach is analogous to the time series quasi-experimental design suggested by Campbell and Stanley (1966). As such you need to carry out similar kinds of checks for threats to validity and eliminate any other possible causes for the effect you have found. This will inevitably involve a lot of browsing nodes and reading the text. However, again, if you have created sets of documents you can use Node Lookup (in the Search Tool) with the scope restricted to documents related just to courses before the change (or just those after the change) to compare text from courses before and after. Do this on nodes you think might offer information about other possible causes of the change.

Grounded theory

Grounded theory, popularized by Glaser, Strauss and Corbin (Glaser and Strauss 1967; Glaser 1978, 1992; Strauss 1987; Strauss and Corbin 1990, 1997), has proved to be one of the most popular approaches to qualitative analysis. There is some debate, not least between Glaser and Strauss, about whether grounded theory should be seen as an iterpretative approach or whether it is more fundamentally a realist approach. Certainly the early descriptions of grounded theory were an explicit attempt to formulate a realist, inductive technique, grounded in the data to an extent that would convince 'hard-nosed' quantitative researchers of the soundness of the approach. However, more recent discussions by grounded theorists, notably Strauss and Corbin (1990) and Charmaz (1995), have formulated an interpretative or social constructionist version that has much more in common with phenomenology. It is this version of grounded theory that I will discuss here.

Grounded theory has been used extensively across a variety of social science disciplines. Its central focus is on inductively generating novel theoretical ideas or hypotheses from the data as opposed to testing theories specified beforehand. In so far as these new theories arise out of the data and are supported by the data they are said to be grounded – hence the title of the method. As Strauss and Corbin (1990: 24) put it: 'the grounded theory approach is a qualitative research method that uses a systematic set of procedures to develop an inductively derived grounded theory about a phenomenon'.

The design of NVivo was strongly influenced by grounded theory and therefore the program gives good support for the method. Table 8.1 summarizes the stages of a grounded theory analysis.

Table 8.1   Stages of analysis showing the chief components of grounded theory

1 After some exposure to the field setting and some collection of data, the researcher starts to develop 'categories' which illuminate and fit the data well.
2 The categories are then 'saturated', meaning that further instances of the categories are gathered until the researcher is confident about the relevance and range of the categories for the research setting. There is a recognition in the idea of 'saturation' that further search for appropriate instances may become a superfluous exercise.
3 The researcher then seeks to abstract a more general formulation of the category, as well as specifying the criteria for inclusion of that category.
4 These more general definitions then act as a guide for the researcher, as well as stimulating further theoretical reflection. This stage may prompt the researcher to think of further instances which may be subsumed under the more general definition of the category.
5 The researcher should be sensitive to the connections between the emerging general categories and other milieux in which the categories may be relevant. For example, can categories relating to the dying in hospital (Glaser and Strauss's main research focus) be extended to encapsulate other social settings?
6 The researcher may become increasingly aware of the connections between categories developed in the previous stage, and will seek to develop hypotheses about such links.
7 The researcher should then seek to establish the conditions in which these connections pertain.
8 At this point, the researcher should explore the implications of the emerging theoretical framework for other, pre-existing theoretical schemes which are relevant to the substantive area.
9 The researcher may then seek to test the emerging relationships among categories under extreme conditions to test the validity of the posited connections.

Source: (Bryman 1988: 83–4)

However, as Bryman and Burgess point out, much research that claims to be using grounded theory does not adopt the full set of procedures recommended by its developers. Usually the term merely signifies that theory has emerged from the data without necessarily involving all aspects of the approach (Bryman and Burgess 1994). For example, grounded theorists argue that initial data collection and preliminary analysis should take place before consulting and incorporating any research literature. This is to ensure that analysis is grounded in the data and that pre-existing constructs do not shape the analysis and subsequent theory formation. Existing theory is not completely omitted, its integration is only delayed, since it forms an important part of later theory development. However, few users of grounded theory are absolutely strict about keeping out theoretical presuppositions at the start of analysis.

To some degree I, too, am taking a loose definition in this section, since the full grounded theory approach requires the researcher to undertake data collection and analysis side by side. As new theoretical ideas emerge, the researcher should collect more data to test out the limits of applicability of the theory and to fill out particular concepts and theoretical points. The analysis is modified and extended as the new data require. This is a form of theoretical sampling, where the choice of the next source of data is determined by the emerging theory. Specifically, the method suggests that researchers should seek out those settings or respondents or data sources that are distinctive or different according to the emerging theory. The new data thus provide the research with information that can increase the 'density' and 'saturation' of the emerging categories and themes. These terms refer to what might be called the vertical and horizontal elements of the concept or idea behind the theme. Density refers to the vertical dimension, the idea of a richer, more detailed and theoretically sensitive concept. The concept is said to be saturated when no more data collection or analysis of further examples reveals any more information, including contrary information. The assumption of this book, generally, is that you already have a data set that you need to analyse. Nevertheless, a limited version of saturation is possible within such a fixed data set. For instance, a case-by-case examination of themes and ideas (similar to that of analytic induction) can be undertaken to attempt to saturate concepts.

Strauss and Corbin (1990) give a very accessible account of grounded theory. They present many specific ideas and techniques for achieving a grounded analysis that can be supported well using NVivo. They divide analysis in grounded theory into three stages:

- open coding, where the text is read reflectively to identify relevant categories;
- axial coding, where categories are refined, developed and related or interconnected;
- selective coding, where the 'core category', or central category that ties all other categories in the theory together into a story, is identified and related to other categories.

Open coding

This is essentially the kind of coding I covered in Chapter 4. You examine the text for salient categories of information (nodes) by making comparisons and asking questions. These categories are labelled (the node is given a name), but, as Strauss and Corbin suggest, it is important to avoid a label that is merely a description of the text. You need to try to formulate theoretical names. For example, if the text is 'my mates told me about job vacancies' then the node should be called something like 'Word of mouth' or

'Networking for job finding', not just 'Mates told respondent' or some such. To put it another way, the actual text is always an example of a more general phenomenon, and the node title should indicate this more general idea.

An alternative approach mentioned by Strauss and Corbin is the use of in vivo terms. These are concepts used by the participants themselves to organize their world. Notice, though, that these are concepts, not just the respondent's words. For example, in my university, staff often refer to 'level 7'. Although in one sense it simply refers to those managers (the vice chancellor etc.) who have offices on level 7 of the central administration building, it means much more than that. For instance, many important university meetings happen in the conference rooms on level 7, and the term serves to distinguish the central university management from that in the schools and services – an important issue in a decentralized university. 'Level 7', although it is an in vivo term, also has theoretical weight.

Strauss and Corbin suggest that a central part of open coding is identifying properties and dimensions for the nodes. By 'properties' they mean multiple perspectives or aspects of the node. Two examples of this can be seen in the node tree developed in Chapter 7, reproduced again as Figure 8.4. The node 'Strategy' has two types, 'Haphazard' and 'Routine', and the node 'Activities' has several aspects, 'Company internal bulletins', 'contacting people', 'Former work colleagues' and so on. In NVivo it is easy to organize these nodes. You just use the node tree and put property nodes as children of the node they refer to.

Figure 8.4 A tree fragment illustrating node properties

By 'dimensions' Strauss and Corbin mean to those kinds of properties that can be presented on a continuum. For example, colour has properties like hue, tone, shade and intensity, and shade has dimensions such as dark, light and so on. Typical dimensions include frequency, duration, extent, intensity, amount and manner. Again there is an example in the node tree discussed in

Chapter 7. A further development of this is shown in Figure 8.5. The node 'Job Searching' has three properties: it can have a 'Strategy', an 'Activity' or a 'Breadth'. The last node has the dimensions 'Local', 'Regional' and 'National'.

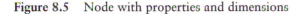

```
]- 🎥 Job Searching
    ⊞- 👤 Strategy
    ⊞- 👤 Activities
    ⊟- 👤 Breadth
            👤 Local
            👤 Regional
            👤 National
```

Figure 8.5   Node with properties and dimensions

Thus, as you construct new nodes, you should be asking yourself whether they have properties or dimensions. Often you will find that other nodes in your tree or free nodes are examples of properties or dimensions of the node in question, and, as we saw in Chapter 7, you can move them to form children of the node.

Strauss (1987: 30) recommends that you 'move quickly to dimensions that seem relevant to given words, phrases, etc.' during open coding. As you are reading through the text identifying nodes, you may not want to get diverted into thinking about properties and dimensions immediately; however, you don't want to lose the thoughts about them that you have at that point. In this case it might help to highlight the relevant terms in the text coded at the node that is suggestive of a property or dimension. Do this by selecting the terms in the Browser and colouring the words using the pull-down menu in the toolbar. If that colour doesn't show up well, try putting the text in bold as well. Later you can browse the node and the words you have coloured will stand out to remind you. If that is not enough of a reminder, then try linking an internal annotation DataBite to the text you have coloured and jot some additional ideas in the annotation.

Strauss and Corbin recommend that you should open-code by going through the texts line by line or sentence by sentence looking for ideas and text to code. As you read you should constantly ask questions of the text: who, when, where, what, how, how much, why and so on? This is designed to alert you to the theoretical issues lying behind the text and to give you a sensitivity to the deeper theoretical levels in them. To assist with this they suggest a variety of other techniques, mainly using comparisons. In fact grounded theory has been referred to as the method of constant comparison plus theoretical sampling. The techniques are especially useful at the early stages of analysis and if you are finding it hard to decide what to code. They include the following.

- *Analysis of word, phrase or sentence.* Pick out one word or phrase that seems significant. List all possible meanings. Examine the text to see which apply here. You may find new meanings that weren't immediately obvious.
- *Flip-flop technique.* Compare extremes on a given dimension. For example, if someone mentions age as an issue in finding work, try to contrast this with what it would be like for someone very young, just entering the job market, and someone else near the end of their working life. You may discover dimensions or issues you hadn't thought of before, such as the interaction of age and skills. Older people may lack new skills, but young people lack general work experience skills. If you have already done a fair amount of coding, you could achieve this contrast using attributes to restrict the scope of a node search and compare the results using different attributes.
- *Systematic comparison.* Ask a series of 'what ifs' to explore all the dimensions of two phenomena. How do they differ, how do people respond differently? Again, if you already have some coding, at least one node for each of the two phenomena, then you can use node intersection searching. Search for the intersection of the node for one phenomenon with any other node that might be a possible dimension. Repeat for the node for the other phenomenon. Browse the resulting nodes to compare their texts.
- *Far out comparisons.* Take one element of the concept you are examining and think of the most remote or different example of some other phenomenon that shares some characteristics with that concept. Then work through all the other elements of both phenomena to see if they shed any light on the original. For example, you might compare the unemployed with those who have lost limbs. Both suffer loss. Those without limbs experience stigma – is it the same for the unemployed? Those experiencing stigma deal with it by avoiding public places (hiding away), passing it off as others' problem and so on – do the unemployed do the same? Alternatively, you might compare the unemployed who talk about bad luck in finding work with gamblers' talk of a run of bad luck. Gamblers overestimate the extent to which they can control events – do those looking for work do the same? In these cases the point about the comparison is to generate more nodes that form dimensions, properties or aspects of the original idea. You can set these up in the node tree and then later use text searching or browsing and reading to look for relevant passages to code.
- *Waving the red flag.* Be sensitive to phrases like 'Never', 'Always', 'It couldn't possibly be that way'. They are signals to look more closely. It is rarely the case that they are actually true. They usually mean things *shouldn't* happen that way. You need to find out what would happen if that situation actually did occur. It is fairly easy to use Text Search to look for these terms, though you may need to do some more data collection to get an answer to what happens if they do occur.

Axial coding

The second stage of Strauss and Corbin's model is axial coding, where you begin to explore the relationship of categories, making connections between them. In NVivo this can be done, to start with, by rearranging the node tree in the way discussed in Chapter 7. Strauss and Corbin suggest a particular model for doing this in which you identify six types of category or node. These are listed in Table 8.2, along with a short explanation and a few examples taken from the Job Search project. The idea is that each element in turn has a causal influence on the next. Thus the causal conditions produce the phenomenon which in turn causes the strategies in the contexts. These are mediated by intervening conditions and produce actions and interactions that result in consequences.

There are several ways you can use NVivo to help you organize your thinking about axial coding. You could use the node tree to set up a root node for each model element and group all the actual instances as child

Table 8.2   Elements of the axial coding model

Model element	Explanation	Examples from Job Search project
Causal conditions	What influences the central phenomenon, events, incidences, happenings	Job market, conflict at work, child rearing, company failure
Phenomenon	The central idea, event, happening, incident which a set of actions or interactions is directed at managing or handling, or to which the set of actions is related	Living with unemployment, finding work
Strategies	Addressing the phenomenon Purposeful, goal-oriented	Networking, selling skills, part-time work, waiting
Context	Locations of events	Home, job clubs, local employers
Intervening conditions	Shaping, facilitating or constraining the strategies that take place within a specific context	Personal contacts, local job market, work skills, marketing skills
Action/interaction	Strategies devised to manage, handle, carry out, respond to a phenomenon under a set of perceived conditions	Handling disappointment, hard luck stories, job-finding courses, career-change training
Consequences	Outcomes or results of action or interaction, result from the strategies	Jobs, frustration, compromise, leave job market

nodes (see Figure 8.6a). Or you could set up a subtree for each phenomenon and include only relevant model elements as its children (see Figure 8.6b). Alternatively, or in addition, you could create sets of nodes for each of the model elements. An advantage of using sets is that they don't involve moving nodes from their original positions in the node tree. However, if you wish you can set up trees as in Figure 8.6 where the child nodes are copies of the originals. There are two problems with this, though. First, it breaks the rules about repeating nodes discussed in the previous chapter (no big deal as long as you know what you are doing). Second, if you change any coding or attributes of the original node, these aren't reflected in the copy (a big problem if you continue coding throughout analysis as most people do). Using sets doesn't suffer from this second problem as set members are aliases of or shortcuts to the original nodes. A combination of sets and nodes is often the best solution. Start by using sets, one for each model element – causal conditions, phenomena etc. – to gather up candidate nodes. You can do this while you are still open-coding. Then create root nodes for each central phenomenon you identify, with placeholder parent nodes as children as in Figure 8.6b. Move (don't copy) nodes and subtrees from elsewhere in the node tree to appropriate places in the new trees. These will become the main place where you develop your node structure and the corresponding model of what is happening in your study. Use the constructing of these trees as an opportunity to explore the nodes further. Try to establish for each their properties and dimensions (if you have not already done so). Look for confirmations of the causal linkages in the text by browsing the nodes. Pay particular attention to possible exceptions. As I argued earlier, exceptions do not mean you have to reject the causal linkage and the theory. Instead, by reading the text carefully, you may be able to modify or extend the theory.

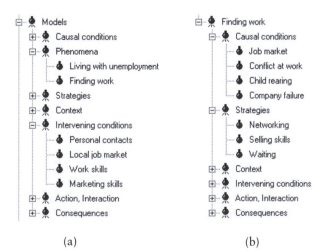

(a)   (b)

Figure 8.6   Two ways of handling axial coding

This may mean creating new nodes to code the new circumstances, or it might even mean constructing new, alternative models.

You may find it useful to create a diagram of relationships between the elements of the model. These will probably not be captured entirely by the node tree structure. This can be done with pen and paper, but there is a facility in NVivo for diagrams that we shall look at in the next chapter. In addition, you can record linkages in NVivo using NodeLinks, but there is no way of labelling them and there is no visual representation of them. So they are really only useful here for recording what is in your pen-and-paper diagram.

Selective coding

This can be both the easiest stage and the hardest. It is the easiest because if you have already done lots of axial coding, most of the work you need to do at this stage is already done. It is the hardest because it often involves some hard choices. As you develop your axial coding a small number of phenomena or themes will begin to emerge as central in your study. You will recognize them because they are linked to many other elements of your model or because they appear high up in the coding tree. Selective coding begins with the selection of one of these as the central phenomenon. Even if you have two good candidates, Strauss and Corbin (1990) recommend that you select just one. That is often hard to do. The point is that around the central phenomenon you construct a story that brings together most of the elements of your study. This will be your thesis, your argument or your position, and you can't have two. Think of yourself writing a paper about your study for a journal. The central phenomenon is what the title of the paper will refer to. For example, in the Job Search project, two central phenomena suggest themselves: the use of personal and network resources to find work, and how the unemployed handle the disappointment of not finding work. These actually define two very different studies. The former is very much in the area of practical issues of job finding and would be of great interest to those trying to help the unemployed find work (as well as of possible help to the unemployed themselves). The latter addresses a set of issues centred more in the psychology or lived experience of unemployment. It would focus on the language people use to describe their experience, the stories they tell and the psychological mechanisms and behaviours they use to overcome the pressures and stresses of unemployment. These two phenomena therefore define two very different theses or stories. A good, focused analysis and write-up would have to concentrate on only one of them.

Once you have selected your central phenomenon, selective coding consists in systematically relating it to other nodes. This may indicate some further refinement needed in other nodes and require filling out their properties and dimensions. By this stage much of the work you do involves manipulating nodes: moving them, creating new ones, amalgamating or dividing them. Compared to open and axial coding there is much less reference back to the text. The reason is that by this stage most of your activity should be analytic and theoretical. Just as with axial coding, you may find using a diagram is useful, especially as a diagram can not only show a variety of linkages but also name them and allocate them to different types.

Narrative, life history and biography

The analysis of narratives, stories and biographies allows us to examine the rhetorical devices that social actors use and the way they represent and contexualize their experience and personal knowledge. Narratives involve the personal dimension, and are usually related from the individual's point of view. For some they include just about anything respondents say. For others they are just those discourses where individuals recount events they have experienced, things they have done or that were done to them, or perhaps things others have experienced. Sometimes it seems as if everything is narrative. If that were so then the term would be pointless. In my view there is still a narrative use of language that is different from other uses – for example, explanation, commands, requests and descriptions. In contrast, 'story' is a narrower term and denotes a genre that has a specific form and/or content, including protagonists, events, complications and consequences. As Riessman (1993) points out, during research interviews, respondents often include stories in their responses.

Another example of narrative is the autobiography or life history. Whereas people spontaneously use narratives when telling us about themselves and regularly include short stories in their discourse, biographies and life histories are usually the result of a specific request. The ancient mariner of Coleridge's poem is the exception, not the rule. Either the researcher requests this from the respondent or a publisher requests it of an author. Data can come from interviews, biography, autobiography, life history interview, personal letters, diaries etc.

Biographical content

The most obvious way to get a narrative is to ask someone to tell you the story of their life, their autobiography. This is a particular form of the interview and the focus is on how people organize the account of their life through stories and thus make sense of what they have experienced and done. The general approach people take when telling their life history is 'how it happened' or 'how I came to be where I am today'. Life histories or biographies have several key features. They are almost always chronological. The events are recalled in the order they happened, although at times respondents may refer back to a previous event to fill in more detail which is now relevant to the current point of the story. People usually identify key events and key social actors. These are events and people that have made a difference to them, without which they wouldn't be the people they are now. A particular example of a key event is the turning point or what Denzin (1989a, 1989b) refers to as the epiphany, the event that leaves a mark on the person. This is something people say has made them, in their eyes, a different person. Often described in terms like 'before X I used to do Y (be a Z kind of person), but now I do A (or am a B kind of person)'. Key events and persons are good indicators of how a person conceives of their life, what it means to them. Other common features of life histories include planning, luck and other influences. Often events or people are discussed in these terms – as people who they were lucky to meet, who influenced them (e.g. partners, spouses, mentors), or as events they had always planned (e.g. getting married, having a family).

Life histories usually exhibit themes and these, along with the features just discussed, can be coded at nodes in the usual fashion. Themes vary enormously depending on the person's experience and they may only apply at one stage of the person's biography. Sometimes themes are significant by their absence. The kinds of things to look out for are the following:

- The relational story – constantly referring to others, what they did with people, to people or people did to them.
- Belonging and separateness – two contrasting themes that may be important for people for whom identity is an issue.
- Closeness, remoteness and experience of moving – a theme often expressed in the context of a highly mobile life (either socially or geographically mobile).
- The idea of occupational or other social roles – e.g. parent, children, patients. Often a central life concept.
- Relations with opposite sex – the absence of discussion may be as significant as its inclusion.
- A focus on early life as determinant of later actions – what made me the way I am.

It is likely that you will only have a few life histories to deal with in a study. Even so, some case-by-case comparison may be revealing. You might compare different participants' views on some event they were all involved with or you could compare how people experience similar transitions in their lives. Single node lookup, possibly with some use of attributes to divide up the data (e.g. into male and female) is probably sufficient.

As I noted above, life histories are usually chronological. It might therefore be possible to mark transitions in the story using section headings. If the text is not strictly chronological then it still will be possible to code sections of the story at appropriate thematic nodes. It might be sufficient to use fairly obvious and broad nodes such as 'childhood', 'professional training', 'early occupational career', 'parenthood', 'national service', 'management', 'career change' and 'retirement'. These can then be used to assist with node searching at a finer detail. For example, you may want to look for transitions between themes. Use co-occurrence or sequence in the Proximity Search tool and define the scope of the search using one or two of the broad nodes. Choose the definition of co-occurrence or sequence as 'within the text coded at the scope node(s)'. This way you can examine text on different kinds of transitions such as the move from, for example, professional training to early occupational career. It's probably best to opt to retrieve text from the first and last items as well as text between them. You can use a similar scope in a node lookup to find text expressive of a particular theme used at specific stages of the biography. For example, are relationships with the opposite sex something respondents only mention at certain stages of their life history?

Another important phenomenon worth looking for is episodes that seem to contradict the themes in terms of content, mood or evaluation by the narrator. Assuming you have coded text by content, mood or evaluation, then a Boolean intersect (and) search with the broad thematic nodes will find such text. One special attitude narrators can take to an issue is to fail to mention it. Again, you can use Boolean search to display the text for specific themes for those people who did not mention something others did. Use the themes as scope nodes as before. Then do a Boolean negation (not) search on the node coding the issue other people mentioned. You should opt to return the results as a node if you just want to read the text coded at the theme for those not mentioning the issue. Choose to return the results as a set of documents if you want to be able to read all the biography for those not mentioning the issue. (Note that you can do this from the node of finds anyway by simply selecting some text and choosing **Browse/Edit/Code Document** from its contextual menu 🔖.)

Narrative structure

As well as examining the thematic content of biographies we can look at the narrative structure of people's stories. Such stories are offered not just as a whole life biography, but also, in shorter versions, as part of normal conversation. In responding to interviews and the like, people often include short stories, the content and structure of which can be revealing. As has been recognized since at least classical antiquity, a story has a beginning, a middle, an end and a logic. Events are not just temporal, they have a causal sequence – one event leads on ineluctably to the next. We can treat the stories people tell as having a plot and categorize them like plays. Table 8.3 gives a fourfold classification of stories based on dramatic themes. I have underlined terms that you might consider setting up nodes for. In the Job

Table 8.3   Dramaturgical classification of stories

Romance	The hero faces a series of <u>challenges</u> en route to his <u>goal</u> and eventual <u>victory</u>.
Comedy	The goal is the restoration of social order, and the hero must have the requisite social <u>skills</u> to overcome the <u>hazards</u> that threaten that <u>order</u>.
Tragedy	The hero is defeated by the <u>forces of evil</u> and is <u>ostracized from society</u>.
Satire	A <u>cynical perspective</u> on <u>social hegemony</u>.

Search project the stories people told seemed to fall mainly into the romance type (those people being entrepreneurial and active in looking for work) and the tragedy type (those seemingly defeated by the difficulty of finding work). A few, you could say, fell into the satire type on account of their cynical perspective. Life stories progress, they advance or regress, depending whether the story moves on to better things or to worse things, or they stay stable when the 'plot' is steady. If things steadily advance then the story is said to

Table 8.4   Labov's narrative elements

Structure	*Question*
Abstract	Summary of the substance of the narrative. What was this about? Initiates the narrative, summarizing the point, or gives general proposition which narrative will exemplify. In interviews, interviewer's question may do this. Sometimes omitted.
Orientation	The time, place, situation, participants of the story. It tells us who, what, when or how, giving the cast, setting, time period etc. Typical phrases used are 'It's like when . . .' or 'That happened to me when . . .'.
Complicating action	The sequence of events, answering the question 'then what happened?'. The major account of the events that are central to the story or the bones of what happened. Labov suggests these are commonly recalled in the simple past tense. The action can involve turning points, crises or problems, and show how they were made sense of by the narrator.
Evaluation	Answers the question 'so what?'. Gives the significance and meaning of the action, or the attitude of the narrator. Highlights the point of the narrative.
Resolution	What finally happened? The outcome of events or the resolution of the problem. Typical phrases used are 'So that meant . . .' or 'That's why . . .'.
Coda	This is an optional section. It marks the end of the story and a return of speech to the present tense. It marks the transition to other narrative.

ascend. If things progressively worsen then the story is descending. Others stories may ascend then descend or descend and then ascend as things turn from good to bad or the reverse.

Several researchers have focused on the kinds of stories that people introduce into their ordinary discourses, including interviews. Labov (see Labov and Waletsky 1967; Labov 1972, 1982) suggests that a fully formed story has six elements (see Table 8.4).

By analysing narratives and stories in this way to see how they are constructed, we can begin to understand the functions the story performs. The structure helps us understand how people give shape to events, how they make a point, their reaction to events and how they 'package' them. All of these can be used as a starting point for further exploration and analysis.

Many of the respondents in the Job Search project told short stories as part of the responses they gave in the interviews. These stood out from the rest of their responses. They were often about issues of central concern to them, which they returned to at other points in the interview, and they often involved longer responses than was usual in the interview. They also fitted into the structure given by Labov in Table 8.4. For example, at one point in her interview, June was being asked about how she came to be unemployed. This is how she replied:

INT_HELEN

And what happened?

JUNE

I left them. There had been quite a bit of aggravation between me and the man that was brought in to be my boss, because he decided that he wanted to do the work that I was employed to do, and for me to do other things. Although it was a nice job – I ended up doing the customer relations, which I really enjoyed – he was brought in as Sales Director and he couldn't do the selling, he liked to do the administration side of it – which I'd always done. He carefully removed the guy that was my helper, my assistant, and took him onto his staff. I thought 'I'm not going to have this, not after 15 years', so I upped sticks.

INT_HELEN

That must have been quite a wrench for you?

JUNE

It was, because the company had been very good to me. . . .

Figure 8.7   June's reply

In this case the initial stage of the story was started by a prompt from the interviewer, Helen, to which June replied with the abstract – it's almost a title in this case – for her story, 'I left them'. The rest of the story can be fitted into Labov's structure as in Table 8.5.

This is a very simple example, but it illustrates quite well how people tell stories and how they seem implicitly to recognize the conventions of how to tell the tale. Not all stories will fit quite as well into the categories, but most do to a large degree. Looking at those points in their interviews where respondents broke into a story, it is quite clear that these are important issues for the narrator. One could almost say that they are defining instances of how they see themselves or how they explain how they got to be 'one of the unemployed'. In the case of June, it is significant that a little later in the interview she again told a story and it was again about the moment she quit her job after a dispute at a meeting. One issue that is indicated in the story

Table 8.5   June's story

Structure	Text
Abstract	INT_HELEN
	And what happened?
	JUNE
	I left them.
Orientation	There had been quite a bit of aggravation between me and the man that was brought in to be my boss, because he decided that he wanted to do the work that I was employed to do, and for me to do other things.
Complicating action	Although it was a nice job – I ended up doing the customer relations, which I really enjoyed – he was brought in as Sales Director and he couldn't do the selling, he liked to do the administration side of it – which I'd always done. He carefully removed the guy that was my helper, my assistant, and took him onto his staff.
Evaluation	I thought 'I'm not going to have this, not after 15 years',
Resolution	so I upped sticks.
Coda	INT_HELEN
	That must have been quite a wrench for you?
	JUNE
	It was, because the company had been very good to me. . . .

and that she repeated at other points in the interview is that she had many friends at the company and was well treated. Her leaving is explained solely in terms of the relations between her and the Sales Director. The theme of the importance of good social relations at work was not something that all respondents mentioned. In fact, only one or two others did. The obvious question is what marked these people out. A table of which of the relevant documents (or cases) are coded at the appropriate nodes will help here. This can be done by assaying the scope of a search in the Search Tool.

To assay a scope

1 Open the Search Tool window.
2 Use the scope to set up the things you want to assay. These can be documents or cases where you want to see how they have been coded, or nodes where you want to see what they are coding. In this example I used a set of likely nodes that I had set up earlier. If you are using nodes as your scope make sure you don't have any documents showing in the custom scope area – click on **Remove All** (and vice versa if your scope is documents).
3 Click on the **Assay Scope** button. This opens the Assay Scope window (see Figure 8.8).

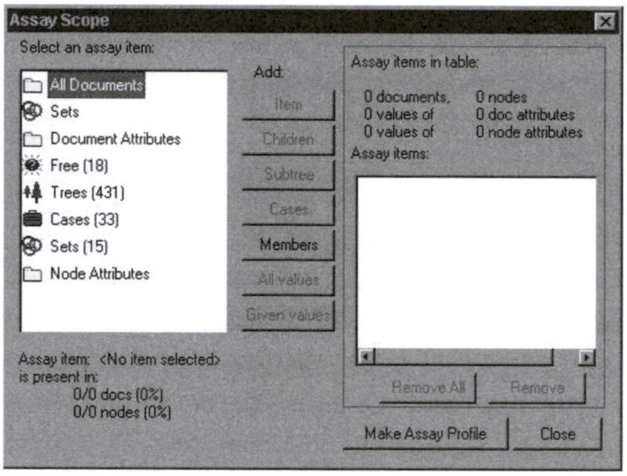

Figure 8.8   The Assay Scope window

4 Use this to select the items you want to assay. As the scope in this example is nodes, it makes sense to assay documents. In other words, we are asking what documents the scope nodes code. If the scope were documents, we could ask what nodes code these documents or what attributes are assigned to them.
5 If you select a set then you can include all its members by clicking on the **Members** button (see Figure 8.9). Likewise, if you click on a parent node

in the node tree then you can include all its children by clicking on the **Children** button and so on.

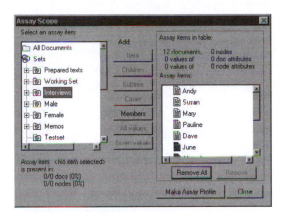

Figure 8.9   The Assay Scope window showing adding all set members at once

6 When you have added all the documents needed, click on the **Make Assay Profile** button.
7 This opens the Assay Profile window (see Figure 8.10). I have resized the columns so that the scope items show on one line and the document columns are only as wide as need be to show the document names.

Scope Items	Pauline	June	John	Mary	Jim	Harry	Susan	Ahmed	Tom	Dave	Andy	Sharon	Totals	Percent
/Job Searching/Activities/Company internal bulletins	1									1			2	16.67
/Job Searching/Activities/Use of newspapers	1	1	1	1						1		1	6	50.00
/Job Searching/Activities/Mates & relatives - work	1	1				1	1	1	1	1	1		8	66.67
/Job Searching/Strategy/Type/Entrepreneurial	1	1	1										3	25.00
/Job Searching/Activities/Job Centres	1	1		1					1	1	1	1	8	66.67
/Work background/Mangerial - professional	1	1											2	16.67
/Job Searching/Activities/contacting people			1				1				1	1	4	33.33
/Job Searching/Activities/Former work colleagues							1			1			2	16.67
/Job Searching/Strategy/Type/Haphazard							1	1	1	1	1	1	6	50.00
/Work background/Manual					1	1	1	1	1	1			6	50.00
/Job Searching/Breadth/Local							1		1				2	16.67
/Work background/Routine office		1		1	1								3	25.00
/Job Searching/Breadth/Regional		1	1	1						1			4	33.33
/Job Searching/Activities/Job Finder							1		1	1			3	25.00
/Job Searching/Breadth/National													0	0
/Job Searching/Strategy/Type/Routine				1	1	1							3	25.00
/Work background/No previous job												1	1	8.33
/Job Searching/Strategy													0	0
/Job Searching/Activities/Word of mouth					1	1	1		1	1	1		6	50.00
Totals	**6**	**5**	**6**	**3**	**6**	**7**	**4**	**6**	**8**	**7**	**6**	**5**	**69**	
Percent	**31.58**	**26.32**	**31.58**	**15.79**	**31.58**	**36.84**	**21.05**	**31.58**	**42.11**	**36.84**	**31.58**	**26.32**		

Figure 8.10   The Assay Profile window

8 This table shows which documents are coded at nodes from the list in the leftmost column. A '1' in the cell means the document is coded, an

empty cell means it is not. The row totals column shows how many documents are coded at each node, and so on.

9 Examining the table becomes easier if you reorder the rows and columns. Click on a column title to reorder the rows so that those that code the document appear sorted to the bottom. Click again to reverse this order. The same can be done with rows by clicking on the row title. I got the order shown in Figure 8.9 by clicking twice on the '/Job Searching/Strategy/Type/Entrepreneurial' row and then twice on the 'Pauline' column.

10 By inspection of the table you can see there is some suggestion that Pauline, June and John are different from the others in their approach to job searching. Also notice that those with a manual job background tend to be haphazard searchers and that two of those with routine approaches used to be in routine office jobs!

Scope items appear as rows in the assay table that is finally produced. The table is more readable if nodes (tree nodes often have long names) appear as rows, thus their names appear in the first column. The table shows scope items in rows and assay items in columns. So it often makes sense to make nodes the scope items as in the example above.

The answer to the question about those who had stories about good relations at work (Pauline, June and John) in the Job Search project seems to revolve around the fact that the individuals were mostly in managerial posts (browsing the text coded for June shows she was a solicitor's clerk), were quite entrepreneurial in looking for work and at the point of interview were optimistic about their success in getting back into a job.

How can NVivo help with the identification and analysis of stories? You could do a text search to look for key phrases of the 'It's like when . . .' kind, but, as you can see from June's story, these are not found in all cases. So you have to keep an eye open for the appropriate passages while reading the documents. Use a node to code text that is telling a story, and you might also want to colour the text so that it stands out next time you are reading the document. You could break up the text as I have done in Table 8.5 and insert the appropriate headings; however, it is probably best not to edit the original documents too much. Instead, you can cut and paste the story into another document, perhaps one specially for stories from your data. In this new document you can break up and caption the text. If you bring all the stories together into one document you can easily start doing some comparative analysis. As we shall see in a moment, this can be useful. Don't forget to set up links from each story in this document back to the original document. Click at the beginning of the copy of the story and click on the document link button to insert a small icon showing the document link (see Figure 8.11). The icon's contextual menu 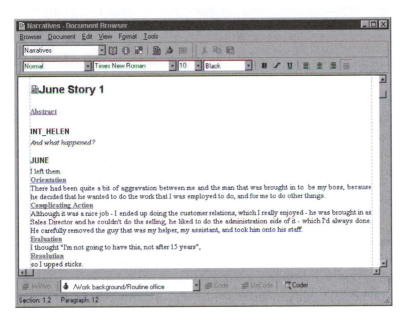 shows the name of the linked document. Select this to go straight to the original document. (The story part headings are in red in the original shown in Figure 8.11 so they show up quite well. I have underlined them here so you can see them in black and white.)

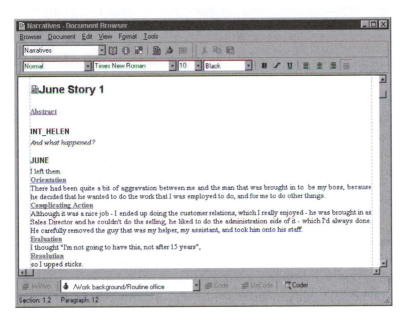

Figure 8.11   A new document with stories' parts categorized

Functions of stories

In the case of June's story, paying attention to the occurrence of stories in the interview and looking at what might lie behind her use of the form at strategic moments can give an insight into what are important themes for the interviewee and suggest ideas for further investigation. Respondents order their careers and memories into a series of narrative chronicles, marked by key happenings. These can show how the actor frames and makes sense of a particular set of experiences. Typical examples of this are how people measure success, how they overcome adversity, what they think of as good and bad practice and explanations of success and failure. As we have seen earlier in the Job Search project, people are also often concerned with luck and planning, and use stories to talk about these issues.

Stories can also have an ethical or moral dimension. Respondents use them to indicate good and bad practice, both to the researcher and to their peers. A typical example of this is the cautionary tale that recounts accidents or disasters in the organization where they work or the setting they are in. Such stories act as a collective reminder of what not to do and how not to be. Moral tales are usually about others, but if the tale is about the narrator this is often because it is an example of overcoming adversity or a key turning point or epiphany. In many cases moral tales are a way of passing on cultural heritage or organizational culture, though these functions are also achieved by stories other than moral tales. Examples are atrocity stories, morality fables in organizations, fables of incompetence (such as, in medical settings, giving warnings of what not to do), the oral culture of schoolchildren and urban legends.

Another important use for stories is to structure our ideas of self and to establish our identity. This can be achieved at the social level by the kind of moral tales and cultural stories I have just mentioned. Such shared stories can define a subgroup or subculture, especially to those in the group. Being inducted into such groups often includes being told the key stories for the group. But stories can be used to establish identity at an individual level too. Stories present a narrator's inner reality to the outside world. We know or discover ourselves and reveal ourselves to others by the stories we tell.

Stories have other psychological functions too, such as giving people a way to deal with particularly sensitive or traumatic times or events such as divorce or violence. You could say that stories about job loss or failure at interview that were given by respondents in the Job Search project are examples of this too. As we shall see below, analysis of the language used in such stories can reveal much about what a narrator feels.

Linguistic characteristics

Another way of analysing stories is to focus on the language used, the stylistic conventions and the metaphors. Zilber gives an example of this using linguistic features of a narrative to identify and analyse its emotional content, especially in emotionally charged stories (Lieblich *et al.* 1998: 154–62). Zilber looked for a variety of discrete linguistic or stylistic characteristics that a variety of psychological literature suggested was indicative of underlying emotional issues. A partial list of these is shown in Table 8.6.

The method consists of finding a possible emotionally charged story, going through it and highlighting just the text that tells the bare facts about the events portrayed. What remains can then be analysed for evidence of the kinds of linguistic features listed in Table 8.6. This can easily be simulated in NVivo by coding the complete story at a node, say, 'Emotive story'. Then read through the story to find the text that is just giving the straight factual content. Code this at another node, say, 'Facts'. To highlight just the factual parts, open the Coder (if not already open) and, with the story showing in the Browser, select the node 'Facts' in the Coder. This will highlight the text. Alternatively, if you just want to see the non-factual (i.e. emotive) content,

Table 8.6 Possible emotionally charged linguistic features of a narrative

- Adverbs such as 'suddenly' 'unfortunately' may indicate how expected or unexpected events were.
- Mental verbs such as 'I thought', 'I understood' and 'I noticed' may indicate extent to which an experience is in consciousness and can be remembered.
- Denotations of time and place may indicate attempts to distance an event or bring it closer.
- Past, present and future tense in verbs, and transition between them, may indicate a speaker's sense of identification with the events described.
- Transitions between first-person, second-person and third-person verb forms may indicate difficulty of re-encountering a difficult experience.
- Passive and active verbs may indicate speaker's perception of agency.
- Breaking chronological or causal flow with digressions, regressions, leaps in time etc. may indicate attempts to avoid discussing a difficult experience.
- Repetition may indicate that the subject under discussion elicits an emotional charge for the narrator.
- Detailed description may indicate reluctance to describe difficult emotions.

Source: adapted from Lieblich *et al.* (1998: 156)

then do a Boolean difference search on the nodes 'Emotive story' and 'Facts'. Browse the resulting node and this will show only the non-factual part of the story. You can now go through looking for the kind of stylistic features listed in Table 8.6 and code them at new nodes for emotive content. This will partly help you look closely at the text to try to identify the underlying emotions – but also, having coded the text, you can also undertake some comparisons with other stories and other people using the node search tool.

Conclusion

It is, I hope, clear that there are many ways in which NVivo can be used to support a range of techniques and approaches in qualitative analysis. The approaches I have discussed here in no way exhaust those that can be supported by NVivo. I have touched on some other approaches such as phenomenology and discourse analysis in other chapters. If you want to follow up these or the methods I have covered in this chapter then the further reading (below) suggests some places to start.

Further reading

Brewer, J.D. (2000) *Ethnography*. Buckingham: Open University Press. (A recent text with discussion of ethnographic analysis.)
Denzin, N.K. (1989) *Interpretive Biography*. Newbury Park, CA and London: Sage.

(Short introduction by one of the originators of biographical approaches in social sciences.)

Glaser, B.G. and Strauss, A.L. (1967) *The Discovery of Grounded Theory: Strategies for Qualitative Research*. Chicago: Aldine. (The original text on the grounded theory approach.)

Gomm, R., Hammersley, M. and Foster, P. (eds) (2000) *Case Study Method: Key Issues, Key Texts*. London: Sage. (An excellent recent collection that includes the classic Robinson paper on analytic induction.)

Hammersley, M. and Atkinson, P. (1995) *Ethnography: Principles in Practice*, 2nd edn. London: Routledge. (A classic and well-tried text. Contains discussion of analysis in ethnography.)

King, N. (1998) Template analysis, in G. Symon and C. Cassell (eds) *Qualitative Methods and Analysis in Organizational Research*. London: Sage. (A very accessible template approach derived from a phenomenological and interpretivist position.)

Lieblich, A., Tuval-Mashiach, R. and Zilber, T. (1998) *Narrative Research: Reading, Analysis and Interpretation*. London: Sage. (Examines a wide range of narrative and biographical techniques with extended examples.)

Moustakas, C. (1994) *Phenomenological Research Methods*. Thousand Oaks, CA: Sage. (One of the best texts on how to do phenomenological research.)

Riessman, C.K. (1993) *Narrative Analysis*. Newbury Park, CA and London: Sage. (A readable summary of narrative approaches.)

Robson, C. (1993) *Real World Research: A Resource for Social Scientists and Practitioner-Researchers*. Oxford, UK and Cambridge, MA, USA: Basil Blackwell. (A general text, but Chapter 12 contains a useful discussion of the structured approach.)

Smith, J.A. (1995) Semi-structured interview and qualitative analysis, in J.A. Smith, R. Harré and L. Van Langenhove (eds) *Rethinking Methods in Psychology*. London: Sage. (An introduction to the thematic approach of the author's interpretative phenomenological analysis.)

Strauss, A.L. and Corbin, J. (1998) *Basics of Qualitative Research: Techniques and Procedures for Developing Grounded Theory*, 2nd edn. Thousand Oaks, CA: Sage. (Good, clear, step-by-step introduction to the interpretivist version of grounded theory.)

Willig, C. (2001) *Introducing Qualitative Research in Psychology*. Buckingham: Open University Press. (Good, practical advice in chapters devoted to case studies, grounded theory, phenomenology and discourse analysis.)

Yin, R. (1994) *Case Study Research: Design and Methods*. Thousand Oaks, CA: Sage. (A short book but with useful chapters on analysis.)

9 Visualizing the data

Matrices and tables

Tables are commonly used in quantitative analysis, where they are usually called cross-tabulations. They are a convenient way to make comparisons across different subgroups of the data set and between different attributes of individuals. Tables of data, also referred to as matrices, can be used in similar ways in qualitative analysis. To some extent their logic is similar, but there are some important differences. To understand this, let us start by examining a simple quantitative table. Table 9.1, for example, summarizes

Table 9.1 Example quantitative cross-tabulation: males and females with degrees

	Has science degree	Non-science degree	Totals
Male	Cell 1, 1 36	Cell 1, 2 54	90
Female	Cell 2, 1 17	Cell 2, 2 78	95
Totals	53	123	185

into one of four categories the numbers of individuals with degrees in a sample. Cell 1, 1 is the number of males with science degrees, cell 1, 2 the number with non-science degrees, cell 2, 1 the number of females with science degrees and cell 2, 2 the number of females with non-science degrees. (To refer to cells in the table I have used pairs of numbers, the first indicating the row the cell is in, the second the column it is in. Thus cell 1, 2 is in the first row and the second column. This nomenclature is used in NVivo, so I shall continue to use it in the examples here.)

There are two ways of reading the data in this table. We can compare columns, that is, compare the characteristics of those with science or non-science degrees. Thus we can say that although there are about equal numbers of males and females with degrees, about two-thirds of those with science degrees are male. Likewise, of those with non-science degrees, almost two-thirds are female. We can also compare rows, that is compare the characteristics of males with females. Thus we can note that of the males, 40 per cent have science degrees whereas only about 18 per cent of the females do.

We can use a similar kind of logic in qualitative analysis, only instead of counts of numbers of cases in each cell we can use qualitative data such as sample passages of text or characterizations or attributes of the individuals represented by that cell. This is an important difference. We might, for instance, still compare two columns, but what is compared is not the numeric profile but the actual content of the cells. The other difference is that whereas in quantitative cross-tabulations rows and columns are variables, in qualitative tables, rows and column can be cases, nodes, attributes or documents. Table 9.2 shows an equivalent qualitative table.

Notice that in this case the contents of the cells are summary descriptions – ways in which respondents described men or women with science degrees or with non-science degrees taken from the texts collected in the study. Notice also that there are no row and column totals, as this makes no sense when the cell contents are passages of text and not counts. What the table provides is four summary descriptions, one in each cell. Some row-by-row and column-by-column comparison can be made, though in this case it is

Table 9.2   Example qualitative table: descriptions of people with degrees

	Has science degree	*Non-science degree*
Male	*Cell 1, 1* Reliable, steady, dull, numerate, traditional, clever, laddish	*Cell 1, 2* Artistic, sociable, ordinary, unreliable, unworldly
Female	*Cell 2, 1* Individualistic, dogmatic, clever, masculine, inspirational, numerate	*Cell 2, 2* Arty, feminine, bookish, traditional, radical

less revealing than in the quantitative table. Thus we can note that for both males and females there was a similar numerate–artistic distinction made by respondents, but that whereas men with science degrees are seen as dull and traditional, women with science degrees are seen as individualistic and inspirational. Looking at cell 2, 2, you can see that not all the descriptions are consistent. Women with non-science degrees are seen as both traditional and radical. This is not a contradiction, it just reflects the fact that the responses from several people are represented in this one cell and at least two of them made different comments.

Case-by-case comparisons

A common use for tables is to facilitate cross-case comparisons. For example, in the Job Search project we might compare respondents by their work background, their vacancy searching accounts and where they were looking for work. This produces something like Table 9.3. The cells contain a combination of selected, representative quotations and researcher's summary. Table 9.3 is just for illustration, and I've made it small enough to fit on the page. Typically a table of this kind would have many more rows for all the respondents in the study and possibly more columns. With a larger table further manipulation can be done. Miles and Huberman (1994: 177–86) suggest that it is often possible to partially order the cases. This will

Table 9.3   Example of a comparison between cases

	Work background	Vacancy searching accounts	Job search breadth
Harry	Cell 1, 1 Caretaker	Cell 1, 2 '[The] other applicant . . . had a car and it were funny hours working and he had advantage of being there on time, so that's why he got it.'	Cell 1, 3 'Not really away from town.' (local)
Pauline	Cell 2, 1 Supply teaching	Cell 2, 2 'I got the interview, so I treated it as a trial run. Really, I didn't think.'	Cell 2, 3 'Bonstreet' (local)
June	Cell 3, 1 Clerk at a solicitors	Cell 3, 2 'when she told me how much they were paying . . . it would be like going back to square one'	Cell 3, 3 'I told them, "I'm quite willing to relocate, but only to North East England." '

be particularly appropriate if you have been dimensionalizing your concepts in the manner suggested by grounded theory. For instance, the last column, 'Job search breadth' might be ordered by how broad the search was, varying from local to national. You can then reorder the rows in the table so that this column is in ascending (or descending) order. This is easily done using cut and paste in a word processor. Then look back to the other columns to see if a matching pattern appears in them. If there is then this might be preliminary evidence for a relationship between the two phenomena. In the case of Table 9.3, for example, you might expect to find a relationship between the kind of work background and job search breadth – certain kinds of jobs are associated with geographically wider searching.

As we saw in the previous chapter, case-by-case comparisons of this kind are a central part of the structured, analytic induction approach to analysis. A table like Table 9.3 can form a first look at the data in order to identify possible issues, causal relations and patterns for investigation in the structured way. Inspection of the table might also suggest further ideas for coding. For example, in Table 9.3 we might, on the basis of comparison with 'job search breadth', consider a new node combining work background with search breadth that refers to the kind of job market people were searching in.

Node and attribute analysis

Yet another common use for tables is for whole-case or whole-sample comparisons. In such tables the content may come from the whole data set or from a subsample created by the documents that meet the criteria defined by the rows and columns of the table, that is to say, those documents for which there could be entries in the table cells. Typically, rows and columns are nodes or attributes. The cell contents are generated from those passages of text that relate in some way to both the row and column type. For example, in the Job Search project we have seen that respondents adopted different job searching strategies: routine, haphazard or entrepreneurial. We might want to see how the strategies adopted by women compared with those used by men. Table 9.4 shows the resulting table. Unlike Table 9.3, cells in this table may contain text taken from more than one case or respondent. It is thus even more important to think carefully about what examples to include and how to summarize them if you give your own explanations.

The obvious way to use this table is to compare columns – thus comparing male and female. For example, we can note that women mentioned childcare and fitting in with a working partner's schedule, whereas men didn't. Before concluding this is a true gender difference, however, you need to check for alternative explanations. One might be that the women were younger, on average, than the men and therefore more likely to have young families and working partners. Another possible explanation is that the

Table 9.4 Job search strategies by gender

	Female	*Male*
Routine	Cell 1, 1 'My routine's determined by childcare requirements' (Pauline). 'I get the paper every day, without fail' (June). 'I used to go down Racetrain a lot, . . . I also joined Job Club . . . I kept a file and a record of all the letters I received' (Sharon).	Cell 1, 2 'I used to spend mornings going through the papers. I either used to buy papers or go down to the library. Afternoons writing off to places for information or filling application forms in, and then evenings for the evening papers, again' (Jim). 'Just the same pattern all through the week' (Harry).
Haphazard	Cell 2, 1 'Not really, I just do it. It happens' (Susan). 'Not really, because my husband works shift work' (Mary).	Cell 2, 2 'No routine, but I keep meself busy, like – keep meself occupied – I've plenty of gardening to do' (Dave). 'No, not really. I usually go down and have a look Monday, Wednesday, Friday, something like that' (Andy).
Entrepreneurial	Cell 3, 1 'Personal approaches to firms and through friends' (June).	Cell 3, 2 'I . . . spend . . . a couple of days every week with a company. I make sure that they know that I'm there' (John).

pattern arises purely from the way respondents and quotations were selected for inclusion in the table. To guard against this you need to check back to the original text for all respondents – especially those who do not appear in the table.

Chronological comparisons

It is clear, then, that tables are good devices for making comparisons between cases or groups of cases. But they can also be used for examining relationships *within* cases. Table 9.5 gives one example of this. Here all the information comes from one case, a person with a chronic illness who was interviewed on three separate occasions in a piece of biographical research. The rows are significant aspects of their life, and the table affords an easy comparison of how their views about these aspects changed (or not) over

Table 9.5 Example of a comparison within a single case

	First interview	*Second interview*	*Third interview*
Pain management	Cell 1, 1 'At first I was worried I might run out of pain killers.'	Cell 1, 2 'I try to avoid taking pain killers because of the side effects.'	Cell 1, 3 'There are times when I find the drowsiness better than the pain.'
Help from relatives	Cell 2, 1 'My husband did his best to help, but he's never done much cooking.'	Cell 2, 2 'Fred went to evening classes on cooking. I think he quite enjoys himself now.'	Cell 2, 3 'I don't know what I'd do if Fred got ill, my children live so far away.'
Independence	Cell 3, 1 'I think I was so self absorbed with the illness that I didn't worry about getting help.'	Cell 3, 2 'I find it very frustrating having to get Fred or someone else to move and lift things for me.'	Cell 3, 3 'With the new equipment I feel a lot more in control.'

time. The cell contents are just illustrations. In a real study they would typically be longer and you might have several passages in each cell.

The obvious approach to examining the data in this table is to do a chronological comparison by reading across each row. Thus we can see how this respondent's views about taking pain killers changed as she became familiar with their use. The same can be done with other rows. Nevertheless, there is also something to be gained from comparing rows up and down the table. For instance, comparing cells 2, 2 and 2, 3 with 3, 2 and 3, 3, we can see that notions of independence are not separate from the issue of how relatives help. Having to be cooked for has a clear impact on feelings of dependence in a couple where there was a strict division of labour ('My husband . . . never did much cooking').

What cells can contain

As is clear from the tables discussed above, the cells can contain a variety of things. The most obvious is direct quotations from respondents, as in Table 9.4. However, this is rarely possible because that would mean too much text in the table. The table becomes too large and/or too unwieldy. Some researchers deal with the size issue by covering the walls of their office with tables! But even so, too much text makes it hard to make the kind of between-cell comparisons tables are meant to support. In most cases it is better to sample what respondents are saying and include just particularly salient or representative passages. Alternatively, you can summarize or rephrase in your own words or even start

Table 9.6 What to put in the cells of tables

Possible cell contents	Examples from the Job Search project
Direct quotes, extracts from written-up field notes	'I thought what I'd better do would be start off by contacting people I'd worked with, outside the company, and these people would know what capabilities I had.'
Summaries, paraphrases or abstracts	Emphasizes family more than having a job. Resigned to long period of unemployment.
Researcher explanations	Focus on personalized explanations (bad luck, prejudice) cf. structural explanations (changing job market, recession).
Ratings or summarized judgements	Job searching activities – high Level of training undertaken – low.
Combinations of the above	[Routine?] 'Well, in the sense of taking them at 9, picking her [daughter] up at 11.30, and at about 3.30. Monday's Brownies, Thursday's swimming, Saturday's gym, Wednesday's Junior Club, Sunday's Sunday School.' Regular/routine pattern, little job searching.

Source: adapted from Miles and Huberman (1994: 241)

to express what has been said in terms of explanations or theories. As we shall see below, one advantage of creating tables or matrices using NVivo is that you can preserve, in a set of nodes, all the original text and go back and inspect it whenever you want. In this way you can continually check your interpretations of the table. Table 9.6 summarizes the various options.

Matrix searching in NVivo

In NVivo the way to generate tables such as Tables 9.4 and 9.5 is to use matrix searching. This assumes that you have already done a considerable amount of coding and creation of attributes. The idea behind matrix searching is that one group of nodes or attributes is compared, pairwise, with another group of nodes or attributes. Unless the nodes and attributes have been fully coded, the results of this search won't make a lot of sense. In a simple case, such as that in Table 9.4, matrix search will take three nodes, 'Routine', 'Haphazard' and 'Entrepreneurial', and do a pairwise search with the two attributes, 'Female' and 'Male'. Thus the first node 'Routine' will be searched with the first attribute, 'Female', then with the second, 'Male'. Then the second node, 'Haphazard' will be searched with the first attribute, then with the second, and so on. Each pairwise search produces a node the name of which will contain the two-number cell reference I have used in the example tables. For example, the node named 'Matrix intersection [3,2]' will code the text found by searching the third node with the second attribute.

What kind of search is carried out on each pair and thus what found text is coded at each of the nodes created depends on what you choose. Just as there are Boolean and non-Boolean searches (as we saw in Chapter 7), so there is a similar choice of matrix searches. There are two kinds of Boolean matrix search – intersection and difference – and three kinds of non-Boolean matrix search – co-occurrence, sequence and inclusion (surrounding). For example, assuming you have coded nodes for type of job search and coded attributes for gender, then Table 9.4 can be created using a matrix intersection search. The found text coded at each cell is that which is coded at both the item defining the cell's matrix row and to the item defining the cell's matrix column.

To do a matrix intersection search

1 Open the Search Tool.
2 Click on the **Boolean Search** button. This opens the Boolean Search dialog.

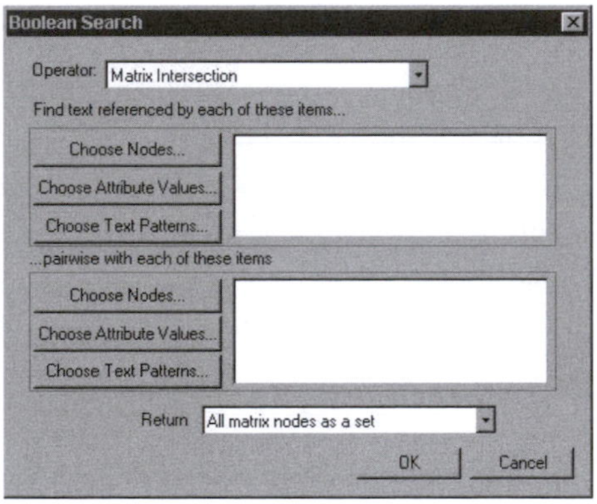

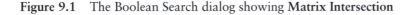

Figure 9.1 The Boolean Search dialog showing **Matrix Intersection**

3 Using the pull-down menu at the top of the dialog, choose **Matrix Intersection** (see Figure 9.1).
4 You now have to select items for the first list and items for the second list that define the matrix. Items in the first list define the rows of the matrix and items in the second list define columns of the matrix.
5 To produce the matrix that supports Table 9.4, click on the **Choose Nodes. . .** button against the first list and use the dialog that opens to

choose the nodes you need. In this example the nodes required are all children of the placeholder node 'Type' itself a child of 'Strategy'. Figure 9.2 shows these nodes in the Node Explorer. Therefore you can select the node 'Type' and then click on the **Children** button to transfer all three children nodes at once.

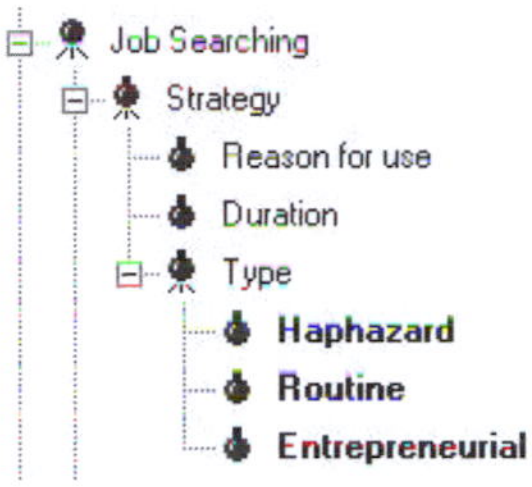

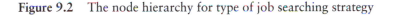

Figure 9.2   The node hierarchy for type of job searching strategy

6 Repeat this for the second list by clicking on the **Choose Attribute Values. . .** button and selecting the values 'Female' and 'Male' from the attribute 'Gender' (see Figure 9.3). Click **OK**.

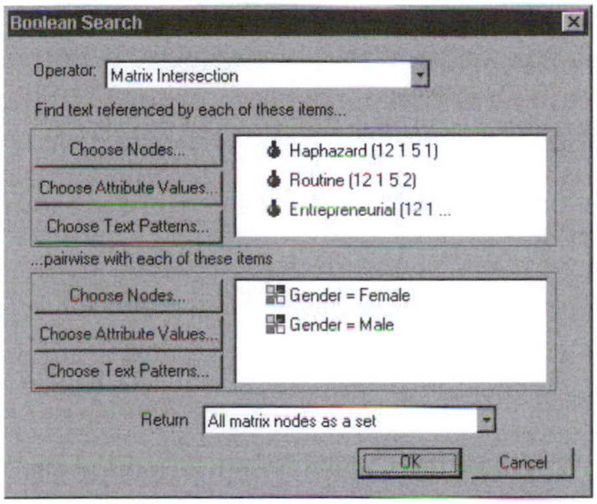

Figure 9.3   Nodes and attributes chosen for a matrix intersection search

7 If you have not already done so, select an appropriate scope for the search (e.g. all interview documents).
8 You don't have to, but it usually makes sense when doing matrix intersection searches to customize the result. Spread the resulting finds to at least the surrounding paragraph. Intersection search only finds text coded at both items in the pairwise search. In this example that is not an issue as the whole document will have been assigned the attribute values 'female' or 'male'. However, if you are searching a node intersection with another node then the found text might be quite short. It then makes sense to spread the find to a larger passage of text so that browsing the

node produces a meaningful passage. While you are customizing you might as well give a name to the new nodes that will be created. In this example I used 'Search strategy by gender' but left the new node to be created as a child of the root node 'Search Results'.

9 Click on **Run Search**.

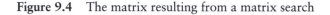

Matrix Table	1: Gender =...le	2: Gender =...le
1:/Job Searching/Strategy/Type/Haphazard	1, 1	1, 2
2:/Job Searching/Strategy/Type/Routine	2, 1	2, 2
3:/Job Searching/Strategy/Type/Entrepreneurial	3, 1	3, 2

Figure 9.4 The matrix resulting from a matrix search

10 Unless you have changed the option when customizing results, when the search is done (and assuming you have elected not to show the node in the Node Browser) a window opens showing the search matrix (see Figure 9.4). I have resized the first column so that you can see the node titles in full. Unfortunately, resizing the other columns does not make the column titles more readable. As you can see from Figure 9.4, it is difficult to tell which is which. To see the full attribute title, move the mouse over the column title and leave it there for a second or two. A small box pops up showing the title in full (see Figure 9.5). The same procedure works for row titles too.

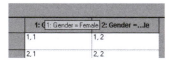

Figure 9.5 The pop-up full name of a column

11 You can browse the found text for each of the cells in this matrix using each cell's contextual menu ⌂.

12 You can also browse the found text from the Node Explorer. A new parent node called 'Search strategy by gender' (or whatever you have opted to name it) is added as a child of the root node 'Search Results' – see Figure 9.6. (You may have opted to save it somewhere else; 'Search Results' is the default.) Use the parent node's contextual menu ⌂ to open the matrix window (Figure 9.4) if you need to come back to it at a later time.

- Search strategy by gender
  - Search strategy by gender[1,1]
  - **Search strategy by gender[1,2]**
  - Search strategy by gender[2,1]
  - **Search strategy by gender[2,2]**
  - **Search strategy by gender[3,1]**
  - **Search strategy by gender[3,2]**

Figure 9.6   The subtree resulting from a matrix search

13 The matrix display can be changed to show several other results. These include the number of characters coded at each node, the number of documents coded and the number of coding references (see Figures 9.7, 9.8 and 9.9). Use the pull-down Display menu at the top of the window to access these. Cells in these displays are shaded to give a quick impression of the size of the numbers in them. The shading can be turned off using the **Matrix** menu in the Matrix dialog window. The numeric information in the matrices can also be displayed together with other information by selecting **Profile Matrix Nodes' Information** from the **Matrix** menu.

Matrix Table	1: Gender =...le	2: Gender =...le
1:/Job Searching/Strategy/Type/Haphazard	1116	1583
2:/Job Searching/Strategy/Type/Entrepreneurial	560	5561
3:/Job Searching/Strategy/Type/Routine	2693	2751

Figure 9.7   Matrix showing the number of characters coded

Matrix Table	1: Gender =...le	2: Gender =...le
1:/Job Searching/Strategy/Type/Haphazard	2	3
2:/Job Searching/Strategy/Type/Entrepreneurial	1	1
3:/Job Searching/Strategy/Type/Routine	3	3

Figure 9.8   Matrix showing the number of documents coded

Matrix Table	1: Gender =...le	2: Gender =...le
1:/Job Searching/Strategy/Type/Haphazard	2	3
2:/Job Searching/Strategy/Type/Entrepreneurial	2	2
3:/Job Searching/Strategy/Type/Routine	3	3

Figure 9.9   Matrix showing the number of coding references

The numerical matrix displays such as those in Figures 9.7–9.9 may be used to provide some idea of how often or frequently an issue was referred to. If an issue was talked about more or by more people, this might suggest that it had more importance or salience. It can also indicate whether an issue was a majority view or a minority one. However, counts of this kind in qualitative work need to be treated with caution. Samples are rarely drawn on a random basis and therefore frequency of response is no warrant, on its own, for generalizing to a wider population. Bear in mind the words from Coffey and Atkinson (1996: 181) I quoted at the end of Chapter 7: 'Analytic significance is not guaranteed by frequency . . .'. In qualitative research what is left unsaid can be just as significant as what is said. Nevertheless such numbers can be used to check hunches about correlations and causal relationships.

Matrix searching is therefore a way to generate the text that might go into a table such as Table 9.2, 9.3, 9.4 or 9.5. Sample text or summary text can be generated by browsing in turn each of the nodes (or cells) created by the matrix search. You can cut and paste this text into a new document (such as a memo) within NVivo or, if you want to set up a table like those above, you will need to cut and paste the text into a word processor such as Word.

 Any matrix search can search for text as well as for nodes and attributes. However, it is probably best to do a simple text search first that creates a new node and then use the new node in the matrix search. This means that you can tidy up the coding of the new node in the manner described in Chapter 6 before doing the matrix search.

Several of the examples of node searching mentioned in Chapters 7 and 8 can be done in one stage using matrix intersection. For example, in Chapter 7 I suggested searching on the node 'Application experience' to see whether men consistently talk differently (or less) about the experience of looking for work than women. A matrix search with the node 'Application experience' in the first list and the two attribute values 'Male' and 'Female' in the second list would produce the results in one go.

Matrix difference

This is the other available Boolean matrix search option. It will find all the text referenced by the first list of items specified in the Boolean search dialog, pairwise, less any text referenced by items in the second list. The most common use for matrix difference is for searching nodes against nodes. You need to ensure that nodes in the first list code relatively large passages since what you are doing is effectively subtracting from them any text coded at nodes in the second list. For example, matrix difference on nodes A, B and

C against nodes X and Y (in the second list) would return text coded at node A that is not coded at node X, text coded at node B that is not coded at node X, text coded at node C that is not coded at node X, then text coded at node A that is not coded at node Y and so on.

Something you need to remember about both of the Boolean matrix searches is that if none of the text actually overlaps then what is found is nothing in the case of matrix intersection and just the text coded at first list of nodes (A, B, C etc.) in the case of matrix difference. Sometimes such a null result is useful. For instance, in the Job Search project it would be significant if we could show that none of the text coded at 'vacancy searching', 'interviews' or 'using formal help services' was also coded at the node for 'ageism'. Actually just a partial result would be interesting too, if, for instance, only text coded at 'interviews' was also coded at 'racism' but neither text coded at 'vacancy searching' nor 'using formal help services' was. This would be evidence that the area where racism was significant was at interview and possibly not elsewhere. However, in many cases a null result has no great significance other than that the text coded at first list and second list nodes simply does not happen to overlap appropriately. This is a very common situation and in this case the non-Boolean searches are more useful.

Matrix co-occurrence, sequence and inclusion

These are the non-Boolean versions of matrix searching. You set up the search in exactly the same way as matrix intersection, but of course the basis of the pairwise comparison is different. These matrix searches use the same criteria as the non-matrix versions. Taking each pair of items in the two lists in turn,

- matrix co-occurrence looks for text coded at the first item that is near text coded at the second item;
- matrix sequence looks for text coded at the first that is followed by text coded at the second;
- matrix inclusion looks for text coded at the first that completely contains text coded at the second.

As in the non-matrix versions, you have the choice of what text is coded at the new nodes: text coded at the first item, text coded at the second item, or, if appropriate, text coded between them (along with combinations).

When to use matrix intersection and when to use matrix co-occurrence

The pros and cons of matrix intersection and matrix co-occurrence are very similar to those for non-matrix searching. Matrix intersection works well if items in at least one of the lists code quite large passages. The search can be used to focus in on those passages that are coded at (or have attributes for) both. Examples of suitable items include document attributes (that by definition code the whole document) and nodes that code lengthy passages. The latter will tend to be quite high-level and broad concepts. Examples from the Job Search project include 'Application Experience', 'Job Searching/Strategy/Type', 'Work Background' (if not set up as an attribute) and 'Work finding service/Evaluation'. Intersection search will recover all those passages that are coded at, say, various job searching strategy types and are coded at, say, 'Use of personal networks'. This works well as long as we can be sure that all the relevant passages of text are coded at both an item in the first list of nodes and at one in the second list. Spreading the finds to, say, the paragraph might be enough to cover those cases where text coded at a node from the second list is not entirely contained in that coded at the node from the first list. One way to think of matrix intersection search is as a way of dividing broadly coded nodes into narrower and more tightly defined passages.

However, if you cannot be sure that, for instance, all the text coded at 'Use of personal networks' is also coded at one of the job searching strategy types then matrix intersection search will not find all the text you might want. If, for example, you want to recover text about use of personal networks from cases or documents where the person uses a specific job searching strategy, even if the text coded at that node does not contain that coded at 'Use of personal networks' then you will need to use matrix co-occurrence. (As mentioned in Chapter 7, you could set up a new attribute, but matrix co-occurrence is usually quicker to do.) As the text coded at the two search items may not actually overlap, co-occurrence search cannot be used to divide up text coded at nodes in the way that matrix intersection can. However, very often that is not strictly what is needed. A matrix co-occurrence search with nearness defined as overlapping and set to return text from the second item only will return everything that a matrix intersection search would, but without the need for a messy spread of finds in order to retrieve any text coded at the second item but not coded at the first.

Consequently, as in the case of non-matrix searching, you will probably find yourself using matrix co-occurrence more often than not. It can find all the text intersection search does but in addition return all text coded at the second item (or the first if that is more appropriate) and not just that coded only at both the first and second list items.

Charts and diagrams

Tables are an important visual device in qualitative analysis, but are only a part of the wide range of charts and diagrams that researchers use. Many of these can be created easily with a pen and paper, and their main function is to aid in clarifying ideas and thinking. Some are more complex, and software can help in their production. They can be used throughout the project to summarize thinking and conceptualization and to record the development of theoretical ideas. Some are suitable for definitive summaries of data and can be included in final reports. Below I shall examine a selection of such charts. NVivo contains facilities for the production of models and certain kinds of charts and diagrams. We shall look at these features, and I will make some suggestions about how some of the charts and diagrams can be produced in NVivo.

Charts or diagrams can be used to represent a wide variety of relationships in your data. Typically charts contain images that refer to things or items and visual indications of relationships or links between them. The Model Explorer in NVivo comes with a variety of icons that represent nodes, documents, sets and so on. But you can also use your own. For example, you can use different icons or different shapes to represent different ideas or different properties. Likewise, you can use different kinds of lines between these items to represent different kinds of linkage. In the Model Explorer, the links can be coloured, can have direction, a name and different thickness. To distinguish positive or negative influences in links, you can use a + or − sign in the link's title.

The model in Figure 9.10, produced using the NVivo Model Explorer, shows the use of some of these ideas. For example, one of the linkages is shown in grey to indicate its tentative nature. The icon of a cloud is used to indicate an item representing an idea. Some linkages have arrows to indicate causal direction or flow.

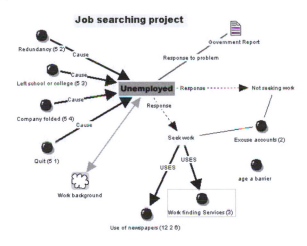

Figure 9.10 A sample chart produced in the NVivo Model Explorer

In many ways the arrows and connecting lines in a chart can represent the same kinds of relationships as those summarized for tree nodes in Table 7.1.

For example, in Figure 9.10 some of the links are labelled 'Cause' or 'Response'. To that extent, therefore, a chart can be another, more flexible, way of displaying the relationship between nodes. However, charts can represent many more things. One important, additional category of linkage is that of flow. Flow can refer to a variety of circumstances. For example, it can represent the flow of time and in this case it is very close to the notion of causal connection. But it can also represent the flow of objects. For example, charts can show the movement of people or organizations through a variety of events and experiences. The event–state network I shall examine in a moment is an example of this. Flow can also represent a flow of logic. The most important example of this is the flow chart or decision chart. Here the linkages represent the 'flow' of decisions or actions that show how people or systems decide what to do or how they operate. (Flow charts of this kind are commonly used in computer programming to show the logical flow in software.) Linkages can also be used to represent the actual relationships given by people, for example in categorizing things or in a hierarchy. Examples of this usage of linkages are the taxonomy, where the links represent the idea 'is a kind of', and the organizational chart, where the links represent a variety of things such as 'is subordinate to', 'reports to', 'is the manager of' and 'sends minutes to'.

Charts thus allow a much greater variety of ideas to be represented than the node tree and enable the free flow of your imagination as to what is portrayed and what it means. As we shall see later, you can use the Model Explorer in NVivo to produce many of these charts. Sometimes you might think it is easier to produce a chart with pen and paper (or even in a computer graphics program). The ease of pen and paper can be exploited for a first draft. However, there is a very big advantage in using NVivo for modelling and producing charts. All the elements in a chart can be connected with items in the main project. Not only can items from the project such as nodes, attributes, documents, cases, sets and memos be used in the model, but new items and links created in the model can be connected back to items in the main project. For example, a tentative idea about a link between two items in the model can be connected with a newly created memo in the project where you can type in your initial thoughts about the link. You can quickly go from the item or link in the model to browse the text of the original node or document or the text of the items you have connected it with.

It is also very easy, in the NVivo Model Explorer, to modify the arrangement of items and linkages in charts and to keep copies of charts at earlier stages of their development. Charts and diagrams produced in the Model Explorer are thus a powerful way of exploring and analysing your data and of recording or auditing the development of your ideas. If you are following the grounded theory approach discussed in Chapter 8, then you will find constructing charts and models in the Model Explorer a very useful way of doing axial and selective coding. For example, the relationships between the elements of the axial coding model summarized in Table 8.2 can be represented in a chart or diagram. Doing this in the Model Explorer means you can investigate these links while still having rapid access to the original data on which the elements are based.

Summed indices and cluster plots

As we saw earlier in this chapter when discussing case-by-case comparisons, it is possible to take a set of responses coded at a node and order them. This was done with the node 'Job Searching: Breadth' in the Job Search project (see Figure 8.5). It is also possible to create some other quantitative variables based on simple counts from the data set. For example, in the Job Search project respondents were asked what services for the unemployed they had used. This information was saved as a set of attributes with the values true (T) or false (F), indicating that they had or had not used the service. Figure 9.11 shows the resulting values. These were combined into a new variable 'Number of services used', also displayed in Figure 9.11. With a small data set like that used in the example Job Search project it is a simple job to set up the attributes in NVivo and to calculate the totals by hand. However, with a large data set you may well find it easier to create the attributes in a

	Ahmed	Andy	Dave	Harry	Jim	John	June	Mary	Pauline	Sharon	Susan	Tom
Adult Training	F	F	F	F	F	F	F	T	F	F	F	F
BCETA	T	F	F	F	F	F	F	F	F	F	F	F
Business Access Scheme	F	F	F	F	F	F	F	F	F	F	F	F
Careers and Education Advice Service	F	F	F	F	T	F	F	F	F	F	F	F
Careers Information Service	T	F	F	F	F	F	F	F	F	T	F	F
Number of services used	3	0	0	0	2	0	1	2	2	1	0	0
Redundancy Counselling	F	F	F	F	F	F	F	F	F	F	F	F
Start Up Business Units	T	F	F	F	F	F	F	T	T	F	F	F
Training Access Points	F	F	F	F	T	F	T	F	T	F	F	F
Workers' Co-operatives	F	F	F	F	F	F	F	F	F	F	F	F
Worklink	F	F	F	F	F	F	F	F	F	F	F	F
Youth training	F	F	F	F	F	F	F	F	F	F	F	F

Figure 9.11 Attributes showing use of services for the unemployed by respondents in the Job Search project

statistics package such as SPSS, and create the new summed variable there. Then all the attributes can be imported into NVivo. See the Reference Guide provided with the program for details of how to do this.

We might now be interested in the relationship between use of services and how geographically wide people's searching was. A cluster plot is one way of showing this. In Figure 9.12 I have displayed the 12 respondents in the Job Search project by the number of services they used and their categorization on the node 'Job Search Breadth'. I have used ellipses (labelled A to D) to indicate what might be clusters of respondents. The next step would be to go back to the data for those respondents in a cluster and see if they have any characteristics in common. For example, cluster A contains the two youngest members of the sample, and cluster B contains older respondents with family responsibilities. Perhaps these facts might explain why they cluster together on the number of services they used and how widely they are looking for vacancies.

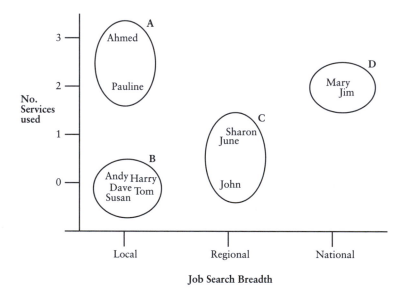

Figure 9.12   Cluster plot showing number of services used against job search breadth

Domain analysis

This is the examination of what some term or concept means for a culture or subgroup. Often it involves working out what are the referents of a term used by respondents or how they classify the objects and concepts they are using. Often such classifications of things can be expressed as a taxonomy. This is a way of ordering objects and ideas such that types have child subtypes that are mutually exclusive. Taxonomies capture the relationships between things and are often expressed as charts. The appearance of these is rather like the node tree in NVivo except that items in the taxonomy cannot appear twice. Figure 9.13 gives an example from the Job Search project that was created using the NVivo Model Explorer. It classifies the various organizations and other forms of help for those looking for work. Taxonomies like this can be a way of either capturing how respondents order their world or organizing one's understanding of concepts from the setting being studied.

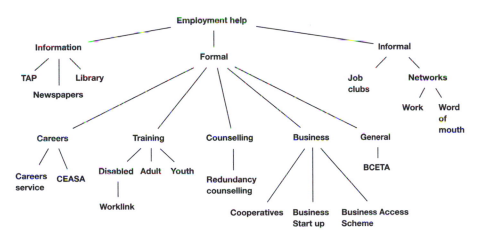

Taxonomy of help for the unemployed

Figure 9.13   Taxonomy produced in the Model Explorer

Event–state networks

An important subgroup of charts are those showing causal influence or temporal flow between items. Perhaps the simplest of these is the event–state network diagram. Research data often identify a variety of events and states, and these can be usefully presented in relation to each other in a chart. Events are one-off occurrences, usually of short duration. In comparison, states normally last some time. People do them or are involved in them on several or many occasions. The distinction is rough and ready, and sometimes it may not be clear whether something is an event or a state. This usually doesn't matter. What is more important is the work that goes into thinking about the phenomena that are categorized as events or states and how they are arranged together in a chart. Miles and Huberman (1994: 115–17) suggest that event–state networks are fairly easy to construct from an event listing and are often a helpful first step towards a more worked-out and substantiated understanding of the causal dynamics in the setting you are investigating.

For example, in the Job Search projects the following events and states could be identified (typically they would be nodes in the node tree):

Events

Quit job
Redundancy
End of short-term contract
Leave school or college
Interview
Careers advice
Training
Job offer

States

Unemployed
Routine searching
Entrepreneurial searching
Looking for work
Half looking for work
New social relations
In work

These events and states can then be entered into a chart, each in its own box. Miles and Huberman (1994: 115) suggest using rectangles for events and ovals for states. The boxes can then be linked by arrows to indicate time sequence. An event linked to a state by an arrow suggests that the event precedes and perhaps even causes the state. The events and states from the table above might be arranged into the chart shown in Figure 9.14. Here the thickness of the tails in the arrows is used to indicate the frequency with which people moved from the event to the state or from event to event or from state to event. The construction and inspection of the chart should produce new questions to investigate. For example, at the bottom of the chart there are two states connected to each other. The formation of new social contacts seems to lead to entrepreneurial searching by some people. You might therefore ask what events triggered the move to the latter state, entrepreneurial searching. This will take you back to the original data to examine text about new social contacts and entrepreneurial searching to see if you can identify any such events.

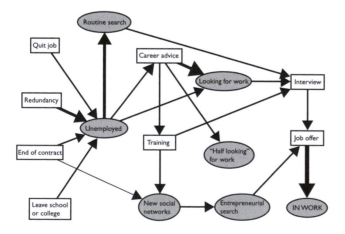

Figure 9.14   Event–state network diagram

Diagrams in grounded theory

In the discussion in Chapter 8 of axial and selective coding in grounded theory we saw that the analytic process focused on the search for certain model elements (summarized in Table 8.2). The model suggested you should identify some core phenomena and some related actions and interactions, and then look for other things that were causal conditions, strategies, contexts, intervening conditions and consequences of the phenomena and actions. It can be very useful to set up a diagram or chart to represent the relationship between these elements. For example, in Figure 9.15 I have produced a chart that displays some of the elements from the phenomenon of finding work. This was produced in NVivo, and most of the items are nodes from the project. The tree in Figure 8.6b shows how the nodes were organized in the node tree. The links in Figure 9.15 have been labelled to show the relationships are, for instance, 'Causal conditions for . . .', 'Intervening conditions of . . .', 'Strategies for . . .' and so on. This diagram is at a very early stage of development but clearly shows that a richer and more complex set of linkages can be represented than the node tree. Different types of lines are used for links to indicate different kinds of relationships, and some of them are very tentative or have an ambiguous status. For example, I have used a thin line to link items, like 'Work skills' and 'Selling skills', that might need some further investigation. 'Work skills' codes those skills respondents had that acted as an intervening condition on what kind of work searching they would do, and 'Selling skills' coded those passages in which respondents talked about how they 'marketed' or 'sold' themselves in job applications etc. Although, analytically, these are different items in the model, browsing the text showed that for some respondents, the skills they acquired or used at work (before losing their job) included the skills of being able to market and sell themselves later

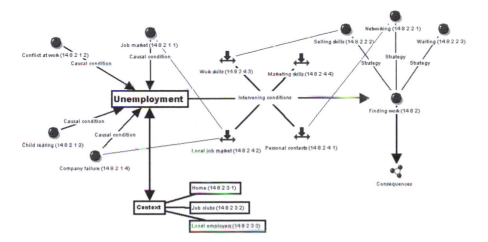

Figure 9.15 Partial axial coding from the Job Search project

when looking for work. It therefore raised the question of whether an important strategy for getting back to work quickly is making sure that while in work you acquire the skills, knowledge and contacts that will enable you to find work quickly should you become unemployed. The link was inserted to suggest this idea (and in the NVivo Model Explorer it can be linked with a memo document summarizing these thoughts).

Flow charts

The event–state model discussed above can be seen as a kind of flow chart. Among other things, it records the flow of individuals through a set of events and states. Indeed, the example above emphasized that by using different thicknesses of lines to indicate the frequency of flow. More generally, flow charts contain items that indicate inputs and outputs and connect them with a series of decision points where the inputs are processed to produce the outputs. The flow through the chart can be of individuals, people or cases or even simply logic. For example, a chart could show how people with different backgrounds (the inputs) go to different kinds of service for the unemployed, move on to other services (the processing) and then eventually get jobs or remain unemployed (the outputs). Figure 9.16 shows this done in the Model Explorer with people from the Job Search project. Links are shown with different thicknesses of line and are labelled with a number to indicate how many people followed that route. Such charts can be used not only to advance the analysis where they can show things like where the key processes are and what the most common routes are, but also in the final report where they can give a very clear picture of what can otherwise seem a very complex phenomenon.

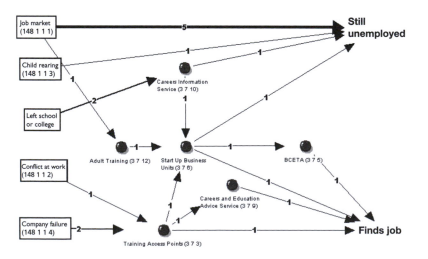

Figure 9.16   Flow of people through job finding services

One of the most common uses for flow charts is to illustrate decisions. Figure 9.17 shows this for one of the respondents, Susan, in the Job Search project, who gave a lengthy account of the decision process she went through when trying to buy household goods while receiving state unemployment benefits. I have left the final outcome as unknown (??) as the point of her explanation was that very often it was not possible to buy what she needed. Such charts can be used, case by case, to highlight contrasts between respondents' different ways of making decisions about issues or for demonstrating a commonly followed (or even mandatory) set of procedures in institutions and organizations.

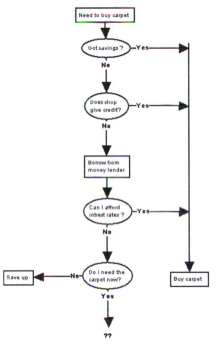

Susan decides how to pay for a carpet

Figure 9.17   Decision flow chart

The NVivo Model Explorer

The facility in NVivo for producing charts and diagrams is called the Model Explorer. This supports a variety of graphic items and links so that you can produce a diagrammatic representation of your thinking. Most of the example charts and diagrams just examined were produced in the Model Explorer. Of course you can create charts with pen and paper and with other computer-based graphics packages, and sometimes simple pen and paper is best. Some charts, such as Figure 9.12, are hard to do in NVivo and pen and paper can be quicker in getting your ideas down. However, as I mentioned above, the key advantage of the Model Explorer in NVivo is that all items in the model can be linked with items in your project, such as nodes, documents and memos. Unlike pen and paper charts or those produced in graphics programs, elements of the model can be continuously recontextualized as you check back to the original text or images that they represent.

To use the Model Explorer

1 From the Project Pad click on the **Create & Explore Models** button.
2 The Model Explorer opens (see Figure 9.18).
3 Use the **View** menu to open the Group, Layers and Item Styles palettes.

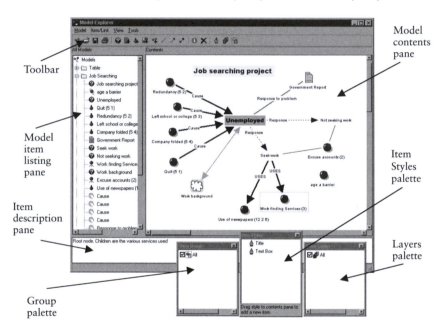

Figure 9.18 The Model Explorer

To create a new model

1 In the Model Explorer click on the new model button 🌳.
2 This adds a new model icon (a small folder) to the bottom of the model list pane and opens an empty (blank) model in the right-hand pane.

Model components may include documents, nodes, cases, sets and attributes from your analysis and other models (which can be effectively embedded within a model). All these items have default icons similar to those in the rest of NVivo. (Note that, by default, free nodes, tree nodes and cases all have the same blue circular icon in models, and memos and documents share the same document icon.) Other items can be added too, and these can have their own customized icons or no icon at all (see pages 214–15). All items can be renamed with a name that is particular to the model. If, say, you change the name of a node item in the model this does not affect its name in the rest of the project. Where model items refer to objects elsewhere in the NVivo project you can access their properties and text using the first two items in the model object's contextual menu 🖿.

To add items to the model

1 Either:
   (a) drag the item from the Document or Node Explorer to the model (works for nodes, documents, cases, node sets but not document sets and attributes); or
   (b) click on the appropriate button in the Model Explorer button bar (works for everything including other items).
2 Optionally rename the item. Double-click on the item name under its icon and type in the new one.

Items can be rearranged in the model by dragging them around. They can be linked with lines or arrows and these can be in various styles and colours. Links can have an optional title that appears across the line. Links can be used to indicate a wide variety of connections between model items, such as 'causes', 'belongs to', 'influences', 'might be related to', 'is a type of', 'leads to' and 'correlates with'. Use style of line and arrow, colour and title to indicate the type of link.

To link two items together in the model

1 Select one item in the model (Click once on the icon or the name).
2 Click on the appropriate link button in the button bar. You can choose just a line, an arrow or a double-headed arrow. If you select the single headed arrow it will point from the first selected item to the second.
3 Click on the item you want to link the first with.
4 A line or arrow now links the two items. As you move one item around the model the link follows it.

The appearance of items and links can be changed using the Properties dialog. It is important to note that this is different from the Properties dialog for items that appear elsewhere in NVivo. Thus, if you move a node from the Node Explorer into a model then it will have two sets of properties, the original set it had in the Node Explorer (and nothing you do to the model will change the contents of this) and a new set peculiar to the Model

Explorer. Properties in the model control what the item or link is called and how it appears on screen – for example, its colour, icon (if applicable), background and shape.

To change item properties

1 Select the item or link in either the right-hand or left-hand pane of the Model Explorer.
2 Select **Properties** from the item's contextual menu . Note that if the item is a node or document this is *not* the first properties item on the contextual menu. The first item gives you access to the properties you would get from the Node or Document Explorers.
3 This opens the Item – Properties or Link – Properties window.
4 Use the tabs and the buttons to change the appearance of the item or link. For example, use different shaped boxes and colours to indicate different kinds of item such as events and states. Use colour, line style and thickness of line to indicate different kinds of linkage, such as a grey or dotted line for a tentative link, or thick lines for strong causation and thin lines for weak causation.

 To use the contextual menu on model items you must first select them with the left mouse button.

Links and items that do not already represent nodes, documents etc. in the rest of the NVivo project can be made to represent these objects. This is very useful as a link in a model can be made to refer to, for example, a memo where you have discussed your ideas about the linkage.

To refer a link to another item in the NVivo project

1 Use the link's contextual menu to select **Represents** and the kind of object you want to refer to.
2 Select the object (e.g. a memo) from the dialog.

Now when you use this object's contextual menu two extra items appear at the top so you can inspect the properties and text of the document, node etc. it represents.

Don't use the delete button in the Model Explorer toolbar. It is far too easy to delete the whole model by mistake. To delete items in a model, use its contextual menu 🖱. That way there is no ambiguity about what you are deleting.

Dealing with large models

Most of the examples of charts discussed above have relatively few items and links. That is generally a reflection of the small size of the Job Search project on which they are based. Normally, projects are much bigger than this and consequently the model can get very large and complex. There are several facilities in the Model Explorer to help with this: styles, groups and layers.

Styles bring together a combination of item or link properties under one name and allow the consistent and easy formatting of items and links in a model. They operate in very much the same way as the styles in Word. Styles in the Model Explorer can combine information about an item's icon or shape, colour, line colour, line thickness and text style and a link's colour, arrow style, line style, line thickness and text style. Styles can be set up and edited using the Item Styles. . . editor or the Link Styles. . . editor accessed from the **Tools** menu. Once you have set up a style, you can apply it to an item or a link using its contextual menu 🖱. The contextual menu lists all the available styles in a hierarchical menu. See pages 214–15 for some ideas on how to use styles.

Groups are a way of collecting together items so that they can all be selected in one go. Selecting several items at once is useful when you are rearranging the model since they can all be moved together without altering their mutual positions. As you move the group, all links adjust to the items' new positions. Using groups is also a way of quickly highlighting items that have something in common (e.g. all the documents relating to female respondents). You can, of course, shift-click to select more than one item at a time to achieve the same effect, but setting up a group and selecting it from the Group palette is usually quicker, especially if you end up selecting the items several times. Items can be members of more than one group.

Layers are the most powerful way of dealing with large, complex models since they allow you to hide and show items and links. Any item or link can be assigned to one or more layers; then, using the Layers palette, you can hide and show any combination of layers. When you show a layer all links in that layer that connect visible items will be visible, but links that link to items that are not showing are hidden. You can, for instance, put the link between two items from one layer (e.g. layer A) into another layer (e.g. layer B). Then if only layer A is showing the link is hidden, if only layer B is showing then both items and the link are hidden, and if both layer A and layer B are showing then both items and the link between them will show. Layers can be used in a variety of ways to hide and show parts of your model. For example, if you have too many links to follow then put links of a certain kind on to a separate layer so they can be hidden to make the rest of the model clearer. If you have too many items then put collections of items on different layers so they can be shown or hidden as you choose. You can use layers to keep a record of previous versions of the model. Just put old links (and/or items) on to a new layer and then hide it. You can use layers to show and hide different kinds of relationships between the items, for instance, links as seen by one respondent or as seen by another, or, if you are working collaboratively, links suggested by one researcher and those suggested by another.

A fourth way of controlling the size of a model is to encapsulate parts of it into a 'submodel'. An example of this can be seen in Figure 9.15, where the icon at the bottom right, labelled 'Consequences', indicates another model. All the elements of this submodel can be displayed separately, including being displayed in a new Model Explorer window. Use the contextual menu ⌂ of the model's icon to open the Explorer. Thus, with a large enough monitor, you can have two models on screen at once and move between them as you wish. The drawback of putting part of your model into a submodel in this way is that you can only have a single link from one model to the other. None of the separate items in one model can be linked to a specific item in the other.

Two useful styles

Styles bring together a range of properties of items and links, including shape, colour, icon and name. If you want several items or links looking the same it is worth setting up a style. Below are two examples you might find useful in your project.

Styles can be edited, renamed and deleted using the Item Styles. . . tool (**Tools:Item Styles. . .** from the menubar).

To set up a new style

1 Select **Item/Link:Style:New Style** from the menubar.
2 This opens the Item Style – Properties dialog. This has two tab panels, **General**, shown on the left in Figure 9.19, and **Appearance**, shown on the right.
3 Fill in these two panels in the following ways.
   (a) If you are a dab hand with paint programs and know how to save

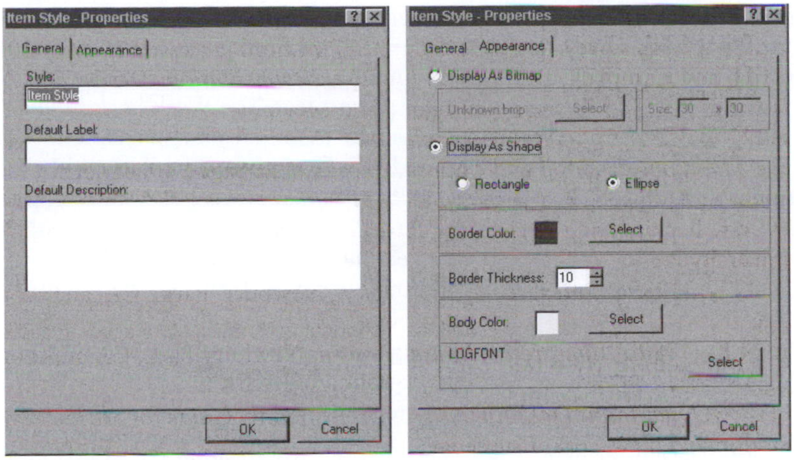

Figure 9.19   The Item Style – Properties dialog **General** tab (left) and **Appearance** tab (right)

a file in Windows bitmap format (.bmp extension, 32 × 32 pixels or slightly larger) then you may want to create your own icons. Creating a style that includes this icon makes it easy to add them to your model by dragging the style from the icon palette. Set up the new style with Style = your name, Default Label = untitled, Default Description = whatever you want, and under **Appearance** set the **Display As Bitmap** and select your new bitmap.

(b) It is very useful to have the ability just to enter some text into the model without any icon or box. Set up a style for plain text by creating one with Style = Plain text, Default Label = untitled, Default Description = blank, and under Appearance set the **Display As Shape** with Shape = Rectangle, Border Color = white, Body Color = white and LOGFONT = MS Sans Serif, regular, 8 point (this is the same as that used for items with icons, but you might prefer something else). When entering text into a text box item you can use the ↵ or **Enter** key to force a new line. There is no ordinary word wrap in text items.

With a bit of imagination you can produce quite a wide variety of model and diagram types using the Model Explorer. Most of the charts discussed earlier in this chapter were produced in the Model Explorer. Table 9.7 shows how I did them.

Table 9.7 How figures 9.10–9.17 were generated

Figure 9.10 Sample chart	The node and document items were imported from the project. The Work background item was a new item that was then assigned the cloud icon from those that come with the software. Linkages were customized to get different colours and widths along with the dotted line. Some were given titles. The Unemployed item in the middle is a new item and, using the Properties dialog, it was changed to display a rectangle with new background colour, line colour, line thickness and font.
Figure 9.12 The cluster plot	This was not produced in the Model Explorer. However, you could do something like this by importing all the relevant documents (or cases) from the project and then changing their properties to display a rectangle with line colour and background colour both white. Create the axes using empty text boxes (described in the explanation for Figure 9.17 in this table). Use text boxes to label the axes. You cannot create variable size ovals like those in this example in NVivo; however, you could just connect items in a cluster using the simple line link.
Figure 9.13 Taxonomy	Items in this chart are either nodes from the project or new items. All were given the plain text box style. (See pages 214–15.) A link style for thin line was also created and applied to all the links.
Figure 9.14 Event–state network	Items were a mixture of nodes from the project and new items. Two styles were set up. One, for events, was a rectangle box with plain text and background coloured yellow. The other was an oval box with plain text and background colour blue. These were applied to appropriate nodes or new items in the model. The thickness of links was changed using the Properties dialog for each link. You could also use colour to indicate different kinds of events and states and also make some of the links represent documents, nodes etc. in your project.

Table 9.7 continued

Figure 9.15 Axial coding example	Almost all items were nodes from the project, but their appearance was changed by displaying as boxes or using different icons. The icon for nodes representing intervening conditions was created in a paint program and saved with the other node icons. Then a new items style was set up using this new icon. Lines were coloured and their thickness changed using the link Properties dialog. Nodes for consequences were entered into a separate, new model and this was introduced into the model as a model item using the model display pane's contextual menu ⌂. The name of the link between the Unemployment and Finding work items is not actually the link title. It is in fact an item displayed as a rectangle with white line and background moved over the link. The advantage of this is that it can be linked with the four items representing the intervening conditions making it look as if they are linked to a link. Links were connected with documents (e.g. memos) that explained the developing concepts they represented. In some cases a brief description of items and links was entered using the Properties dialog. (Note that the description pane at the bottom of the Model Explorer window can be edited, but this is not saved. Use the Properties dialog.)
Figure 9.16 Flowchart	All the services and most of the starting points (on the left) were nodes and were dragged into the Model Explorer from the Node Explorer. Links were all given the same style and their appearance was changed where necessary using the link Properties dialog. Items were moved around the chart until the clearest and most informative picture emerged.
Figure 9.17 Decision flow chart	By convention, flow charts use diamonds to represent decisions or 'either/or' points. As the Model Explorer can't produce diamonds, I used ovals in this example. Two item styles were set up. Both had no icon, a white background and black line. One was a

Table 9.7 continued

	rectangle and the other an oval. A link style with line thickness of 5 and a suitable font (e.g. Arial bold) and a single pointed arrow was also set up. All items were new and were given one of the two item styles. The links on the right, which appear not to link two items, actually do. I used a plain text item (white line and background) with no text entered as a dummy item at the end of these links. Suitable arrangement simulates the link shown.

Conclusion

Tables can be a very powerful way to make comparisons between collections of qualitative data. The text coded there can be quickly browsed using the contextual menu ⌂ of each cell in a table generated by a matrix search. Thus comparisons of text across cases, time periods and between nodes can easily be made. Beware however: tables of this kind, generated from searches, are only as good as the coding and nodes on which they are based. The absence or presence of text in a table, although probably strongly suggestive of a pattern or providing good evidence for a relationship, is not definitive. It may merely reflect the way you have coded the text.

Many researchers, frustrated by the restriction to hierarchical node relationships in software like NUD•IST, find the facility for producing charts and diagrams in NVivo a revelation. A key point about models in NVivo is that the elements can be connected directly with items (nodes, attributes, documents etc.) in the NVivo project. The Model Explorer not only enables you to use a wide variety of objects and relationships to express your ideas, but also keeps you close to your original data as connected items can be easily browsed using their contextual menus ⌂. The Model Explorer is thus not just a neat way of displaying your analytical ideas, but can also be used as a way of building up your analysis. By moving from the model to the coded text and back again, you can check the nature of the relationships expressed in the model and if necessary refine the coding, nodes, memos, attributes etc. in your project. Models can even be used in this way as a key element of your writing about your project, as we shall see in the next chapter.

Further reading

Gladwin, C.H. (1989) *Ethnographic Decision Tree Modeling*. Newbury Park, CA: Sage. (A short but detailed discussion. Of particular interest to ethnographers.)

Miles, M.B. and Huberman, A.M. (1994) *Qualitative Data Analysis: A Sourcebook of New Methods*, 2nd edn. Beverly Hills, CA: Sage. (Many of the methods examined involve the use of tables, matrices and charts. A very useful collection to pick and choose from.)

Padilla, R. (1991) Using computers to develop concept models of social situations, *Qualitative Sociology*, 14: 263–74. (Recommends the use of commercial computer drawing packages for qualitative model building.)

Richards, T.J. and Richards, L. (1998) Using computers in qualitative research, in N.K. Denzin and Y.S. Lincoln (eds) *Collecting and Interpreting Qualitative Materials*. Thousand Oaks, CA and London: Sage. (Contains discussion of use of diagrams in CAQDAS.)

Werner, O. and Schoepfle, G.M. (1987) *Systematic Fieldwork. Vol. 2: Ethnographic Analysis and Data Management*. Newbury Park, CA: Sage. (Examines a very wide range of charts and diagrams that will be of interest to more than just ethnographers.)

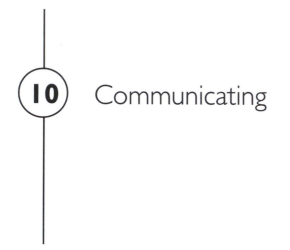

10 Communicating

In many methods books you will find a chapter like this at the end titled something like 'Writing up'. This is common enough in books on quantitative analysis, where, after a lot of data collection and data analysis, the time inevitably comes to write up the results. But there are at least two reasons why I wanted to avoid such a title in this book. First, it can be extremely difficult to get started in writing if it is all left to the end of the project. The pile of work can seem insurmountable. Second, as I have suggested several times already, in qualitative research you ought to be writing all the way through the project, not just at the end. If you have been keeping a research diary and if you have been keeping memos, annotations and other theoretical metadocuments of the kind discussed in Chapter 5 then you should already have a large body of writing about your project and the data in it. I titled this chapter 'Communicating' not only because some of these documents might have been used to communicate analytical ideas with co-researchers but also because in working on them and 'writing up' your project you will be communicating with others as well. These will include yourself – as you try to sort out your analytic and theoretical ideas, your sponsors and other stakeholders and, of course, readers of your final report. Nor should you forget the need to communicate with later researchers who may use your data and your notes to undertake further analysis. Writing in qualitative research therefore involves communicating (potentially) with a wide range of 'audiences'.

The need to write

It is never too early to start writing. You can even start writing before starting data collection and certainly before data collection and data analysis are finished. In some ways writing before you have started data collection is like constructing a node hierarchy before coding. It will encourage you to set down your ideas and hunches even though, in all likelihood, these thoughts will get extensively altered as you proceed through your project. You may be tempted just to write notes (in memos etc.). Sometimes that may be all you have time for, but try to avoid leaving the ideas as notes. Go back and 'write them up' into a narrative as soon as you can, preferably using a word processor or NVivo. There are two reasons for this. Notes that make sense to you as you write them may not when you come back to them months, if not years, later. Why this happens – and the second reason for writing up notes – is that writing is thinking. It is very easy to believe that thinking comes first (perhaps as captured by your notes) and then your writing merely reflects it. However, most of the time the opposite is true. Having to communicate your ideas is an excellent test of how far you have a clear understanding and how coherent your ideas are. As anyone who teaches or lectures will testify, the ability to communicate ideas and theories to an audience is a sure test of how much you really understand the topic you are teaching. Writing is an ideal way of doing this. Such communication does not even have to be written at first. You can discuss ideas with your supervisor, your co-researchers or your colleagues. Such discussions are often very important in team research. But even here it makes sense to capture in writing the essence of any discussion so that important points made are not lost and forgotten later on in the project.

Naturally, the task of producing a final report or thesis is a whole lot bigger than that of writing memos and other analytical notes. For a start, it will almost certainly be longer than any of the notes and drafts you have written before. However, if you have been writing throughout your project, the task will be much less daunting. You will already have many passages and perhaps whole chapters that can form part of the report. If this is so then the question of where you should start writing makes no sense – you have already started writing, and it probably won't be at the beginning. This is fine – you do not need to start with the first chapter or section. The same is true if you are starting from scratch. Getting started is always an issue for writers. It's amazing how jobs like cleaning the house and doing the ironing become more important and more attractive when you need to start writing. Start with the easiest section in order to try and build up some momentum. You will find that progress comes more easily, and the more writing you have done the better you will feel about the project and the more confidence and clarity you will have about the rest of your analysis.

Table 10.1   The two golden rules

---

1 Write early and write often:
   (a) The more you write, the easier it gets.
   (b) If you write every day, it becomes a habit.
   (c) Tiny bits of writing add up to a lot of writing. Break the writing up into
       small bits. Write 100 words on X, 200 words on Y and then file them safely.
       It all mounts up.
   (d) The longer you leave it unwritten, the worse the task becomes.

2 Don't get it right, get it written:
   (a) Until it is on paper no one can help you to get it right. Draft, show the draft
       to people, redraft.
   (b) Drafting is a vital stage in clarifying thought.
   (c) Start writing the bit that is clearest in your head: *not* the Introduction, but
       Chapter 4, or the appendices, or the conclusions, or the methods. As you
       draft, other bits become clear.
   (d) Drafting reveals the places where 'it' isn't right (yet) in ways that nothing
       else does.

Source: adapted from Delamont *et al.* (1997: 121)

Some writers start with a sequence or outline of what they want to say and
then proceed through it filling out the ideas. Others start with a table of contents, and then progressively expand it and fill in the details. Yet others just
start with a statement of purpose or objective for their work and then write
on from there. Some writers like to produce one sentence at a time, getting
each perfect before moving on to the next. In contrast, others prefer to free-
write. They get it all down and then go back and tidy it up. It matters not a
jot which you do or which you prefer. Choose whichever approach suits you,
even whatever suits you on the day. All that matters is that you start writing
and continue writing. Table 10.1 presents the two golden rules which you
should follow.

Organization

No matter how early in your project you have started writing and irrespec-
tive of how much you have been writing notes, memos and criticisms
throughout the analysis, there comes a time when you need to bring it all
together to write a report, thesis or paper so that you can communicate your
results to others. You need to organize your thoughts and get a focus.
Getting organized means finding a structure that can bring together all your
disparate jottings into a coherent 'story'. Such a structure will often be presented as chapters or sections in your report. For example, in the simplest
case you might give a chronological account where each section is an episode

Table 10.2   Organizing the qualitative report

1 A set of individual case studies, followed by a discussion of differences and
  similarities between cases.
2 An account structured around the main themes identified, drawing illustrative
  examples from each transcript (or other text) as required.
3 A thematic presentation of the findings, using a different individual case study to
  illustrate each of the main themes.

Source: adapted from King (1998)

in what you have studied, or a case-by-case account, where each section
discusses one case. Alternatively, you can organize your work thematically.
Such themes might be in vivo or emic notions – suggested by ideas used by
those you have studied – or they might be theoretical or etic ideas, more
abstract and derived from the literature. You might even mix emic and etic
themes. Again, each theme might be a separate chapter or section. Table
10.2 summarizes the options.

The expanding drop file

If you have lots of notes in NVivo then a simple way to organize them into
such themes or cases is to use document and node sets. Just create a set for
each theme and then drag the relevant documents on to them. This is the
electronic equivalent of what Wolcott (1990: 38) refers to as the 'expanding
drop file' approach. As Wolcott describes it, the approach consists of keeping a file in which there is a folder for each topic, case, theme and so on, into
which you can put any notes, documents, memos etc. The idea is that you
can return to the folder at any time and there you will find most of the
material you need to write the section it supports. As time passes, the contents of each folder can be worked up gradually from notes into first draft
and thence via revisions to the final version. Folders develop at different
rates and it is not necessary to work on them in the order the topics they represent will appear in the final report. At any time you can look in the folder
and get a good idea of progress (or lack of it).

In NVivo sets are the obvious analogue of Wolcott's folders. Create sets
for each topic or chapter and just drag all the relevant documents or nodes
on to the appropriate set. You can even establish sets of documents or nodes
for *ad hoc* purposes such as writing an interim report or a paper on a subset
of your material. However, in NVivo there are alternative approaches that
achieve the same end of organizing your writing, but do so in ways you
might find more conducive.

The first of these is using a key document as the mechanism for linking all
relevant texts and nodes together. The disadvantage of sets is that their contents have no structured relationship. They merely contain a collection of

items. However, by using DocLinks, NodeLinks, annotations and DataBite links from a key document, you can establish a collection of nodes and documents and, at the same time, in the key document from which they are linked, you can start to develop an understanding of how they are related. At its simplest this might be a set of headings or an outline of the document you are trying to write. At first just link these headings to documents, memos and nodes of relevance. Gradually, as you develop the key document and begin to fill out the details, you can cut and paste sections from your theoretical and conceptual notes into it and then edit them there. If cut and paste are not available from the menu (or the Edit menu is not available) you will find that the keyboard shortcuts Ctrl-X, Ctrl-C and Ctrl-V for cut, copy and paste, respectively, will work. Keep the links back to the originals so you can recall how your thinking started if you need to. Links to relevant nodes will give you material for suitable quotations from your respondents or for tables in your report.

The second NVivo equivalent of Wolcott's folders is to use charts in the Model Explorer. Simply drag documents or nodes from their respective explorers on to a chart. This is the equivalent of dragging them on to a set. However, in the chart you can arrange them on the page to indicate groupings and then even make them into specific Model Explorer groups. You can also use the model item links to show how they relate to each other. Use the ability to associate items in the Model Explorer to items in the project to connect links with documents in which you can write down your ideas about the relationship. Such use of charts is the electronic equivalent of using small file cards with notes on to write a chapter. Researchers using this method select out relevant cards and then shuffle them around on their desktop to get a structure that they can then write up from. Moving icons around in a chart is the NVivo analogue. One disadvantage of using the Model Explorer in this way compared with using a key document with document and node links is that the document you are trying to write has to be kept elsewhere. Its contents cannot appear on the chart. For this reason, you might prefer the key document approach. However, a disadvantage of that approach is that it is easy to 'get lost in hyperspace'. So many documents are linked to others and to nodes and so on, that in following a link you forget where you came from and why you were following the link. If you use a chart to represent these links then the route through them is more obvious. The chart acts as a map.

Given the pros and cons of each NVivo approach, you will probably find that a mixture of the three approaches – sets, documents with links, and charts – works best. There is no denying that creating charts or key documents with links is a lot of work. However, the effort of constructing and keeping them up to date pays off in the end because, like the work that goes into writing, this is the effort of thinking and especially of conceptual thinking.

Focus

Part of the intellectual effort of writing up the project will be that devoted to getting a focus. Typically this is unclear when you start work, and only gradually emerges as you analyse your data and write. You will know you have a focus when you can complete the sentence: 'The purpose of this study is . . .'. Getting to that point is the issue. You may find that talking over your research with colleagues or friends helps you to recognize what the focus should be, since in order to explain your work you will need to find some central point around which your description can cohere. An alternative is to try free writing, where you just write on the topic without stopping for 10 minutes or so. This makes writing a way to resolve the problem of focus rather than a source of the problem.

If you have followed the grounded theory approach I discussed in Chapter 8, then the stage of selective coding where you identify a central phenomenon is the equivalent of finding a focus. For Strauss and Corbin (1990), the core category or central phenomenon is something around which narrative and conceptual description can be woven. It takes some time and considerable development of the coding scheme before the one or two candidates for the central phenomenon become clear, they argue. Table 10.3 summarizes the criteria suggested by Strauss and Corbin. However, Glaser, who co-developed grounded theory with Strauss, parts company with his colleague on this issue. For him, the core category is a central and recurrent conceptual entity, substantially and richly connected to other categories and with considerable analytic power. It accounts for much of the variation in a pattern of behaviour 'which is relevant and problematic for those involved' in

Table 10.3   Criteria for choosing a central category

1 It must be central; that is, all other major categories can be related to it.
2 It must appear frequently in the data. This means that, within all or almost all cases, there are indicators pointing to the concept.
3 The explanation that evolves by relating the categories is logical and consistent. There is no forcing of data.
4 The name of the category and the concept behind it should be sufficiently abstract that it can be used to do research in other substantive areas, leading to the development of a more general theory.
5 As the category is refined analytically through integration with other concepts, the theory grows in depth and explanatory power.
6 The concept is able to explain variation as well as the main point made by the data; that is, when conditions vary, the explanation still holds, although the way in which a phenomenon is expressed might look somewhat different. One should also be able to explain contradictory or alternative cases in terms of the central idea.

Source: adapted from Strauss and Corbin (1990: 147)

the situation studied (Glaser 1978: 93). For these reasons, Glaser thinks, it is actually not very difficult to uncover it.

The dispute between Glaser, on the one hand, and Strauss and Corbin, on the other, seems to revolve around the degree to which the focus of analysis should be concepts that arise out of the concerns of the respondents themselves, the emic concepts, or how far they should be informed by social science theory and concepts, the etic. This dispute will run and run, but in my view the deciding factor is what is right for your project. That depends as much on your predilections as on the requirements of the sponsors of the analysis you are undertaking.

Redrafting

Becker points out that one of the bad habits a lot of undergraduates get into is thinking that the first draft is the final draft. In his book on writing in the social sciences (Becker 1986) he is at great pains to show how much redrafting, editing and tightening is necessary in order to write a decent final report. The aim of redrafting is to re-express your writing to make it clearer, read better and flow more easily. One of the most important aspects of this is to cut out redundant material. Look for needless repetition and delete it. For example, where points are supported by multiple examples and one will do, take out the extras. Sometimes you can cut out illustrations without losing meaning and reliability, though beware of compromising the credibility of your report. One characteristic of many first drafts is that they have lengthy beginnings – as if the writers had taken their time to get into the flow of things. It's often easy to cut the first sentence or so of every beginning. Another trick is to consider moving some of your material to an appendix. If you can do that, then it's often a sign that the material could be cut altogether. To summarize: when redrafting, cut out what you can and, above all, when in doubt, leave it out.

Good writers are able to redraft their work on their own but all writers, no matter how experienced, can gain from getting feedback from others. Get friends or colleagues, preferably those who have at least a little knowledge about your topic, to read your drafts. It will help them, and you, if you tell them what kind of feedback you want. Is the draft too long, so you need advice on how and where to cut it? Is the writing at the right level for the intended audience? Do you need the contents checked for accuracy and detail (rather than style)? Do you want the reader to mark detailed typos? If you tell your reader what feedback you want they won't waste their time picking up all the small spelling mistakes when all you need is to know what passages of the text you could cut out.

The corollary of the need for redrafting is that the first draft can be pretty rough and ready. That should make the task of producing it less pressured. As long as you can revise and improve the text there is no problem. As

Becker (1986: 21) notes, 'the only version that counts is the last one'. On the other hand, don't start editing too soon. Wait till you have a complete first draft. Borrowing some instructions he found for assembling a lawnmower, Wolcott (1990: 47) puts it nicely: 'Make sure all parts are properly in place before tightening'.

If you are writing using a word processor or NVivo then it makes sense to make a copy of the previous draft that can be kept in case you need to refer back to it. In fact I do this every time I redraft. Once I ended up with 12 versions of a paper, reflecting 12 drafts. In NVivo you could save a copy of the whole project and then keep this somewhere safe (e.g. on a removable drive such as a Zip or CD-RW). Alternatively, you could just copy the files you are working on and then move the originals into a set called something like 'Version 1'. Keeping a copy serves two purposes. Psychologically it makes it easier to change the text as you can always tell yourself that you can go back to the saved version if you need to. Practically, you may move large sections around and delete parts you think are redundant. If later you change your mind, the originals are still available for you to reinstate them.

Style

Traditionally, the style in which reports, papers, theses and so on have been written has been a rather dry, technical one. Writers presented the basic story using the passive voice and the past tense. Respondents' own words were used, but only to a limited degree and usually only in illustrative quotations. This reflected the predominant scientific and realist stance taken by social scientists. Research could reveal the true underlying nature of social reality and the write-up could represent that reality in a simple, straightforward and objective manner.

The realization that there might be problems with these beliefs came first in anthropology. This discipline had the job of trying to make societies and cultures that might seem strange, bizarre and illogical look rational and understandable to Western readers. The identification of the issues involved in this can be traced back at least to the critique of Evans-Prichard by Winch (1974). Evans-Prichard was one of the leading ethnographers of the day and famous for his study of the Azande, an African people. Winch argued not only that Evans-Prichard illegitimately applied the standards of Western science to his description of Zande cultural practices, but that the task of writing an ethnography was essentially one of translation from one culture to another and hence fraught with difficulties. In the following decades there has been a realization that these issues apply not only to the relatively exotic cultures and societies studied by anthropologists but also to any attempt by social scientists to give an authoritative account of any social reality. As I suggested in Chapter 1, for some writers this means the complete rejection of any attempt at producing an objective and realist account of the object of study.

The upshot of this has been a widening of the standards expected of social science writing and in some cases experimentation with radically different forms of reporting such as dialogues and debates. It has engendered a growing awareness of the range of styles in which qualitative analysis can be reported. For instance, Van Maanen has distinguished three basic forms of presenting research findings in ethnography. These are summarized in Table 10.4. Although these illustrate a greater variety of possible approaches, in most areas of the social sciences realist tales are still by far the most common.

Another consequence of recognizing the difficulties of writing in qualitative research is the realization that writing can be a form of research itself and not just a report about research. An aspect of this is the intertextuality of research reports, that is to say, the way that research texts relate to other texts. The importance of this for those writing about qualitative data is that readers generally expect texts to follow a genre or style. Examples include the community studies report, the anthropological monograph, the evaluation report, the scientific paper and the popular magazine article. It is important when writing up your analysis that you make yourself aware of the traditions and styles of writing in your field and make clear how your text relates to the other – even if you have chosen to reject the dominant

Table 10.4   Van Maanen's Tales of the Field

Realist tales
Observations are reported as facts or documented by quotations from respondents or texts. Typical or common forms of the object of study are presented. The views and beliefs of those being studied are emphasized. Sometimes the report may try to take a position of 'interpretive omnipotence' (Van Maanen 1988: 51). The author goes beyond subjective viewpoints to present wider, more general and more theoretical interpretations.

Confessional tales
A more personalized account. The authors' views are made clear and the role they played in the research and in the interpretations is discussed. Authors' viewpoints are treated as an issue, as are all the problems encountered in getting 'into the field' and in gathering data. Naturalness in presentation along with an account grounded in the data collected are used to show how what happened was a meeting between two cultures.

Impressionist tales
These take the form of a dramatic recounting of events, often in chronological order. The writer attempts to create, by the inclusion of all the details associated with remembering, the sense of hearing, seeing and experiencing what the researcher did. Like a novel, the writer tries to make the audience feel they are in the field. Narratives are often used.

Source: adapted from Van Maanen (1988)

forms. It is therefore important that you are aware of the audience you are addressing. The audience, the potential readers or listeners, will have a set of expectations about what they read or hear and how it is expressed. You will need to be aware of the impact of such expectations, not only on the overall form and style of your writing, but also, to return to a point made earlier, on the detailed way you express yourself when redrafting the text.

Evidence

In discussing his 'tales of the field' Van Maanen makes it clear that in every case the writer has to demonstrate as well as possible how the account being given is grounded in the data. In other words, it is the author's job to show that any claims made or descriptions given truly represent what happened. A key facet of this in qualitative research is the inclusion of quotations from your data.

Including quotations in your report helps give the reader the feel for the aesthetic of the settings and the people you studied. It enables the reader to get closer to the data and enables you to show exactly how the ideas or theories you discuss in your main text are expressed by those you have studied. And, of course, it constitutes evidence that your analysis is valid and accurate. Given all these functions, it might seem that more and longer quotations are better. Given that you can cut and paste quotations from your NVivo project into your report, this is easy to do. However, the greatest danger when including quotations is if you use them to make analytic points rather than using your own words. This is, perhaps, the most common misuse of quotations in undergraduate work. It is tantamount to making readers do the analysis for themselves. You need to keep a balance between quotations and your analysis. Moreover, long quotations can be problematic as they will include many analytic items and the reader will have problems identifying which the quotation is meant to be illustrating. Short quotations (a sentence or two) can serve as simple illustrations for analytic points being made in the text. Longer quotations (longer paragraphs) should be used sparingly and will probably need an explanation of their own to tell the reader how to interpret them and how to relate them to the analytic points in your report. On the other hand, you need to guard against making the quotations too short as they may become decontextualized. You can put the quotation into context in your own text, but then it may hardly be worth including it unless it is showing some particular or unusual use of words (an in vivo concept perhaps). Table 10.5 summarizes guidelines for including quotations in your report.

Table 10.5   Guidelines for reporting quotations

1 The quotes should be related to the general text – for example, to the respondent's 'lived world' or to your theoretical ideas.
2 Each quote should be contextualized – for example, what question was it a response to, what came before and after (if relevant).
3 Each quote should be interpreted – explain what viewpoint it supports, illuminates, disproves etc.
4 There should be a balance between quotes and text. No more that half the text of any results section or chapter should be quotes.
5 Quotes should usually be short. Try breaking up long passages of quotation into smaller ones linked by your own commentary.
6 Use only the best quote. Say how many others made the same point. Use several quotes if they illustrate a range of different answers.
7 Interview quotes should be rendered in a written style. Except where the details are relevant (e.g. sociolinguistic studies) it is acceptable to tidy up the text, especially in longer excepts. The full details of hesitations, digressions, dialects and so on can make for very heavy reading. Use [. . .] to indicate where you have deleted digressions.
8 There should be a simple signature system for the editing of the quotes. Say at the end of your report how you edited your quotes (e.g. that you substituted names to preserve anonymity – but obviously not the actual substitutions) and give a list of symbols used for pauses, omissions etc.

Source: adapted from Kvale (1996: 266–7)

Quality

As I discussed in Chapter 1, validity and reliability refer to the degree to which the research represents a true picture of the setting under investigation and how far similar results would be obtained if the work were repeated even if different researchers were involved. In quantitative research there are agreed techniques and methods, such as random allocation in experiments and probability sampling in surveys, that will ensure validity and reliability. The situation in qualitative research is less clear. As we have seen in previous chapters, there are some techniques (constant comparison and the search for negative cases are two) that help ensure validity and reliability and, at various points, I have suggested ways of ensuring consistency and reliability in your analysis. However, these are not so much techniques that will guarantee validity as processes or states of mind on the part of the analyst. Just as the recognition of the problematic nature of the text constituting the research report has produced a new focus on writing, so the lack of simple techniques for validity and reliability has focused attention on to how the results of qualitative analysis are presented. As Flick (1998: 247) puts it, 'where trustworthiness and credibility replace reliability and validity . . . the problem of grounding is transferred to the level of writing and reporting'.

As I suggested above, one of the ways in which you can persuade the reader of the trustworthiness and credibility of your work is by demonstrating how it is grounded in your data. The use of appropriate quotations is one way of doing this. Another is by referring to cases and examples in your narrative. However, there are dangers in the way you do this. One is the temptation to overgeneralize. It is all too easy to write 'those searching for work . . .' when what you actually mean is 'one of those searching for work . . .'. You might think the words 'some of' are implicit in the phrase 'those searching for work' but it will give your reader much more confidence in your analysis if you say 'a small minority' or 'more than half' or even '60% of those searching for work' (whichever is appropriate). The use of such terms will also help you guard against what has been called 'selective anecdotalism'. This is the use of particular examples to try to make a general point. There is a great temptation, when writing up qualitative research, to pick out particularly fascinating or even exotic examples to illustrate your analysis. The danger is that you will use these to build a more general picture than is warranted. You can guard against this in the same way by using references to frequency. At the same time, be aware that your anecdotal examples may in fact be negative instances – in which case, report them as such.

You can quickly obtain the information you need for making such qualifications in NVivo by generating a node coding report or by profiling the coding in a set.

To produce a node report with counts

1 Open the Node Browser on the appropriate node.
2 Select **Node:Make Coding Report. . .** from the menu bar.
3 Click on the **Choose. . .** button to select an appropriate set of documents to report on. For example, All documents or All interviews in the Job Search project.
4 In this case you are not interested in reporting the text so uncheck the **Show text** box.
5 Click on **OK**.
6 A Text Editor window opens showing the report (see Figure 10.1). If you wish, this can be saved to disk. The program will prompt you as you close the window.

To profile the coding in a set

1 Open the Node Browser on the appropriate node.
2 Select **Node:Profile Coding into a Document Set** from the menu bar and then select either **Character Counts. . .** or **Number of Passages. . .** from the hierarchical menu.

```
NVivo revision 1.2.142                                      Licensee: Graham R Gibbs

Project: Job Search              User: Administrator         Date: 23/10/00 - 13:00:36

                        NODE CODING REPORT


          Node:  /Search Results/Children work break
   Treenode address:  (1 1)
             Created:  16/4/00 - 15:42:49
            Modified:  23/10/00 - 12:58:59
        Description:
Text Search: text matching the pattern 'children'

Scope: { June, Mary, Pauline, Sharon, Susan }

Result is a node coding all the finds: (1 1) /Search Results/Single Text Lookup (n)
Document finds are spread to (no spread). Node finds are spread to (no spread).


   Documents in Set:  Interviews
      Document 1 of 12  June
         Passage 1 of 2  Section 3.8, Para 120, 411 chars.
         Passage 2 of 2  Section 3.18, Para 140, 643 chars.

      Document 2 of 12  Mary
         Passage 1 of 1  Section 0, Para 229, 187 chars.

      Document 3 of 12  Pauline
         Passage 1 of 7  Section 0, Para 33, 178 chars.
         Passage 2 of 7  Section 0, Para 65, 145 chars.
         Passage 3 of 7  Section 0, Para 77, 699 chars.
         Passage 4 of 7  Section 0, Para 158, 47 chars.
         Passage 5 of 7  Section 0, Para 174, 580 chars.
```

Figure 10.1   A node coding report showing passages and character counts

3 This opens a new window showing either the number of characters coded at the selected node (see Figure 10.2, left) or the number of passages coded at that node (see Figure 10.2, right) for each document in the selected set.

Coding Character Count	(1 1)	Totals
Documents		
Ahmed	0	0
Andy	0	0
Dave	0	0
Harry	0	0
Jim	0	0
John	0	0
June	1054	1054
Mary	187	187
Pauline	2236	2236
Sharon	0	0
Susan	6692	6692
Tom	0	0
Totals	**10169**	**10169**

Coding Passage Count	(1 1)	Totals
Documents		
Ahmed	0	0
Andy	0	0
Dave	0	0
Harry	0	0
Jim	0	0
John	0	0
June	2	2
Mary	1	1
Pauline	7	7
Sharon	0	0
Susan	14	14
Tom	0	0
Totals	**24**	**24**

Figure 10.2   The number of characters coded profile and the number of passages coded profile

From each of these results you can quickly calculate appropriate percentages if you want.

Teams

Many qualitative projects are now undertaken by more than one researcher and sometimes at more than one site. There are two ways in which the qualitative analyst may operate in such teams. In the first case there may be a division of labour in the team. Different researchers may be working on different parts of the project, examining different settings, or they may be taking different roles in the project. For instance, one may be co-ordinating and writing, one doing interviews, one undertaking observations and another doing the analysis. The major issues here are how to co-ordinate the work being done by these researchers and how to ensure good communication between them. NVivo has some good tools to manage such co-ordination. At the most basic level, you can use the project to store all documents that record the activities of the team. This will include both online and proxy documents for all the data being collected, e-mails, letters, drafts and so on produced by team members, along with records of meetings, discussions and so on that are aimed at furthering the research and analysis. These can all be dated using **Edit: Insert Date & Time** from the menu bar in the Document Browser. Use NVivo's powerful search tools to find material and to categorize and organize it.

Using the reports options in the program, you can produce computer files or paper copies that can be shared with other researchers. For example, you can produce coding reports on documents to show co-workers how the text is being coded. Use the procedure described above to produce reports on the coding of documents. To get the report to cover more than one node, create a set of the relevant ones. Use the Node Set Editor or drag nodes from the right-hand Node Explorer pane to the set (Ctrl-click or Shift-click to select several nodes at once). In this case your colleagues will want to see the text, so select this option in the Node Coding Report Setup dialog, and they will probably need to see paragraph numbers and DataLinks so make sure these are selected too.

You can also produce summaries of how documents and nodes have been assigned attributes. Choose **Explore Set's Attributes** from either a document set's or a node set's contextual menu ⌂. The resulting table can be saved in tab-separated text format or in SPSS format or printed.

Another clever way to communicate within the research group is to use NVivo for presentations. Link up a computer with a projector device and you can use the Model Explorer to produce some useful images. Use the layers facility to reveal parts of a model, progressively, just as you might in a PowerPoint presentation. You can even use the Model Explorer to co-ordinate a theoretical discussion among team members, adding to and changing the model as they make suggestions.

You may want team members to be able to access the actual NVivo project files themselves. Assuming all the appropriate members have a copy of

NVivo, there are two ways you can do this. At appropriate points you can produce a copy of the project. This can be locked to read-only so that it constitutes a snapshot of the project at the time of saving. As well as enabling you to share the current state of analysis with co-workers, this procedure will act as a form of auditing of the project. By going back through the various stages you will be able to reconstruct how you arrived at the final version of the analysis. This ability to backtrack the development of analysis can also play a part in reassuring those reading your project report that your analysis is sound, since you can explain what process of analysis led to your final interpretation.

To save a read-only copy of the project

1 In the Project Pad, select **Project:Save Project As. . .** from the menu bar. This opens the Save Project As dialog (see Figure 10.3).

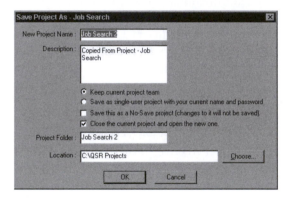

Figure 10.3 The Save Project As dialog

2 Give the copy a name. By default the program adds a '2' after the original name.
3 Add to the description. For auditing purposes it is a good idea to put the date and time in here.
4 Check the box labelled **Save this as a No-Save project**.
5 Choose a location if you want to save the project somewhere different.
6 Click on **OK**.

NVivo projects can become rather large so you might find it convenient to compress the files. Use a program like WinZip to do this. I found that a 2 MB project compressed into a file of about 600 kB. Make the compressed file a self-extracting archive so that members of your team do not need a copy of WinZip to decompress it.

The alternative way of sharing files is to allow other users access to the original project. They can then either access the files from your machine (e.g. when you are not there) or, more conveniently, they can access the files over a local network. You may need to get your local computer network manager to put the files on to a networked drive, and you may also want access to these files restricted to read-only or at least blocked so that only one user can use the project at one time. In addition, you will need to set up user accounts for the team members in NVivo.

To set up extra user accounts in NVivo

1 Open the Properties dialog by selecting **Project:Inspect/Change Project Properties. . .** from the menu bar in the Project Pad.
2 Click on the **Team** tab (see Figure 10.4).

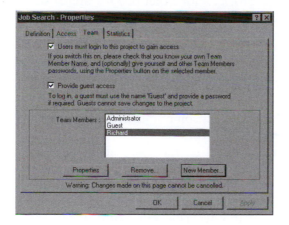

Figure 10.4   The project Properties dialog

3 Click on the check box, **Users must login to this project.**
4 Click on the **Provide guest access** check box if you want to allow guests.
5 Click on the **New Member. . .** button to add new members. Each will need a name and position (optional) and a password (optional). The Team Member dialog opens (see Figure 10.5).

Figure 10.5   The Team Member dialog

6 Complete the details for each team member.
7 Details for each team member can be changed by selecting the name in the team list and then clicking on the **Properties** button.
8 Click on **OK**.

If you are allowing several of the team to write to the project then you may need to set up some way of organizing their access so that they don't interfere with the work of other members. For example, you can make sure that they work on different documents or that they use different nodes for coding. Sets are a convenient way of managing this.

The second way of working as a team is where more than one person is engaged on the analysis at the same time. NVivo can only open one project at a time, so you cannot cut and paste from one project to another. One option here is to have a single project with either one researcher designated as the only person who can enter all analysis, or several people who share write access, but have agreements about when they can edit the project (no two at the same time) and what parts of it they are allowed to change. Alternatively there is a Merge program available so you can have two or more, separate versions of the project and these can be combined into a single file. In this case you can have several people with their own versions of the project (which will be merged at some stage) with agreements about what parts of the project they should work on.

That said, and despite the difficulties, there are advantages in having several researchers analysing the data together. You can check the work of one against the other and thus minimize researcher bias and get a measure of the reliability of coding. For example, you could check the coding of one researcher against the coding of another. This only really makes sense if you have already agreed upon a set of nodes and is a check on both the clarity of the node definitions and how well and consistently the researchers code the text. One simple way to do this is using what I called, in Chapter 3, 'on the beach' coding. This involves marking up a paper copy of documents and forces coders to mark whole paragraphs. If two or more researchers do this independently their results can be entered into two separate node trees, one for each researcher. The coding can be compared in NVivo in two ways. Either use the Boolean search, node difference, on each pair of equivalent nodes. Do this twice, one node first and then the other first, and combine the results using union search. This will produce a node coding all the text that is coded differently by the two researchers. Alternatively, use the Coder to display the text coded at one node while displaying the text coded at the other in the Node Browser. You will find it useful to view the paragraph before and after each passage in the Node Browser. Do this by changing the passage contents display.

In NVivo, however, since coding can be done to the level of one character, this procedure is of less use once coding has been refined. Different researchers may code just a few characters differently, even though they have coded substantially the same passages. Even so, you may find the techniques described in the previous paragraph useful in highlighting those substantive passages that have been omitted altogether by one or more coders. You can then discuss in the team what should be done with them. Don't put too much weight on identical coding as a measure of reliability. It's often rather arbitrary where coding starts and finishes. More important is the concept that lies behind the node. This is what must be agreed within teams. The concept it represents must be clear and unambiguous, and procedures like those just described may help teams focus on that issue.

In both processes for comparing coding you will need more than one copy of the node tree to which the text is being coded. Set up a root node for each researcher and then copy and paste the entire tree (make sure you tell the program to paste all the children too) as a child of each researcher's root node. This is best done before any coding takes place, otherwise you will need to uncode all text from each of the copied nodes. There is no way in NVivo of locking selected nodes for specified users, so you will have to manage this through clear instructions to each co-researcher. You could go further and allow each researcher to set up their own node tree (or at least modify their copy of the original). Again, confine each researcher to nodes under their own root node. Compare similar nodes using the techniques described above and discuss the results, along with any more radically different coding, at team meetings in order to decide what to do with the disagreements.

Conclusion

Having reached the end of this book, I hope it is clear to you how much and in what ways NVivo can support you in the analysis of your qualitative data. Even before you start collecting data, NVivo can help you sort out your theoretical and analytical ideas and act as a database for all your notes, references and memos. The main tasks of coding data, searching text and undertaking analysis through the comparison of nodes and attributes is, of course, well supported in the software. But, if you so choose, even the process of writing about your data and constructing final reports can be done in NVivo. You may feel this is all too much. You may long for the feel of pen and paper and the smell of ink or pencil. Of course the program does have its limits. Sometimes it is just easier to get out a pen and paper and do a quick analysis rather than having to spend a lot of time learning new functions in the software. However, if you need it, the program is there and waiting. There is no doubt that for many forms of qualitative analysis, the use of software like NVivo will make the process more robust, easier to control and in the end, perhaps, more enjoyable.

Further reading

Becker, H.S. (1986) *Writing for Social Scientists: How to Start and Finish Your Thesis, Book or Article.* Chicago and London: University of Chicago Press. (Based on the author's own graduate course and full of sage advice.)

Flick, U. (1998) *An Introduction to Qualitative Research.* London: Sage. (A recent text containing a good summary of debates about writing, theory and expression in qualitative analysis.)

Kvale, S. (1996) *InterViews: An Introduction to Qualitative Research Interviewing.* Thousand Oaks, CA: Sage. (Includes a discussion of how to write up interview studies.)

Miles, M.B. and Huberman, A.M. (1994) *Qualitative Data Analysis: A Sourcebook of New Methods*, 2nd edn. Beverly Hills, CA: Sage. (Several good ideas on how to work in teams.)

Seale, C. (1999) *The Quality of Qualitative Research.* London: Sage. (This is a comprehensive discussion of the issues that affect the quality of research, including issues of validity and reliability as they apply to qualitative research.)

Silverman, D. (ed.) (1999) *Doing Qualitative Research: A Practical Handbook.* London: Sage. (A very accessible text including, *inter alia*, much discussion of writing in qualitative work, such as getting started, writing as analysis and writing proposals.)

Strauss, A.L. and Corbin, J. (1998) *Basics of Qualitative Research: Techniques and Procedures for Developing Grounded Theory*, 2nd edn. Thousand Oaks, CA: Sage. (Includes a chapter on writing from a grounded theory perspective.)

Wolcott, H.F. (1990) *Writing up Qualitative Research.* Newbury Park, CA and London: Sage. (A short and lively discussion of writing for qualitative researchers.)

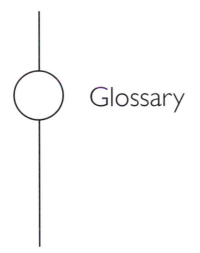

Glossary

Accounts A specific form of narrative in which respondents try to account for, justify, excuse, legitimate etc. their actions or situation.

Alias In NVivo, an icon for a node or document when you construct a set. The actual node or document is not moved into the set. Instead, a new icon alias of (or shortcut to) the original is placed in the set. Deleting an alias does not delete the original.

Analytic induction A way of building explanations in qualitative analysis by constructing and testing a set of causal links between events, actions etc. in one case and the iterative extension of this to further cases.

Annotation A short passage usually commenting on the contents of a document and linked to it as a DataBite.

Assay A process of inspecting the properties of a set or the scope of a search – for example, to see which items contain text coded at a specific node.

Attribute A property of a node, case or document. Very like a variable in quantitative analysis. An attribute (e.g. 'Gender') may have several values (e.g. 'Male', 'Female', 'Not relevant') and any particular node, case or document may be assigned just one value for each attribute.

Autobiography An extended account or narrative by a person of their own life. See **biography**.

Axial coding In grounded theory, the second stage of coding in which the relationships of categories are explored and connections between them are made.

Biography An extended account or narrative of a person's life. It usually has a structure and is expressed in key themes, often with an epiphany or turning point. The narrative is usually chronological.

Boolean search   Named after the mathematician, Boole, this is a search in which the items being searched for are combined by Boolean connectors such as and, or and not. For instance, one may search for text that matches the words 'luck' *and* 'chance' or for text that is *not* coded at the node 'Individual interview'.

CAQDAS   Computer-assisted qualitative data analysis software. Remember that computers only assist, and that the software does not analyse.

Case node   A type of node where all the material relating to one case (a setting, institution, person etc.) can be kept together. Case nodes can be grouped with similar ones under a case type node.

Cell   An element of a **table** positioned in a particular row and column. In qualitative analysis, its contents are usually text data taken from project documents or summaries of them.

Children   In a node tree, all the nodes connected to and below a specified node.

Chronology   The presentation of events, stories etc. in the order in which they actually happened or in which they were experienced.

Cluster plot   A diagram with two axes each of which is a scaled feature or attribute (e.g. from low to high). Cases, settings or people are arranged on the chart to indicate where they fall in terms of the two axes. Cases etc. that fall near to each other are said to be clustered.

Coding   The action of identifying a passage of text in a document that exemplifies some idea or concept and then connecting it to a node that represents that idea or concept.

Coding on   The process of reviewing and recoding the text already coded at a node. This may mean reducing or expanding the coded text to reflect the refinement of the concept the node represents or, additionally, coding some of the text at other nodes.

Coding stripes   Traditionally these are (coloured) stripes down the margin of a text to show how lines have been coded. In NVivo this is shown by vertical, coloured lines displayed (optionally) in a pane to the right of a document. Each is named with the title of the node at which the text is coded.

Constant comparison   The process or comparing, throughout an analysis, the ideas represented by nodes (in NVivo) with the text coded at them to check that the ideas are well grounded in the data.

Conversation analysis   The study of talk-in-interaction to discover how people produce an orderly social world.

Co-occurrence search (near)   In NVivo, a type of proximity search that finds all the text referenced by the first specified item (node, attribute or text string) that is near the text referenced by a second item specified. 'Near' can be variously defined.

Cover sheet   Brief information about a document, its provenance, type, date etc. which the user enters. Traditionally kept on a sheet on the front of the transcript.

DataBite   In NVivo, a short passage written as a note (annotation) about a section of a document or an external computer file (text, image, video etc.) that is linked to a specific place in the document. The text to which it is anchored is green and underlined.

Deduction   The logical move from a general statement to a specific one. Cf. **hypothetico-deductive method**.

Descriptive coding   Coding to nodes that simply refer to surface features of the people, events, settings etc. in a study. Much descriptive coding in NVivo can be done using attributes.

Difference search   A type of Boolean search that finds all the passages referenced by any of the specified items (nodes, attributes or text strings) in one list but referenced by none in a second list.

Dimension   The multiple properties or aspects that a node may have. For example, a node about activities may have a list of the several different kinds of activity as one of its dimensions. Duration, actors, settings etc. may constitute other dimensions. In NVivo, these can be represented by the children of the node.

Discourse analysis   The study of the way versions of the world, society, events and psyche are produced in the use of language and discourse. The Foucauldian version is concerned with the construction of subjects within various forms of knowledge/power.

DocLink   In NVivo, a linkage between a document or node and a document. The link may be from the document or node as a whole or from a specific anchor point in the document.

Document   In NVivo, an editable **rich text file**. It may be a transcription of project data or it may be a summary of such data or memos, notes or passages written by the researcher. The text can be coded at nodes and linked to other documents and files in a variety of ways.

Document description   Information about the document that is kept in the Document Property along with the name, creation date etc., and/or in a linked memo. This information can be extracted from a document when it is imported into a project. See also **cover sheet**.

Document section   Part of a document. In NVivo a document section starts with a paragraph in a heading style and includes all the text up to (but not including) the next paragraph which is in a heading style of the same or higher level. There are nine levels of section, with 1 the highest, and sections are nested in those at a higher level. Level 0 indicates the whole document. NVivo can use sections, for example, by spreading finds in a search to the enclosing section.

Domain analysis   The examination of what some term or concept means for a culture or subgroup.

Ethnography   A multi-method qualitative approach that examines specific social settings. Originally associated with anthropology.

Event–state networks   A diagram showing events and states identified in the study linked by arrows showing time sequence.

Explanation building   A form of analysis also known as **analytic induction**.

Flow chart   a chart or diagram showing the flow of people, objects or logic through states or actions and decisions.

Free node   A node which is not part of a node tree or a case or case type. Free nodes are kept in a simple list but may be moved to the node tree when required. This enables nodes to be created without having to worry immediately about how they relate to other nodes.

Generalizability   The ability to move from explanations and descriptions of particular examples to general populations.

Grounded theory   Originally an inductive form of qualitative research in which novel explanations and understandings of phenomena are developed by close examination of data. Sampling of cases, settings or respondents is guided by the need to test the limits of developing explanations which are constantly grounded in the data being analysed.

Group   A way of bringing together items in a model that are in some way related to each other. Groups may be selected and moved as a whole in the model.

Hypothesis   A testable proposition that captures the researcher's understanding of the situation being studied.

Hypothetico-deductive method   The scientific method in which proposed general theories or conjectures are tested by deducing from them specific statements that are capable of being tested by comparison with empirical evidence. If the evidence conflicts with that predicted, then the theory or conjecture is refuted.

Importing   The process of bringing the contents of a file into the project (in plain text or rich text) as a document or (in spreadsheet or tab-separated format) as attributes.

In vivo coding   A term from grounded theory in which a term, phrase or concept used by people in a setting is used as a name and idea for coding data. In NVivo, an in vivo node can be quickly created using the selected text as its title.

Inclusion search (surrounding)   In NVivo, a search that finds all the text referenced by the first specified item (node, attribute or text string) that surrounds the text referenced by a second specified item.

Induction   The logical move from a number of specific statements, events or observations to a general theory or explanation of the situation or phenomenon.

Interpretive coding   Coding of text in which the researcher interprets the contents to generate some concept, idea, explanation, or understanding. Interpretation may be based on respondents' own views and experiences, the researcher's view or understanding or on some pre-existing theory or framework. Cf. **descriptive coding**.

Intersection search (and)   In NVivo, a search that finds all the text referenced by all of the specified items (nodes, attributes or text strings).

Layer   In an NVivo model, a way of associating items so that they can be displayed or hidden together.

Lexical searching   Text searching that is concerned to find the occurrence of words and phrases used by respondents and investigate their context of use.

Link   In NVivo, a connection between documents and nodes and annotations, external files and other documents and nodes. Or a connection between items in a model, or a connection between nodes in the node tree.

Matrix   A table arranged in rows and columns in which rows represent one set of items and columns represent another. Each row and column defines a **cell**. The contents of the cells can be used to investigate the relationship between the items the rows represent and those the columns represent.

Matrix co-occurrence   In NVivo, a type of proximity search (q.v.) that carries out a **co-occurrence search** on each item (node, attribute or text string) in one list, pairwise, with each in a second list. See **matrix search**.

Matrix difference   In NVivo, a type of Boolean search that carries out a **difference search** on each item (node, attribute or text string) in one list, pairwise, with each in a second list. See **matrix search**.

Matrix inclusion   In NVivo, a type of proximity search that carries out an **inclusion**

search on each item (node, attribute or text string) in one list, pairwise, with each in a second list. See **matrix search**.

Matrix intersection   In NVivo, a type of Boolean search that carries out an **intersection search** on each item (node, attribute or text string) in one list, pairwise, with each in a second list. See **matrix search**.

Matrix search   In NVivo, a search that operates on text coded at one collection of items, pairwise, with that coded at items in another. The items may be nodes, attributes or the result of a text search. The result is a matrix of finds, and these are coded at a list of sibling nodes under a matrix parent node. The content of each cell in the matrix is represented by text coded at one of the nodes in that list. Nodes are numbered to indicate their place in the matrix.

Matrix sequence   In NVivo, a type of **proximity search** that carries out a **sequence search** on each item (node, attribute or text string) in one list, pairwise, with each in a second list. See **matrix search**.

Memo   A document containing commentary on the primary data or nodes of the project.

Merging nodes   In NVivo, the process of combining two nodes so that only one node, which codes all the text coded at one or both the original nodes, remains.

Metadata   Data about data. In NVivo such data can be stored as attributes, document descriptions, memos, linked documents, files etc.

Metaphor   The use of imagery in speech or text as a kind of rhetorical device. Metaphor use may indicate culturally shared ideas or difficulties in expression.

Model   In NVivo, a diagram in which elements that can represent nodes, documents or simply ideas are linked with lines and arrows that show how they relate to each other. Models are constructed in the Model Explorer.

Narrative   Text or speech that tells a story of events and experiences, usually involving the personal dimension and told from the individual's point of view.

Negation search   In NVivo, a search that finds all the text referenced by none of the specified items (nodes, attributes or text strings).

Negative case   A case, event, setting, person, experience, story, etc. that apparently contradicts a theory, explanation or understanding generated earlier in the analysis (or derived from the literature). In qualitative research negative cases are commonly used to revise the theory, explanation or understanding rather than reject it. Cf. **hypothetico-deductive method**.

Node   In NVivo, an object that represents an idea, theory, dimension, characteristic etc. of the data. Text in documents can be coded at a node. Nodes can be linked to other nodes either directly or by position in a **node tree** and linked to documents.

Node description   In NVivo, information about the node that is kept in the node property along with the name, creation date etc. and/or in a linked memo. It describes the idea, concept etc. the node represents.

Node hierarchy   See **node tree**.

Node search   In NVivo, a search for the text coded at a node or nodes.

Node tree   The arrangement of nodes into a hierarchy, and so also known as a node hierarchy. At the top are one or more 'root' or 'top' nodes and arranged below them each may have one or more child nodes, which in turn may have their own child nodes etc.

NodeLink   In NVivo, a DataLink linking a document or node to a node.

Non-Boolean   In NVivo, a type of search that does not use the Boolean terms and, or, not and less. The non-Boolean searches are co-occurrence, sequence and inclusion.

Non-serial coding   Also known as signpost coding. Coding that collects together passages from different documents and different cases that all seem to exemplify the same idea, concept or notion. The size of passage coded may vary from one character to whole documents. Cf. **serial coding**.

Open coding   The first stage of coding in grounded theory, where text is read reflectively to identify relevant categories. New nodes are created and are given a theoretical or analytical (and not merely descriptive) name. Relevant text is coded at the node. The analyst may try to develop **dimensions** for the categories (nodes).

Organization chart   A chart showing the elements of an organization (people, departments, divisions, etc.) and their relationship to each other (often in terms of a hierarchy).

Paragraph   In NVivo, all the text between one hard carriage return and the next. In Microsoft Word the hard carriage return is indicated by the paragraph symbol ¶.

Paragraph Coder   The facility in NVivo to code whole paragraphs by reference to their sequential number in the document.

Paragraph style   See **style (paragraph)**.

Parent (nodes)   In the node tree or case tree system, the node directly linked to the node from above.

Plain text file   A computer file (indicating by a .txt file extension) containing nothing but text characters and a limited selection of punctuation marks etc. A plain text file does not appear in any specific font, font size, colour, style etc. Cf. **rich text file**.

Project   In NVivo, the collection of all the files, documents, nodes, attributes, memos, cases, reports, users etc. associated with a research project. Users may only open one NVivo project at a time.

Project Pad   A window in NVivo, when a project is open, which gives access to all the main functions of the program.

Proximity search   In NVivo, a group of non-Boolean searches in which the closeness or sequence of coded passages is significant.

Proxy document   A document in an NVivo project that stands for some other document or item that may not itself be part of the project. The contents of a proxy document may be used to refer to specific contents of the external item (e.g. pages in a book, meter number on an audiotape) and be linked to it if it is online (e.g. a digitized video file).

Reliability   The degree to which different observers, researchers etc. (or the same observers, researchers etc. on different occasions) make the same observations or collect the same data.

Report   In NVivo, a rich text file which the user may create from within the program. Its contents may record various kinds of data generated by the program from the project.

Rich text file   A computer file (indicated by an .rtf file extension) containing text that may appear in one or more fonts, font sizes, colours, styles etc. Cf. **plain text file**.

Root node   In the NVivo node or case node tree, a node that has no parent.

RTF   See **rich text file**.

Saturation   In grounded theory, the situation where after further instances of the categories are gathered, the researcher is confident about their relevance and range. The search for further appropriate instances seems futile when the categories are saturated.

Scope   The range of items which are searched in a search operation. It is a collection of nodes and/or documents.

Search Tool   In NVivo, a window for setting up and controlling searches.

Section   See **document section**.

Selective coding   The final stage of grounded theory in which a central phenomenon or core category is identified and all other categories are related to it.

Sequence searching (preceding)   In NVivo, a search that finds all the text referenced by the first specified items (nodes, attributes or text strings) which starts before the text referenced by the second specified items.

Serial coding   The coding of all the text for a specific item to one of a series of nodes. The items may be a topic in a structured or semi-structured interview, a whole interview or all the documents associated with a case or a person. Typically all the text in a project is coded at one or other of the series of nodes rather in the manner that the text of a book is divided into chapters.

Set   A collection of nodes or documents. **Aliases** rather than the actual nodes or documents are stored in the set.

Shortcut   See **alias**.

Sibling (nodes)   Nodes that share the same parent in the node tree or case node area.

Signpost coding   See **non-serial coding**.

Splitting nodes   Creating two nodes from the text coded at one. Passages coded at the original node are coded to one or other or both of the new nodes. This is done when inspection of the node definition and examination of the coded passages suggests there are two discrete concepts represented.

Spread   In NVivo, the widening of a selected passage (e.g. one resulting from a search) to include some surrounding text.

Story   A short narrative, often with a regular sequence of elements that people include in interview responses and conversations.

String   Any sequence of letters, numbers or characters.

Style (Model Explorer)   In NVivo, a named collection of visible qualities (e.g. colour, label font, size, thickness) that can be assigned to an item or link in a model.

Style (paragraph)   A named collection of qualities (e.g. colour, font, font size, line spacing) that can be assigned to a paragraph. Styles are preserved in rich text format documents.

Style (writing)   The manner of writing up a qualitative project that takes in to account the audience at which the work is directed and their expectations about how the work should be written, based on their familiarity with other reports.

Subtree   Part of a tree formed by a node and all its descendants (its children and all their children etc.).

System closure   In NVivo, the results of analyses such as searches are presented as nodes and may be preserved as part of the project. They in turn can be the subject of further analysis. This is referred to as system closure.

Table   A diagram, usually arranged in rows and columns. Cf. **matrix**.

Tab-separated format   A format in which data from a spreadsheet or statistics software may be saved. Columns of figures are separated from each other by commas and each line ends with a carriage return. NVivo can import tab-separated data into attributes.

Taxonomy   A strict hierarchical arrangement of items where the relationship between parent and child items is that of 'is a kind of . . .' or 'is a type of . . .'.

Team   In NVivo, the group of users entitled to use the project.

Text search   In NVivo, a form of searching where text is found if it matches a specified string or set of strings of characters.

Themes   A set of ideas or concepts either derived from prior theory (e.g. in template analysis) or from respondents' lived experience (in interpretative phenomenological analysis) which can be used to establish a set of nodes at which text can be coded.

Theoretical elaboration   The stage of analysis in which the patterns into which data have been organized can be clarified, and categorization and coding of the data can be used to test out ideas about what is going on in the study.

Transcription   The process of transferring audio or video recordings of speech or handwritten notes into a typed or word-processed form. In some cases special characters may be used to indicate aspects of how words were spoken.

Tree   In NVivo, the hierarchical, branching structure of tree nodes and case nodes.

Tree node   A node stored in the node tree. Each of these is either a root node or a child of a node (or a child of a root node). Ideally, nodes relate to their parents by being 'examples of . . .', or 'contexts for . . .' or 'causes of . . .' or 'settings for . . .' and so on.

Typology   An arrangement of items into different types.

Union search   In NVivo, a search that finds all the text referenced by any of the specified items (nodes, attributes or text strings).

Validity   The extent to which an account accurately represents the social phenomena to which it refers.

Variable   In quantitative analysis, a general characteristic or quality shared by all cases in the study. Variables have two or more values and usually each case is assigned just one value (or a small number of values). Values may be numeric or categories. In NVivo, this kind of information is stored in attributes, though any particular node, case or document may only have one single value for each attribute.

Wildcard   A character (or term) in text search that controls a special matching process. In NVivo, for example, a full stop (.) stands for any single character.

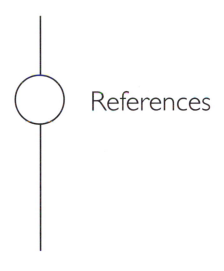

References

Austin, J.L. (1962) *How to Do Things with Words*. Oxford: Oxford University Press.

Becker, H.S. (1986) *Writing for Social Scientists: How to Start and Finish Your Thesis, Book or Article*. Chicago and London: University of Chicago Press.

Bhaskar, R. (1993) *Dialectic: The Pulse of Freedom*. London: Verso.

Billig, M. (1997) Rhetorical and discursive analysis: How families talk about the royal family, in N. Hayes (ed.) *Doing Qualitative Analysis in Pyschology*. Hove: Psychology Press.

Bogdan, R. and Biklen, S.K. (1992) *Qualitative Research for Education: An Introduction to Theory and Methods*, 2nd edn. Boston: Allyn & Bacon.

Bryman, A. (1988) *Quantity and Quality in Social Research*. London: Unwin Hyman.

Bryman, A. and Burgess, R. (1994) Developments in qualitative data analysis: An introduction, in A. Bryman and R. Burgess (eds) *Analysing Qualitative Data*. London: Routledge.

Bulmer, M. (1979) Concepts in the analysis of qualitative data, in M. Bulmer (ed.) *Sociological Research Methods*. London: Macmillan.

Campbell, D.T. and Stanley, J. (1966) *Experimental and Quasi-experimental Designs for Research*. Chicago: Rand McNally.

Charmaz, C. (1995) Grounded theory, in J.A. Smith, R. Harré and L. Van Langenhove (eds) *Rethinking Methods in Psychology*. London: Sage.

Coffey, A. and Atkinson, P. (1996) *Making Sense of Qualitative Data Analysis: Complementary Research Strategies*. London and Thousand Oaks, CA: Sage.

Coffey, A., Holbrook, B. and Atkinson, P. (1996) Qualitative data analysis:

technologies and representations, *Sociological Research Online*, 1. http://www.soc.surrey.ac.uk/socresonline/1/1/4.html (accessed 30 May 2001).

Cook, T.D. and Campbell, D.T. (1979) *Quasi-experimentation: Design and Analysis Issues for Field Settings*. Chicago: Rand McNally.

Creswell, J.W. (1998) *Qualitative Inquiry and Research Design: Choosing among Five Traditions*. London and Thousand Oaks, CA: Sage Publications.

Delamont, S., Atkinson, P. and Parry, O. (1997) *Supervising the PhD: A Guide to Success*. Buckingham: Society for Research into Higher Education and Open University Press.

Denzin, N.K. (1989a) *Interpretive Biography*. Newbury Park, CA and London: Sage.

Denzin, N.K. (1989b) *Interpretive Interactionism*. Newbury Park, CA and London: Sage.

Dey, I. (1993) *Qualitative Data Analysis: A User-Friendly Guide for Social Scientists*. London and New York: Routledge.

Fielding, N.G. and Lee, R.M. (1998) *Computer Analysis and Qualitative Research*. London: Sage.

Flick, U. (1998) *An Introduction to Qualitative Research*. London: Sage.

Giorgi, A. (1970) *Psychology as a Human Science*. New York: Harper & Row.

Giorgi, A. (ed.) (1985) *Phenomenology and Psychological Research*. Pittsburgh, PA: Duquesne University Press.

Glaser, B.G. (1978) *Theoretical Sensitivity: Advances in the Methodology of Grounded Theory*. Mill Valley, CA: Sociology Press.

Glaser, B.G. (1992) *Emergence vs Forcing: Basics of Grounded Theory Analysis*. Mill Valley, CA: Sociology Press.

Glaser, B.G. and Strauss, A.L. (1967) *The Discovery of Grounded Theory: Strategies for Qualitative Research*. Chicago: Aldine.

Guba, E.G. and Lincoln, Y.S. (1989) *Fourth Generation Evaluation*. Newbury Park, CA: Sage.

Hammersley, M. and Atkinson, P. (1995) *Ethnography: Principles in Practice*, 2nd edn. London: Routledge.

Hammersley, M. (1992) Ethnography and realism, in M. Hammersley (ed.) *What's Wrong with Ethnography?* London: Routledge.

Harré, R. (1997) Account analysis and its relatives: An outline of the main methods for social psychology, in N. Hayes (ed.) *Doing Qualitative Analysis in Pyschology*. Hove: Psychology Press.

Kelle, U. (ed.) (1995) *Computer-Aided Qualitative Data Analysis: Theory, Methods and Practice*. London: Sage.

Kelle, U. (1997) Theory building in qualitative research and computer programs for the management of textual data, *Sociological Research Online*, 2. http://www.socresonline.org.uk/2/2/1.html (accessed 30 May 2001).

King, N. (1998) Template analysis, in G. Symon and C. Cassell (eds) *Qualitative Methods and Analysis in Organizational Research*. London: Sage.

Kvale, S. (1996) *InterViews: An Introduction to Qualitative Research Interviewing*. Thousand Oaks, CA: Sage.

Labov, W. (1972) The transformation of experience in narrative syntax, in W. Labov (ed.) *Language in the Inner City: Studies in the Black English Vernacular*. Philadelphia: University of Pennsylvania Press.

Labov, W. (1982) Speech actions and reactions in personal narrative, in D. Tannen (ed.) *Analyzing Discourse: Text and Talk*. Washington, DC: Georgetown University Press.

Labov, W. and Waletsky, J. (1967) Narrative analysis: Oral versions of personal experience, in J. Helm (ed.) *Essays on the Verbal and Visual Arts*. Seattle: University of Washington Press.

Lee, R.M. and Fielding, N. (1996) Qualitative aata analysis: Representations of a technology: A comment on Coffey, Holbrook and Atkinson, *Sociological Research Online*, 1. http://www.socresonline.org.uk/1/4/1f.html (accessed 30 May 2001).

Lieblich, A., Tuval-Mashiach, R. and Zilber, T. (1998) *Narrative Research: Reading, Analysis and Interpretation*. London: Sage.

Mason, J. (1996) *Qualitative Researching*. London: Sage.

Miles, M.B. and Huberman, A.M. (1994) *Qualitative Data Analysis: A Sourcebook of New Methods*, 2nd edn. Beverly Hills, CA: Sage.

Mills, C.W. (1940) Situated actions and vocabularies of motive, *American Sociological Review*, 5: 439–52.

Moustakas, C. (1994) *Phenomenological Research Methods*. Thousand Oaks, CA: Sage.

Popper, K. (1959) *The Logic of Scientific Discovery*. London: Hutchinson.

Potter, J. and Wetherell, M. (1987) *Discourse and Social Psychology*. London: Sage.

Potter, J. and Wetherell, M. (1995) Discourse analysis, in J. Smith, R. Harré and L. Van Langenhove (eds) *Rethinking Methods in Psychology*. London: Sage.

Riessman, C.K. (1993) *Narrative Analysis*. Newbury Park, CA and London: Sage.

Robinson, W.S. (1951) The logical structure of analytic induction, *American Sociological Review*, 16: 812–18.

Robson, C. (1993) *Real World Research: A Resource for Social Scientists and Practitioner-Researchers*. Oxford, UK and Cambridge, MA, USA: Basil Blackwell.

Silverman, D. (1993) *Interpreting Qualitative Data. Methods for Analysing Talk, Text and Interaction*. London: Sage.

Smith, J.A. (1995) Semi-structured interview and qualitative analysis, in J.A. Smith, R. Harré and L. Van Langenhove (eds) *Rethinking Methods in Psychology*. London: Sage.

Strauss, A.L. (1987) *Qualitative Analysis for Social Scientists*. Cambridge: Cambridge University Press.

Strauss, A.L. and Corbin, J. (1990) *Basics of Qualitative Research, Grounded Theory Procedures and Techniques*. London: Sage.

Strauss, A.L. and Corbin, J. (1997) *Grounded Theory in Practice*. London: Sage.

Tesch, R. (1990) *Qualitative Research – Analysis Types and Software Tools*. London: Falmer.

Van Maanen, J. (1988) *Tales of the Field: On Writing Ethnography*. Chicago: University of Chicago Press.

Weaver, A. and Atkinson, P. (1994) *Microcomputing and Qualitative Data Analysis*. Aldershot: Avebury.

Weitzman, E. and Miles, M. (1995) *Computer Programs for Qualitative Data Analysis: A Software Source Book*. Thousand Oaks, CA: Sage.

Winch, P. (1958) *The Idea of Social Science and its Relation to Philosophy*. London: Routledge & Kegan Paul.

Winch, P. (1974) Understanding a 'primitive' society, in B. Wilson (ed.) *Rationality*. Oxford: Blackwell.

Wolcott, H.F. (1990) *Writing up Qualitative Research*. Newbury Park, CA and London: Sage.

Wolcott, H.F. (1994) *Transforming Qualitative Data: Description, Analysis, and Interpretation*. London: Sage.

Yin, R. (1994) *Case Study Research: Design and Methods*. Thousand Oaks, CA: Sage.

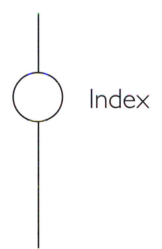

Index